GW00938982

Rüdiger Buck-Emden
mySAP® CRM

 PRESS

Edited by Bernhard Hochlehnert, SAP AG

With SAP PRESS, you have the guarantee of obtaining first-hand SAP knowledge – factual, current, and proven. SAP PRESS is a common initiative of SAP and Galileo Press. The goal is to provide qualified SAP-product knowledge to the user. SAP PRESS combines the know-how of SAP with the publishing competence of Galileo Press. The books offer expert knowledge of technical and commercial SAP topics.

A. Rickayzen, J. Dart, C. Brennecke, M. Schneider
Practical Workflow for SAP
2002, 504 pp., ISBN 3-89842-999-7

Paul Read
SAP Database Administration with MS SQL Server 2000
2002, 312 pp., ISBN 3-89842-998-9

Thomas Schneider
SAP Performance Optimization Guide
2002, 504 pp., ISBN 3-89842-281-X

Sue McFarland Metzger, Susanne Röhrs
SAP R/3 Change and Transport Management
2002, 600 pp., ISBN 3-89842-282-8

Rüdiger Buck-Emden

mySAP® CRM

Solution for Success

Galileo Press

German Edition first published in 2002 as
mySAP CRM. Geschäftserfolg mit dem neuen Kundenbeziehungsmanagement

Translation: Lemoine International Ltd., Ireland
Typesetting: Lemoine International Ltd., Ireland
Printed and bound by Bercker Graphischer Betrieb, Germany
Cover design by department, Cologne

Contents

Foreword

Many esteemed people have helped in the putting together of this book. I would like to thank them for their collaboration and support. They are:

Peter Zencke, who has contributed an introduction to the subject area and made many other suggestions for the book,

Dietmar Saddei for fruitful discussions and many new ideas,

the collaborating authors Achim Appold, Stephan Brand, Christian Cole, Christopher Fastabend, Jörg Flender, Alison Gordon, Tomas Gumprecht, Stefan Hack, Volker Hildebrand, Frank Israel, Fabian Kamm, Stefan Kraus, Mark Layden, Claudia Mairon, Wolfgang Ölschläger, Jörg Rosbach, Ingo Sauerzapf, Thomas Weinerth, Peter Wesche and Rainer Zinow, who apart from their day to day work still found the time and energy to prepare their respective contributions

and Jochen Böder, Michael Brucker, Steve Coombs, Bernhard Drittler, Henrike Groetecke, Carsten Hahn, Ulrich Hauke, Bernhard Hochlehnert, Annette Hofmann, Martin Hofmann, Mark Krimpenfort, Peter Kulka, Dietmar Maier, Heike Matz, Wilfried Merkel, Andreas Muther, Annette Rawolle, Thomas Reiss, Gerhard Rickes, Bernhard Runge, Andreas Schuh, Hans-Heinrich Siemers, Andrea Sudbrack, Erik Tiden, Frank Vollmer and numerous other colleagues who have contributed in so many ways to the realization of this book.

Finally I would like to thank Wiebke Hübner and Tomas Wehren at Galileo Press for their friendly and constructive cooperation.

December 2001

Rüdiger Buck-Emden

1   Introduction: The Customer as a new old Center

Dr. Peter Zencke, member of the board of directors, SAP AG

Customer Relationship Management (CRM) is currently one of the most frequently used terms in strategy discussions in enterprises. The basic idea behind effective management of customer relationships and the specific analysis of knowledge about the customer will become an undisputed principle in determining how a company will be run in almost all industry sectors. Who or what else could be at the focus of a company's actions, if not the customer – both important company equity and the true source of all profit.

However, what exactly is understood by Customer Relationship Management, as far as its IT execution is concerned, has changed greatly in recent years. Until recently CRM referred to a grouping together of a range of isolated Sales Force Automation, Call Center and Electronic Commerce applications. This Front Office Software used innovative technologies for Channel-Management in sales and distribution and customer service. An important step towards customer orientation was made, but the evolution of CRM could not end there.

It was not long before the narrow definition of CRM was broken down. For example, with mySAP Customer Relationship Management (mySAP CRM), SAP not only offers a comprehensive solution with powerful Front Office Applications, covering all sales, marketing and services channels, they have also seamlessly integrated customer interaction with the Backend with fulfillment systems, especially with internal company process development and financial control systems.

SAP's integrated CRM base takes the close interconnection of customer specific processes further with Supply Chain Management (SCM) calculation. Therefore customers' needs do not only drive internal company processes, but they also extend along the supply chain to manufacturers, suppliers and distributors.

These operational CRM functions are developed into analytical applications. They serve to evaluate a large quantity of diverse data that is obtained from interaction with the customer through all phases of the business relationship and, in particular, aspects of customer satisfaction, market penetration and profitability. The information gained in this way supports strategic business decisions and opens the way for additional added value potential.

With consistent use of the Internet, the spectrum of CRM solutions will finally be extended to a new type of collaborative business scenario, based on portals and virtual marketplaces.

Business portals represent an entrance gate for individuals to the user services and information that they need for their various work or consumer roles. As a fundamental part of SAP's CRM solution concept, they make it possible to carry out collaborative processes between employees within a company and also between people working in different companies.

Analogously, electronic exchanges are the central and structured transfer sites for very different collaboration and information services that can be used by a limited number of business partners or an unlimited number of market players. Portals and exchanges form the links around SAP's comprehensive CRM offer.

This book describes the mySAP CRM solution and the associated strategy in full detail. The authors explain how the many collaborative business processes work together and, on the basis of the mySAP e-business platform, show the perspectives that can be opened up by such an integrated approach to business.

2   The new New Economy

Profitable Internet Business Models

Early excitement about the commercial possibilities of using the Internet was often accompanied by the term *New Economy*. Towards the end of the 1990's dotcom companies were mushrooming, in the hope that the Internet would help in the achievement of rapid business success. Many of these companies rose to breathtaking levels on the stock exchange in a very short space of time, without actually making clear how their business model would achieve profitable results. With the correction of stock markets in 2000 and stiff competition from so many dotcom companies, however, it soon became clear that even in the New Economy, it was not excessive share speculation and vision, but rather income and profitability that would finally establish the financial worth of a company. The *new* New Economy was based on this fact. An economy that recalled the traditional basic principles of business development, used in conjunction with a desire to exploit the far reaching possibilities of the Internet for actually *profitable* business models.

New Possibilities for Shaping Business Processes

The Internet has made markets more transparent and has dramatically changed the relationship between companies, and also collaboration between companies and their suppliers and business partners. Never before had it been possible to establish business links so quickly, never before were companies in a position to work together so closely and to expand their activities beyond the boundaries of their own enterprise as in the Internet age.

At the same time the Internet offers enormous possibilities for the consolidation of customer relationships. No shop in the world can register the preferences of their customers as precisely and completely as a Web Shop. The deep understanding of the customer that can be gained from this makes it possible to offer tailor-made products and services and therefore leads directly to economic success.

Basically this means that companies are rethinking their business model for the Internet age, and in doing so they must take into account the new possibilities for customer interaction and cross-enterprise collaboration.

Purchasing and Sales Processes Grow Together

In the Internet economy, companies grow even closer. In order to survive global competition they must no longer rely solely on internal resources. Added value is today increasingly achieved in company networks. Thanks to faster, cross-enterprise communication via Internet people with different roles and from different companies cooperate as though they were working for the same company. As a result, purchasing and sales processes blend together seamlessly.

Today many companies already use SCM (Supply Chain Management) applications to link their purchasing-related processes with the business procedures of their suppliers. Sales-related links with customers are guaranteed by powerful CRM solutions. The association between the two sides is done with the help of a common ERP (Enterprise Resource Planning) System with stock and availability management.

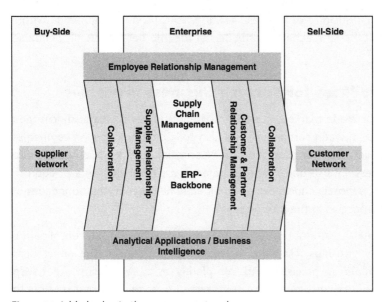

Figure 2.1 Added value in the company network

Purchasing and sales processes are merged together in a single one-step business process which begins with an inquiry. As soon as a buyer gives an instruction, the purchasing company's system generates an order. At the same time, an offer is drawn up in the selling company's system. Both the order processing on the one hand (until delivery and receipt of payment) and the procurement activities on the other hand (up to receipt of goods and payment) run automatically. One-step business means that it is possible for separate companies to fully utilize the potential of Internet to optimize business processes.

Using innovative solutions for the management of the entire logistics chain, enterprises can link their customers, partners and suppliers in a virtual, customer oriented process network. The particular wishes of individual customers become the starting point of the whole logistics chain, along which the partner systems exchange relevant information such as requirements, prognosis, stock availability and production capacity in real time. Two core business tasks – customer relationship maintenance and the optimizing of the logistics chain – are brought even closer together and can no longer be considered as independent processes, as was the case until just a few years ago.

From e-Commerce to e-Business and m-Business

The new New Economy leads to a reshaping of all procurement and sales processes. Whereas the focus of the reengineering initiatives of the 1990's still lay in optimizing internal processes [Hammer 1993], with *e-business* the focus is on redefining and the electronically supported handling of cross-enterprise, collaborative business processes [Kalakota 1999]. Therefore, e-business goes much further than the earlier and, in practice often doomed, beginnings of *e-commerce*, which used the Internet merely for the presentation and sale of products. E-business increasingly promotes the integration of business processes – both within the company and beyond company limits – as a basic maxim. Private or public electronic marketplaces (Private or Public Exchanges), thanks to which many suppliers and purchasers come together in a single (virtual) place, play an important role in this integration. In addition, in the current reshaping of business processes, we have mobile, wirelessly-linked devices such as, for example, mobile telephones and PDAs (Personal Digital Assistants), which change the PC-centered working methods of the previous twenty years in favor of a multi-platform model for mobile users. This new business form, which unites the elements *Internet*, *wireless communication* and *e-business*, is known as *m-business* [Kalakota 2001].

Externalizing Processes

Using the Internet's information exchange services, companies can increasingly develop processes which do not form part of their core skills outside of their traditional company limits, by, for example, using outsourcing services or services on electronic exchanges.

This externalizing process allows for the creation of completely new forms of cross-enterprise cooperation, moving away from isolated data exchange using batch processes or EDI (Electronic Data Interchange) to actual cooperation processes in which information is used collectively and joint access to data is possible in real time. More and more companies already go even further than this and collaborate with other enterprises not only on a data level, but also on the level of processes, from application to application. This makes for rational interaction between partners and generates competitive advantages.

3   Customer Relationship Management in the new New Economy

> *"Intensive customer relationships lay the foundations for a continuous source of income and a considerable basis for further growth. They also produce a lasting barrier to market entry."*
> *[Curry 2000]*

Customer Relationships in the new New Economy

In the Old Economy, the golden rule applied that companies who wanted to achieve long term success had to produce top results regarding at least one of the following criteria:

▶ Close customer relationships

▶ Superior products

▶ First class operative processing and services at an acceptable cost

and offer at least industry standard in the other two. But this rule applied in the past! In today's new New Economy, which is uncompromisingly centered on the customer, companies can only survive in the long term when they achieve top marks in all three disciplines (see also chapter 5, "Cross Industry Solutions" on page 38). The Internet, with its many communications possibilities, brings the world of global competition to even the smallest company, and as a result customers become increasingly demanding. Customers choose their suppliers from all over the world and only become loyal business partners if the particular offer meets their needs exactly – if what they receive is what they want, at the set time and via the agreed means of transport. In order to be able to operate successfully in this milieu in the long term, companies need powerful solutions for the management of all their business processes that directly or indirectly affect customer relationships.

What is Customer Relationship Management?

Customer Relationship Management (CRM) is a collective term for processes and strategies for maintaining relations between the company and customers, business partners and other interested parties. CRM works towards the goal of securing new customers, building up existing customer relationships and increasing competitiveness and company profitability.

In the Old Economy the care of customer relationships was often limited to the communication measures of the marketing department, with the emphasis on imparting information on products rather than on the collection, evaluation and use of information on customers' needs and behavior.

Even today, many companies know far too little about their customers. Who are their customers? What are the needs and preferences of their customers? The Gartner Group assumes that fewer than 10 % of companies have a comprehensive, integrated view of their customers [Close 2001]. In the past, a whole range of projects to improve customer relations failed because companies did not manage to adapt their organizational structure and processes to fit in with the actual demands of their customers (see also "CRM Software Alone is not Enough" on page 23 and chapter 15, "Introduction" on page 239).

Individual Customer Contact by Personalization

Many innovative companies have been quick to recognize the changes associated with the globalization of markets on the Internet and the transition from sellers' to buyers' markets. New, personalized customer care concepts, brought together under the term *One-to-One Marketing* [Peppers 1997], place individual customers and information related to these customers at the center of business processes (see also chapter 9, "One-to-one Marketing" on page 151). This personalization can occur in the following ways, for example:

▶ Customer specific product catalogs or catalog views

▶ Individual pricing and conditions for customers

▶ Customer specific product configurations *(Mass Customization)*

▶ Target group specific product recommendations

▶ Customer specific user interfaces

The goal of this new organization is to use comprehensive information to make all contact channels and business interactions with each individual customer at least as personal as a local salesperson, in order to gain customers and to keep them in the long term. And this is precisely the aim of well-structured and coordinated customer relationship management. CRM is therefore more than just the automation of processes in marketing, sales, service and management. It is also more than a collection of methods to increase the efficiency of these processes. Ultimately CRM means being well-informed when interacting with customers, and, as a result, being well-directed in dealing with their individual needs.

CRM Software Alone is not Enough

Before undertaking a CRM project, enterprises should always be clear on the following: For sucessful customer relationship management the purchase of CRM software alone – of whatever type – is by no means enough. Successful CRM projects are more dependent on the harmonious coming together of four elements (for example, [Brenner 2001], [Homburg 2000]):

▶ Enterprise strategy for Customer Relationship Management

▶ Organizational implementation of strategy in the form of adequate enterprise processes

▶ Enterprise culture that fixes customer orientation as a value within the company and in employees' attitude and behavior

▶ Adequate hardware and software systems

Only when all four areas are brought together to form a consistent enterprise solution, can the potential of innovative CRM concepts be exploited to the full. Another aspect should also be noted: The implementation of customer relationship management is not a one-off, stationary matter. Rather, after the initial setting up, a continuous improvement process must be implemented, driven by service thinking and a growing understanding of customer requirements.

Loyal Customers in the new New Economy

In the new New Economy customer loyalty is a volatile characteristic that must be cultivated carefully, because on the Internet alternative offers are just a few mouse clicks away. Customer loyalty is subject to new rules, to which suppliers must adapt. Basically, it can be said that in the Internet age customer relationships can be maintained in the long term and built up only if the following principles are taken into account in the shaping of customer related business procedures:

▶ **Trouble-free contact possibilities through all interaction channels**
Customers want simple, easy and cost-effective access to their suppliers' services at any time, of any type and via different contact channels. The supplier must always be contactable and give accurate, relevant information, consistent through all channels, independently of whether a customer acts via telephone, fax, e-mail, Internet or pocket PC, or in person.

▶ **Repository of all relevant customer data**
Efficient management of relevant customer data in a central repository is the basic prerequisite for the shaping of personalized business procedures. A customer who has placed an order online via the Internet and later phones the call center to enquire about the delivery date, expects the call center agent to

have direct access to the entire order history. Business procedures with isolated, individual customer data, which means that the customer has to continuously ask or answer the same questions, are a sure way to make a current customer an ex-customer.

However, good data about customers is not enough on its own. If used with inadequate analysis functions it can even be counterproductive – one only has to think of surface marketing campaigns, which flood customers with irrelevant offers again and again with the principle of "equal shares for all". In this way even good customers can be lost. On the other hand, all customers will gladly accept a call from their credit card company if an unusually high amount has been charged to their credit card and there is a risk that there has been unauthorized use or theft.

▶ **A wide choice of products thanks to collaboration between suppliers**

In the new New Economy, enterprises can link their business procedures even closer to those of their customers, suppliers and business partners. Electronic exchanges allow for the seamless merging of purchasing and sales procedures. Collaboration becomes the basis of successful business.

Whereas an important aspect of cooperation between enterprises and their customers lies in the identification of customer needs, collaboration with suppliers and business partners can in some cases help in the preparation of solutions which satisfy these customer needs. If, for example, the purchaser of a new car requests that a particular type of seat be fitted, using Internet-based collaboration the car manufacturer can find out the availability and cost of this type of seat from car seat manufacturers, order the most suitable seat, and supply the car exactly as the customer has requested.

This type of customer-specific production not only raises the degree of customer satisfaction; furthermore, because of the customer's direct participation in the production process, it ensures a close and hopefully long business relationship because a customer who has given detailed requirements to a supplier and, as a result, built up a relationship of trust, will not be so quick to change to another supplier.

Customer Lifecycle Management

Successful business relationships are still viewed from a reduced, punctual perspective by many enterprises. It is however much more important to foster customer relationships over an entire lifecycle *(Customer Lifecycle)*. Within this lifecycle the following phases will, where possible, run several times (see figure 3.1):

- ▶ **Customer Engagement**
  Arouse interest and recognize potential customers
- ▶ **Business Transaction**
  Carry out sales procedure and come to business agreements
- ▶ **Order Fulfillment**
  Fulfill agreed delivery commitments
- ▶ **Customer Service**
  Look after customers

According to the research company META Group, CRM is ultimately a systematic approach to Customer Lifecycle Management, that is, a systematic interaction of enterprises with customers over all four phases of the business relationship [META 1999].

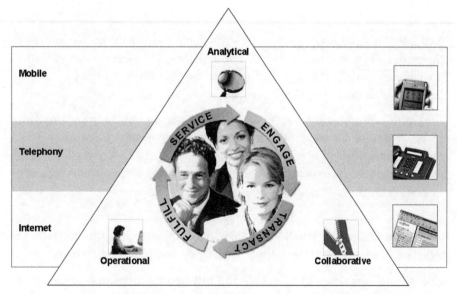

Figure 3.1 Operative, collaborative and analytical CRM in the Customer Lifecycle with mySAP CRM

Integration as a Basis for Business Success

Software solutions for sales and distribution support have undergone meteoric development. The first systems were classified under the term SFA (Sales Force Automation) – in Germany these were also referred to as CAS systems (Computer Aided Selling). The focus of such software lay in the support of sales staff in their day to day work:

- ▶ Contact management
- ▶ Sales activities
- ▶ Management of new sales opportunities
- ▶ Analyses
- ▶ Product and customer information

Above all, it was necessary to improve information management for field sales employees, who spend a lot of time on the road and cannot continuously access the company network. Only in the past few years has it been recognized that it is important not to treat sales as an isolated unit, but that it should be seen in conjunction with all other business organization units that come into contact with customers. The marketing and customer service departments share some of the same information needs and can give important background information to the sales force.

> **Example** After detailed analysis, the marketing department of the company Innovative Products has launched a campaign to improve product 4711's market position by offering a price reduction. However, coordination with Sales only occurs at management level.
>
> Jon Smith, a sales representative, has carefully prepared the long planned visit to one of his most important customers to close a contract for product 4722. Only at the beginning of the meeting does he learn that his customer would like to find out more about product 4711, having had his interest aroused by the marketing brochure that arrived on his desk that same morning.

To avoid this and similar situations, there is an obvious need for the integration of marketing, sales and customer service functions in modern CRM systems.

Although the integration of all people and software solutions that communicate directly with customers and interested parties is already a big step in the right direction, it will not be enough to produce a truly comprehensive and uniform picture of the customer in the company. Areas of the enterprise which have no direct contact with customers must increasingly be taken into account in customer relationship management because they also make a decisive contribution to sales success.

> **Example** Let us presume that the company Innovative Products has now introduced a recognized CRM system. Marketing, sales and customer service applications have been successfully integrated. Jon Smith naturally knows about the campaign for product 4711 and is prepared accordingly. A contract is concluded. However, later it emerges that Innovative Products is unable to deliver on time because, unexpectedly, a supplier is unable to provide the necessary quantity of parts.

It thus becomes clear that sales can only really act in the best interest of the customer if an SCM system is integrated. When the order is accepted, an availability test can be run in real time that considers the entire logistics chain and calculates the possible delivery schedule.

So, all in all, customer relationship management can only be successful if an enterprise really knows its customers, all necessary information is available and the entire customer interaction history can always be accessed.

What Customers Demand of CRM Software

In a recent survey by the Gartner Group market research institute [Nelson 2000] companies cited the following objectives as influential in their decision to introduce a CRM solution:

▶ Increase turnover

▶ Raise profitability

▶ Improve customer loyalty

▶ Gain competitive advantages

▶ Reduce costs

▶ Access to customers via new contact channels

The challenge which companies must set for themselves with the introduction of a CRM solution is to achieve these objectives by means of a harmonious merging of CRM technology, company CRM strategy, and organizational measures.

Because the introduction of a CRM software solution is a long term investment, a company should also check that the chosen software supplier is a stable enterprise, and that the maintenance and further development of the software over its entire life cycle can be assured. Many smaller CRM software providers are at risk in this respect. The Gartner Group predicts that three quarters of the CRM software providers on the market today will be nowhere to be seen by the year 2004 [Thompson 2001].

Demand for More Comprehensive Integration

CRM solutions can only demonstrate their full potential if they are not used in isolation, rather they must be installed with close links to all relevant processes and data within the company and also with links to business partners. This leads to the question of the integration concept of the CRM solution. In answering this question, several dimensions must be taken into account:

▶ Integration of the different contact channels (consistent view of company information and performance, independent of channel)

▶ Integrated merging of operational CRM processes in sales, customer service and marketing

▶ Integration of operational CRM functions with analytical CRM functions

▶ Integration with purchasing and production functions via common stock and availability management

▶ Integration of CRM with backend functions such as invoicing and human resources

▶ Integration of internal and external procedures with the aim of more collaborative business processes with customers and partners.

▶ Integration with public and private exchanges

▶ Integration of information content and applications via a portal and user interface that can be personalized; making it possible to integrate the CRM solution into the portals of different suppliers

▶ Integration of mobile devices (m-business)

Many CRM implementations in enterprises do not yet fulfill the above integration requirements, or they only fulfill them in part. Process integration, in particular, is often poorly developed. As a result there is a risk of automation islands and the implementation of only suboptimal solutions.

Protection of Personal Data

The storing and processing of personal data associated with the more personal One to One marketing must be treated with greater sensitivity. Questions such as:

▶ Which personal data may and should be stored?

▶ Who can be allowed access to what personal data?

▶ How secure is the storage and transfer of personal data against unauthorized access?

▶ What additional security aspects must be taken into account when using different contact channels and end-user equipment?

must be systematically thought out and answered. In addition there is the danger or temptation – stronger in B2C (Business to Consumer) than in B2B (Business to Business) – of passing personal data on to third parties. To avoid a loss of customer confidence, enterprises should take suitable measures and, for example, consider the possibility of giving customers direct access to the personal data stored on them and, if necessary, the possibility of making changes as appropriate.

The Influence of IT

New hardware and software products from IT suppliers act as a continuous catalyst for the development of innovative CRM solutions. Six trends which influence or have influenced the development of innovative CRM solutions can be outlined as follows:

▶ Office productivity tools
▶ Internet
▶ Collaborative software solutions
▶ Analytical applications
▶ Mobile technologies
▶ Multi-channel interaction

Office Productivity Tools

First generation customer relationship management software solutions were developed with the aim of increasing the productivity of sales staff on the road. The orientation towards individual employees soon led to demands for stronger integration of CRM solutions with office productivity tools such as word processing, spreadsheets and project management. This requirement still applies today and was consistently taken into consideration in, for example, the development of mySAP CRM (see also chapter 6, "Integration of Office Functions" on page 54).

Internet as a Dynamic Factor

In the present day the Internet has a decisive influence on the redesigning of customer-oriented processes. E-selling, business partner portals and electronic exchanges bring opportunities but also demands regarding dealings with customers. New and expanded possibilities of automatically collecting, evaluating and using information on customers for personalized customer care is accompanied by the fact that the Internet intensifies competition, something companies can only withstand with deliberate efforts to win customers and consolidate customer ties. Because customers, who are only a few mouse clicks away from a rival supplier's web shop, are very quick to stray if offers do not meet their requirements exactly.

Solutions for Collaborative Value Added Chains

In the last 20 years companies have integrated their backend processes and the flow of information throughout the whole company and replaced function-oriented automating islands with integrated ERP systems. Investments in ERP and process redesign pay off through tighter processes, higher quality information and better decision making processes within the company. More recently, companies further optimize their processes throughout the whole company from the beginning to end of the value added chain with collaborative solutions for Supply Chain Management (SCM) and Customer Relationship Management (CRM).

Software for Data Analysis and Decision Making Support

The falling cost of computer performance and the availability of new software tools for recording and analysing collective data are the main drivers behind analytical solutions and their growing importance both in departments and in the upper echelons of management. Thanks to more powerful hardware and software customer relationships can be understood, used and formed better than ever.

Mobile Technology as the Latest Innovation Thrust

With the spread of wireless, better communicating, and more mobile devices, e-business is increasingly becoming m-business. In contrast to the possibilities offered by today's PCs, applications are becoming more and more oriented to the needs of the mobile user. This also has a sustained influence on applications for selling and buying (for example, *Van Sales*, see chapter 11, "The Traveling Salesman (Van Sales)" on page 185) and as a result, the whole area of customer relationship management.

Multi-Channel Interaction Between Business Partners

CRM solutions today are designed to fit with very different contact channels between companies, business partners and customers. These include Internet, e-mail, telephone, fax, call centers and mobile devices, but also traditional mail and direct contact. The *synchronisation* of all contact channels is crucial because the customer always wants to receive the same information and services from the company irrespective of the contact channel used. Contradictions between information from different contact channels are to be avoided at all costs.

Modern CRM systems are therefore highly integrated systems which enable the supplier to always convey *One Face to the Customer* – irrespective of contact channel (*Touch Point*).

In this respect the simultaneous use of electronic and conventional personal interaction is interesting, for example, the combination of Internet and telephone. Using a Call or Call-me-Back button on the suppliers' Internet site the customer has the possibility to enlist the help or advice of a supplier's call center agent without having to relinquish the advantages of multimedia interactions. Therefore traditional media and the Internet complement each other perfectly.

Against this background it is clear that conventional interaction channels will also play an important role in the future. Ultimately the customer must be able to choose which form of initiating contact he wishes to use in each particular situation. Direct personal contact (face to face) – whether with a field sales representative at the customer's premises or with a member of the sales team in a sales plant – the telephone (call center) and the Internet offer different advantages for the customer so that, essentially, it will come down to a combination of the various different interaction channels.

The Market for CRM Solutions

The market for CRM software solutions can currently be divided into several submarkets with different degrees of maturity:

▶ Solutions for the support of direct and indirect sales organisations. This is a stable market with established suppliers and products.

▶ Call Center solutions. This is also a largely established market. New aspects are currently appearing on the scene with the *Interaction Center* theme and the generally consistent treatment of different contact channels.

▶ CRM solutions on the Internet. A growing market, the potential of which is still by no means fully realized.

▶ Mobile CRM solutions. This is also very much a growing market and it must still grapple with different technology options.

On the whole, the market for CRM solutions will develop in leaps and bounds over the next few years because unlike backend business solutions, comprehensive CRM applications are installed in very few enterprises. Market analysts at Current Analysis [Sprang 2000] estimate that only 5 % of all potential CRM software customers install the appropriate solutions. The market research company AMR Research [Boulanger 2000] states that the world market for CRM solutions will grow from $9.8 billion in 2001 to $20.8 billion in 2004.

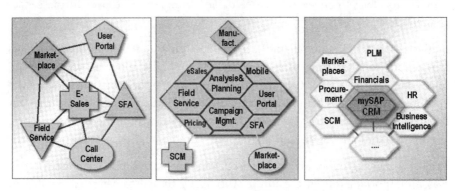

Figure 3.2 CRM Solutions from suppliers of Point Solutions, Suites and Platforms

Regarding suppliers, the market for CRM solutions is currently divided as follows:

▶ Smaller special suppliers selling, for example, products for the area of Sales Force Automation *(Point Solutions)*

▶ Suppliers of comprehensive Front Office solution packages for customer relationship management *(Suite* suppliers)

▶ Software companies who have already been producing successful business application solutions for many years and offer CRM within the framework of their comprehensive solution platform *(Platform* suppliers)

Important CRM software suppliers on the market today include the suite specialist Siebel, the platform supplier SAP, and especially for small to medium sized enterprises, the point solution companies Onyx and Pivotal.

4   The Functional Structure of CRM Solutions

In general, the application services provided by CRM systems can be divided into three functional areas:

▶ Operational CRM

▶ Collaborative CRM

▶ Analytical CRM

This chapter will outline the different task areas.

Operational CRM

The basic foundation for all CRM solutions is an adequately detailed customer data set to which authorized company employees, working in marketing, sales, service and management and, if necessary, customers have access. Operational CRM uses this data for customer oriented services through the entire customer lifecycle.

Important operational CRM services are presented in the following overview:

Marketing

▶ Lead generation and lead management (identification and management of interested prospective buyers)

▶ Telemarketing

▶ Campaign management

▶ Content management (maintenance and preparation of offer related documents on the Internet)

▶ Interaction center or call center with activity and contact management

Sales and distribution

▶ Mobile sales for field sales employees (Sales Force Automation)

▶ Telesales (selling over the phone including Cross-Selling and Up- Selling, that is to say, extending offers and offering higher range products)

▶ Contact management for maintaining customer interaction

▶ Opportunity management (management of qualified interested prospective buyers)

▶ Management of sales and distribution activities and schedules

▶ Product configuration and pricing

▶ Interaction center or call center with activity and contact management

Service and support

▶ Mobile service for field sales employees

▶ Maintenance and management of installation data

▶ Maintenance and management of solution databases

▶ Processing of service inquiries and orders

▶ Interaction center or call center with activity and contact management

Partner Relationship Management

▶ Collaboration with business partners as indirect sales channel

▶ Joint marketing, sales, and service planning and execution for example with dealers, resellers, distribution centers, service providers, marketplace providers, and outsourcing partners

▶ Management of business partners including recruiting, registration, profile management, analysis and monitoring

Top Management

▶ General business planning (finance, sales, capacity requirement)

▶ Balanced Scorecard (tool for management with reconciliation of monetary and non-monetary plan and actual values)

▶ Preparation of Key Performance Indicators (KPIs)

Collaborative CRM

Collaborative CRM supports both long and short term partnership collaboration between different market players using the Internet. One finds examples of collaborative CRM in all areas of marketing, sales and distribution and customer service. The following summary gives an overview of common collaborative scenarios in the area of CRM:

E-marketing

▶ Introducing new products on the market (product launch in close collaboration with customers, producers, dealers and market research companies)

▶ Collaborative planning and execution of marketing campaigns (collaboration with producers, market research companies and marketing service suppliers)

▶ Support of Internet communities (virtual communities of, for example, customers, suppliers and business partners)

▶ Online chats

▶ Personalized product demonstrations and training offers on the Internet

E-selling

▶ B2B Sales (Business-to-Business cooperation of clients' and suppliers' systems) with the direct collaboration of the business partners' processing systems (one-step business). Continuous transparency and optimized processes by means of direct data exchange and interactive query functions between the purchasing process (customer inquiry, purchase order, goods receipt, invoice verification, payment order) on the customer's side and the sales process (customer quotation, order, delivery note, goods issue, invoice, receipt of payment) on the side of the supplier.

▶ B2C Sales (Business-to-Customer) as personalized self service for customers. B2C sales include interactive services such as catalog searches, product configuration, availability check, preparing customer specific price calculation and checking on order status.

▶ Collaborative sales and distribution processes (collaboration with customers, dealers and producers, for example, customer specific product design)

▶ Collaborative key account management (collaboration of producers, dealers and market research companies)

▶ Collaborative sales order management involving different suppliers (Distributed Order Management)

▶ Exchanges as collaborative sales and distribution channels with services for processing RFPs (Request for Proposal), collaboration between customers, main and subsuppliers, RFQs (Request for Quotation), auctions, and so on.

E-service

▶ Collaborative processing of customer complaints (cooperation between customers, service providers, dealers and producers)

▶ Services offered as a 'self-service offer' (collaboration of customers, producers and service companies)

Analytical CRM

The term *analytical CRM* is used to refer to data warehouse and OLAP (Online Analytical Processing) services and analytical, planning and optimizing tools for customer relationship management. The task of analytical CRM is to analyze, evaluate and present all relevant data about customers, their interaction with the company and their behavior in order to

- ▶ Gain improved understanding of customer satisfaction and possible future customer behavior
- ▶ Provide a basis for marketing, sales and distribution, customer service and management decisions
- ▶ Support customer related planning
- ▶ Optimize operative processes such as marketing and promotion activities

Analytical CRM is currently being transformed from an earlier department-oriented initiative to become a management task with direct influence on strategic management decisions. The following key figures are typical basic information that analytical CRM provides as a starting point for the focused control of marketing and sales and distribution activities:

- ▶ *Satisfaction Index* (key figure for customer satisfaction)
- ▶ *Loyalty Index* (key figure for customer loyalty)
- ▶ *Retention Rate* (proportion of customers who buy again, produced at customer segment level)
- ▶ *Share of Wallet* (proportion of total expenditure on a specific product group which a customer spends with a specific supplier)
- ▶ *Response Rate* (Proportion of recipients who react to particular marketing measures)
- ▶ *Customer Lifetime Value* (Overall value which can possibly be obtained with a customer over the entire customer lifecycle)

More detailed questions that can be asked of analytical CRM are, for example:

- ▶ Which customers are the most profitable through the entire duration of the customer relationship?
- ▶ What services can be used to link the customer to the enterprise long term?
- ▶ What services can be used to win new customers?
- ▶ How can a differentiated service offer be drawn up for different customer groups?

5   mySAP.com – SAP's e-Business Platform

mySAP CRM represents a core element of the mySAP e-business platform. The following overview will explain the role of mySAP CRM within the framework of this overall solution.

Elements of mySAP.com

In order to be able to survive profitably and competitively in the Internet influenced business world, companies must be put in a position that enables them to collaborate beyond traditional company limits and operate within virtual networks.

With mySAP.com, SAP makes a comprehensive solution and service offer for all business processes available on the Internet. mySAP.com combines three decades of development experience in the area of integrated business software with the far reaching innovative potential of e-business, m-business, company portals, electronic exchanges and global, collaborative business processes. This organization is reflected in the following definition of mySAP.com:

> The mySAP.com e-business platform is a software and service family which gives customers, partners and employees the means to work together successfully from any place and at any time. (compare with, for example, [Kimbell 2001])

With mySAP.com, users will find a working environment that can be personalized and fitted to suit their current needs, via which they can conduct collaborative business processes, both internal processes and beyond the limits of their own company. Traditional boundaries between companies are therefore increasingly blurred.

The most important characteristics of mySAP.com are:

▶ Comfortable user environment with browser and role-based company portal which can be personalized

▶ Integration of any applications, services and information via portals (user-oriented) and exchanges (process-oriented)

▶ Inclusion of customers, partners and employees in collaborative business networks

mySAP.com comprehensively covers all 'e-business' business processes, both within and between companies. The following solutions form part of mySAP.com:

- ▶ **Cross Industry Solutions** (business solutions irrespective of industry sector)
  - ▶ mySAP Customer Relationship Management (mySAP CRM, optimizing customer relationships)
  - ▶ mySAP Supply Chain Management (mySAP SCM, optimizing the supply chain from suppliers right through to end user)
  - ▶ mySAP Product Lifecycle Management (mySAP PLM, optimizing product data management)
  - ▶ mySAP Supplier Relationship Management (extended procurement solution on the Internet)
  - ▶ mySAP Business Intelligence (mySAP BI, management and evaluation of knowledge and information)
  - ▶ mySAP Human Resources (mySAP HR)
  - ▶ mySAP Financials (mySAP FI)
  - ▶ mySAP Mobile Business (m-business, mobile applications for laptop and hand-held equipment)
- ▶ **Portal and exchange solutions**
  - ▶ mySAP Enterprise Portals (role based enterprise portals)
  - ▶ mySAP Exchanges
- ▶ **Over 20 industry solutions**
  - ▶ mySAP Industry Solutions (business scenarios specific to different industry sectors)
- ▶ **Infrastructure and service solutions**
  - ▶ mySAP Technology (platform technology for all mySAP.com solutions)
  - ▶ mySAP Services (services throughout mySAP.com)
  - ▶ mySAP Hosted Solutions (outsourcing and application service provider services)

All of the mySAP.com elements mentioned will be briefly presented below.

Cross Industry Solutions

The business applications in mySAP.com which can be used across industries are closely interrelated to support a wide variety of business processes. Customer relationship management (mySAP CRM) plays a major role. As a source element for almost all core enterprise processes, it maintains close integration with product development (mySAP PLM) and the operative applications (mySAP SCM, mySAP FI).

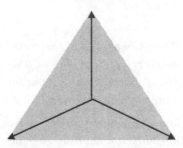

Customer Relationship
Focus on relationship benefits and long
term customer value

Product Leadership
Focus on providing leading edge products
tailored to customer needs

Operational Excellence
Focus on highest convenience
lowest cost to the customer

Figure 5.1 Customer relationship management, product innovation and operative sales order processing working together

The mySAP.com cross-industry solutions are structured as follows:

▶ **mySAP CRM**

Customer-oriented services for planning, developing and maintaining customer relationships with special attention paid to the new possibilites offered by the Internet, mobile devices and multi-channel interaction. mySAP Customer Relationship Management supports customer interaction through all phases of the Customer Interaction Cycle – from the initial contact through contract conclusion, sales order processing and to backend services. mySAP CRM is closely linked with mySAP BI for analytical evaluations and integrates the SAP Business Information Warehouse (SAP BW) functions.

▶ **mySAP SCM**

With mySAP SCM (Supply Chain Management) customers, business partners and suppliers can be linked in cross-company logistics chains. mySAP SCM assures transparency for warehouse stocks, orders, forecasts, production plans and key service indicators and in so doing, improves customer service (meeting deadlines, online calling up of order status information, and so on), production output, ability to respond to changes in demand, order processing times and using production capacities to the full. The planning and optimizing component SAP APO (Advanced Planner and Optimizer) is a core element of mySAP SCM.

▶ **mySAP PLM**

mySAP PLM (Product Lifecycle Management) is SAP's solution for cross-business product planning, product development and asset management on the basis of shared product and project data. Faster, more uniform access to all relevant product information is made possible for all parties involved in product development, service and maintenance such as product designers, suppliers, manufacturers and customers.

▶ **mySAP SRM**

mySAP Supplier Relationship Management is SAP's extended e-procurement solution developed by SAP Markets. With mySAP CRM, cross-company sourcing processes and supplier collaboration are supported for all types of purchased goods and services. Core elements of mySAP SRM are

- ▶ Development and optimization of a global sourcing strategy incl. supplier selection, supplier qualification, and contract management
- ▶ Collaboration with trading partners for example via web-based self-services and distributed content management
- ▶ Operational sourcing, self-service procurement, and supplier relationship monitoring

▶ **mySAP BI**

mySAP Business Intelligence is SAP's solution for the combination and management of internal and external data with the aim of transforming it into business knowledge for decision making support using data, warehouse and analysis tools. Components of mySAP BI include the data warehouse SAP BW (SAP Business Information Warehouse) and SAP SEM (Strategic Enterprise Management) for strategic business management and SAP KM (Knowledge or Content Management) for knowledge management. The components of mySAP BI are closely integrated with the mySAP CRM solution.

mySAP BI is used in the following business scenarios – among others:

- ▶ Customer Relationship Analytics (gauging and optimizing customer relationships)
- ▶ Enterprise Analytics (enterprise evaluation and productivity)
- ▶ Supply Chain Analytics (gauging and optimizing supply chains)
- ▶ Exchange or e-commerce Analytics (analyze online customer experiences and improve competitiveness in e-business)

▶ **mySAP Human Resources and mySAP Financials**

mySAP Human Resources (mySAP HR) and mySAP Financials (mySAP FI) are SAP's well known standard solutions covering all the needs of human resources management and financial accounting (compare, for example, [Brinkmann 2001], [Lübke 2001]). Both are closely tied in with mySAP CRM, for example, on matters of workforce management or invoicing.

▶ **mySAP Mobile Business**

mySAP Mobile Business promotes the further development of mySAP.com beyond the world of desktop-PCs and fixed networks. Mobile devices allow users access to all mySAP.com solutions at any time and from any place. mySAP Mobile Business is the basis for all mobile mySAP CRM applications. Examples for use of mySAP Mobile Business are:

  ▶ Mobile CRM (field employees in sales and customer service)

  ▶ Mobile Business Intelligence (mobile access to analysis and data-warehouse information)

  ▶ Mobile Procurement (direct procurement for employees working externally)

  ▶ Mobile Travel Management (possibility for mobile employees to access central travel management services)

mySAP Enterprise Portals – User Oriented Integration Platform

mySAP Enterprise Portals represent SAP's personalized, role based enterprise portals for all users on the value-added chain. An easy-to-use, easy to understand and personalized browser interface gives users entry to all internal and external enterprise information and to applications and services that they need in their personal working environment. The screen layout of mySAP Enterprise Portal is adapted for the relevant roles of the user in his company or his work center. Each user can represent several roles, between which he can switch at will.

Enterprise boundaries lose their importance with mySAP Enterprise Portals – at least to the extent desired within the framework of business procedures and authorization concepts. Every corner of the world that is linked to the Internet can be reached by mySAP Enterprise Portals using a URL (Uniform Resource Locator). Examples of matters that can be addressed are:

▶ Business transactions

▶ Reports and evaluations

▶ Knowledge-warehouse information

▶ Internet or intranet information

▶ Exchanges

Functionality

mySAP Enterprise Portals are the central points of entry to numerous mySAP.com solutions and to external tools and information, and also to any Internet information and legacy systems. Thanks to their scalability, mySAP Enterprise

Portals guarantee that not only a few but, if necessary, a large number of users can be given access to all required information sources, applications and services.

mySAP Enterprise Portals offer the following functions:

▶ Support of roles and personalization, central user-administration

▶ Navigation tools for looking for and calling up applications, services and data. Each user can activate several roles and the corresponding working environments.

▶ *iViews* (integrated Views, formerly known as *MiniApps*) as a window to any application. According to their role, requirements and preferences, users are automatically offered important content, for example, e-mail, diary, web news, and so on.

▶ *Drag&Relate* a tool with which business tasks can be carried out by simply moving objects in the browser. For example, on the browser a user can use the mouse to move an overdue order over to the symbol for the forwarding agent to automatically display the corresponding delivery information.

▶ *Single Sign-On (SSO):* Users can access internal and external applications and content without having to log on several times with different passwords. After the initial log on all necessary services, applications and data is available without further signing on procedures. Single Sign-On in mySAP Enterprise Portals supports two authentication concepts (see also chapter 17, "Infrastructure Services" on page 274):

  ▶ Single Sign-On with user ID and password

  ▶ Single Sign-On with X.509 client certificate

▶ Integration of non-SAP solutions and external content

▶ Integrated *Knowledge Management* with Web Content Management, text, retrieval and extract functions

▶ *Mobile Portal:* Access to mySAP Enterprise Portals using Internet enabled mobile devices (see also chapter 11, "Standard Architecture" on page 186)

Further details on the presentation of mySAP Technology will be given in chapter 17, "Portal Infrastructure" on page 270.

Role Concept

As a role based portal, mySAP Enterprise Portals offers made-to-measure content and services for employees, partners, customers and suppliers.

A role defines a group of activities – and the data and functions corresponding to them – carried out by a person to achieve a desired business aim. A role and not a person determines how a business process will be carried out and how this process in turn leads to the attainment of a particular business aim. Unlike processes, roles are flexible and can be changed easily. Many companies which may in the past have been organized according to function or process, are now changing to role based organization structures [Vering 2001].

Using role based architecture mySAP Enterprise Portals can, for example, offer a work environment to a head of department which in subareas looks quite different from that of a product developer. On the other hand, both the head of department and the product developer have the role of employee in the enterprise, with the same administration functions, for example, to request leave in the Employee Self Service (ESS) in mySAP HR. mySAP Enterprise Portals address this demand and support several roles per user.

The roles will define the layout of the mySAP Enterprise Portal for each user. Also the services, information and applications required for the particular work environment are established.

The following objects can be taken into consideration in the definition of a role:

▶ Transactions
▶ Reports
▶ iViews
▶ Links to general web sites
▶ Exportable files
▶ Links to Knowledge Warehouse
▶ Links to external systems

mySAP Enterprise Portals generally offer over 200 predefined roles – from work scheduler to sales personnel – that can be further tailored to suit the specific conditions and requirements of a particular company. For example, for mySAP CRM the following roles are available for direct use:

Marketing
▶ Marketing Manager
▶ Marketing Analyst
▶ Campaign Manager
▶ Product Manager
▶ Brand Manager
▶ Category Manager

Sales and Distribution

▶ VP Sales

▶ Sales Manager

▶ Sales Representative

▶ Sales Assistant

▶ Business Sales Analyst

▶ Field Sales Representative

E-selling

▶ Web Shop Manager

▶ E-selling administrator

Customer Service

▶ Contact Center Manager

▶ Contact Center Agent

▶ Customer Service Representative

▶ Customer Service Manager

▶ Knowledge Engineer

▶ Resource Planner for Interaction Center

▶ Field Service Engineer

▶ Contract Administrator

The understanding of the functions to be carried out by the holder of a particular role is subject to a continuous homogenization process and is, as such, congruent to the increasing standardization of buisness management processes. This trend towards standardization will help to make it progressively simpler to develop collaborative business scenarios which go beyond enterprise boundaries.

mySAP Exchanges – Platform for Internet Based Business Transactions

Electronic exchanges serve as platforms for Internet based business transactions between virtual buying and selling communities. They create the prerequisites for dynamic n:m business relationships instead of statistical 1:1 contact between predefined business partners.

mySAP exchanges provide a complete infrastructre for building up virtual markets which can help companies to develop their buying and selling processes as well as other cross-enterprise collaborative processes. The cornerstone is the *MarketSet* product, a common solution of the SAP subsidiaries SAPMarkets and Commerce One which has the following functions:

▶ MarketSet Supply Chain Collaboration (support of collaborative planning, forecasting and stock management involving suppliers, manufacturers and dealers)

▶ MarketSet Lifecycle Collaboration (support of collaborative product development)

▶ MarketSet Analytics (analytical applications for evaluating information from internal and external sources to offer help in decision making for buyers, sales employees and service providers)

▶ MarketSet Catalog (Content management tool for putting together and using an electronic catalog)

▶ MarketSet Procurement (application for procurement on the Internet)

▶ MarketSet Order Management (application for order management on the Internet)

▶ MarketSet Dynamic Pricing (methods for dynamic, trade based price calculation including auctions, markets, and so on)

▶ MarketSet Bulletin Board (information system for fast access to relevant cross-enterprise information such as, for example, auctions, bid invitations)

Users can access mySAP Exchanges via mySAP Enterprise Portals. The buying and selling systems associated with mySAP Exchanges are linked via open interfaces on an XML basis (Extensible Markup Language).

Example: The B2B Exchange EMARO

EMARO AG was set up in 2000 as a subsidiary of Deutsche Bank (60 %) and SAPMarkets (40 %), as a cross-industry exchange for the electronic procurement of MRO (maintenance, repair and operation) goods based on SAP exchange technology. Today, apart from office material, office furniture and hardware and software products, the EMARO exchange offers industrial requirements, tools and standard material. In principle all products in the electronic catalog can be ordered with the click of a mouse.

With the EMARO exchange, customers' and suppliers' goods exchange systems are seamlessly linked with each other. The buyer can choose to install this own purchasing system, such as mySAP E-Procurement, from which purchasers can directly access the EMARO electronic catalog. Alternatively, companies who do not have their own electronic procurement system have the possibility of using the e-procurement system run on the EMARO exchange as a hosting solution. In this case, enterprises only have to provide their buyers with a web browser.

Suppliers can also directly integrate their enterprise applications with the EMARO Exchange. If this is not desired, there is alternatively a web application for order management available on the exchange that, for example, enables suppliers to administer, process and send out sales documents such as orders or order confirmation to customers.

Apart from the technical linking of customers and suppliers, electronic catalogs are a decisive prerequisite for developing business via an exchange. EMARO offers extensive tools and services for creating a catalog.

You can visit EMARO at *www.emaro.com*.

mySAP Industry Solutions

There are special solutions for over 20 industry sectors in mySAP.com *(Industry Solutions)*, which expand the sector-neutral mySAP.com solutions to industry specific functions and developments.

The following industry sector solutions are currently available:

▶ **Discrete Industries**
  ▶ mySAP Aerospace & Defense
  ▶ mySAP Automotive
  ▶ mySAP Engineering & Construction
  ▶ mySAP High Tech
▶ **Process Industries**
  ▶ mySAP Chemicals
  ▶ mySAP Mill Products
  ▶ mySAP Pharmaceuticals
  ▶ mySAP Oil & Gas
  ▶ mySAP Mining
▶ **Financial Services**
  ▶ mySAP Banking
  ▶ mySAP Financial Service Provider
  ▶ mySAP Insurance
▶ **Consumer Industries**
  ▶ mySAP Consumer Products
  ▶ mySAP Retail

- ▶ **Service Industries**
  - ▶ mySAP Media
  - ▶ mySAP Service Providers
  - ▶ mySAP Telecommunications
  - ▶ mySAP Utilities
- ▶ **Public Services**
  - ▶ mySAP Healthcare
  - ▶ mySAP Higher Education & Research
  - ▶ mySAP Public Sector

A more detailed description of SAP's range of products for specialized industries can be found in, for example [Kagermann 2001].

mySAP Technology

All mySAP.com solutions are based on mySAP Technology, the robust and scalable SAP platform for business applications on the Internet. The most important elements of mySAP Technology are:

- ▶ Portal infrastructure
- ▶ Exchange infrastructure
- ▶ SAP Web Application Server
- ▶ Infrastructure services

mySAP Technology meets all technological requirements for business application solutions, which in the Internet age also stretch beyond enterprise boundaries. A technology is available for mobile business development, portal-supported system access, adaptable interfaces and collaborative business networks that can integrate very different platforms across enterprises. The basis for this technology is produced using recognized Internet standards, such as:

- ▶ HTTP (Hypertext Transfer Protocol: application protocol for the transfer of data on the Internet)
- ▶ HTML (Hypertext Markup Language: text description language for Internet pages)
- ▶ XML (Extensible Markup Language: standard information format on the Internet)
- ▶ SOAP (Simple Object Access Protocol: cross-system program-to-program communication on the Internet, which also crosses firewalls, based on HTTP and XML)

- ▶ Java (Programming language for the wide-ranging environment of the Internet)
- ▶ .NET (Microsoft's platform for Internet applications)

Further information on mySAP Technology follow in chapter 17, "mySAP Technology – Platform for Open, Integrated e-Business Solutions" on page 269.

mySAP Services

The installation and running of mySAP.com solutions are accompanied by a wide range of services. mySAP Services offers all services that enterprises need for the transformation of their conventional business processes into cross-enterprise E-Business. These include:

- ▶ Working out the most suitable industry sector specific e-business solution for the company in question (Business Solution Consulting)
- ▶ Implementation strategy for the management of the entire project and optimizing the production operation (Solution Operations Services)
- ▶ User training (Education)
- ▶ Comprehensive service for validity period (Service Infrastructure)

mySAP Services is based on three extensive tools:

- ▶ SAP Solution Architect (Portal for business planning and the implementation of mySAP.com solutions)
- ▶ SAP Solution Manager (Portal for technical implementation and the running of mySAP.com solutions)
- ▶ SAP Service Marketplace (Internet platform for customers who are looking for services from SAP or partner enterprises, wish to access them or order them)

In chapter 15 the range of SAP services related to the implementation of mySAP CRM in an enterprise is presented.

mySAP Hosted Solutions

For some companies the costs of implementation and of changing their technical infrastructure is a considerable obstacle to entering e-business. mySAP Hosted Solutions offers these companies the possibility of using, servicing and administering the hardware and software needed for mySAP.com solutions, whether they belong to SAP or partner enterprises.

The range of mySAP Hosted Solutions extends from individually adapted Application Hosting to the operation of ready to use applications with the One-to-Many model using ASP (Application Service Provider) services right through to marketplace hosting.

▶ **Application Hosting**

Application Hosting is offered to companies that need a fully configured solution according to their individual requirements, yet do not wish to invest in an extensive technical infrastructure. The applications are run and serviced in a central unit. Normally the customer owns the user license.

▶ **Application Service Provider (ASP)**

Application Service Provider offers software and infrastructure services, as well as service, support and implementation services as a ready-to-use solution. Several ASP customers use the same browser-enabled software in the One-to-Many model and in this way reduce the cost of their share of the hardware and software infrastructure. Configuration expense is minimized. The individual customers do not hold any license for the application.

▶ **Marketplace Hosting**

Electronic exchanges for communities of business partners are run with Marketplace Hosting and, where necessary, this can include the implementation of individually-configured solutions which run on the exchange.

mySAP Hosted Solutions are provided by SAPHosting, a subsidiary of SAP which offers the development of Hosting solutions for SAP customers and partners.

6 Basic Principles of the mySAP CRM Solution

Overview

mySAP CRM offers companies a platform for customer relationship management that includes both frontend services for customer interaction as well as all necessary integration interfaces such as production, suppliers and financial accounting. As *the* central business function, mySAP CRM is the starting point for many core procedures in mySAP PLM (Product Lifecycle Management), mySAP SCM (Supply Chain Management) and mySAP FI (Financials).

The following basic goals and principles are essential to the development of mySAP CRM:

▶ Product development based on real, practical business scenarios

▶ Support for collaborative business processes with customers, business partners and suppliers, beyond enterprise boundaries

▶ Preparation of analytical procedures for support with decision making in departments and at top management level

▶ Use of the Internet as a vehicle for new customer relationship management

▶ Use of exchanges as a basis for innovative systems of purchasing, sales and collaboration between business partners

▶ Individual employee environments with user portals that can be personalized for many different roles within customer relationship management

▶ Close integration of CRM applications with Microsoft's office productivity tools

▶ Multi-channel operation with consistent support of all available interaction channels

▶ Integration of mobile business – a bringing together of Internet, seamless communication and e-business – into customer relationship management

▶ Open, standardized interfaces for the integration of the CRM solution with any external applications

▶ Possibility of linking several different backend systems which also enables mySAP CRM to work in combination with non-SAP systems in the backend.

SAP offers mySAP CRM specifically developed for the most diverse sectors of industry (see also chapter 5, "mySAP Industry Solutions" on page 46). Processes, forms and documents in marketing, sales and customer service thus always meet the industry specific requirements of the enterprise.

Portal-based mySAP CRM

mySAP CRM was conceived as a portal-based solution right from the beginning. Here we can see the different portal-related characteristics of mySAP CRM:

▶ Ready-made content: over 20 standard CRM roles offered, as well as ready made iViews to parallel presentation of different CRM subapplications in the corresponding display areas of the portal.

▶ Preparation of CRM-relevant structured or unstructured information on the portal.

▶ Web-enabling of CRM applications

The portal capabilities of mySAP CRM are continuously extended by the use of the most up-to-date technology of SAP portals (see also chapter 5, "mySAP Enterprise Portals – User Oriented Integration Platform" on page 41 and chapter 17, "Portal Infrastructure" on page 270).

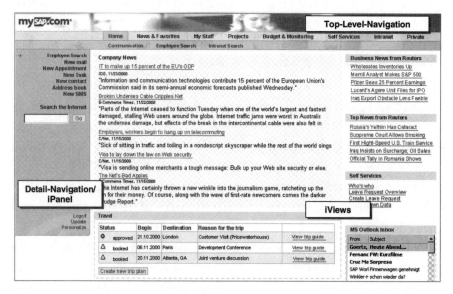

Figure 6.1 Example of portal based mySAP CRM

Role Specific Work Centers

Highly-integrated CRM solutions include different subapplications. Each user has quite specific tasks and looks after individual steps or different sub-processes within the CRM solution. To do so they must, as a rule, have access to different (sub) applications on the Internet and the company intranet. To provide an easy-to-use working environment for each employee that enables them to carry out their specific tasks, it is important to create individual function and information environments. This is done using roles (see also chapter 5, "Role Concept" on page 42). A special user-portal is defined for each role which includes only the functions that are relevant to that particular role in the company.

Each person in the company has several roles. Common to all is the role of *employee*. In addition to this come their task-specific roles. Examples of SAP's CRM user-portals (roles) are briefly described below.

Head of Sales

The head of sales manages a sales and distribution unit. He organizes the sales division and leads his sales personnel. The head of sales implements operative planning. He supports strategic sales planning and must see to it that his sales objectives are in line with company objectives. Important tasks are the analysis and control of all business activities as well as of the sales process. Budget planning and responsibility for the budget also fall within his domain.

Sales Personnel

The sales personnel sell the products and/or services. They initiate contact with customers, work on acquiring new customers and look after existing customers. They see the entire sales process through, starting with the approach of an interested prospective customer or a potential sales lead right through to the closing of a deal, including contract arrangements. The planning of sales activities, the analysis of opportunities (qualified sales leads) and the following up of orders must also be supported by their user-portals.

Service Supervisor

The service supervisor is responsible for the turnover and cost-effectiveness of service measures. He is responsible for service employees and carries out personnel planning. His area of responsibility also includes the strategic planning of services. He initiates and coordinates customer relationship measures in the service department, develops service products and service contracts and analyses satisfaction with service offers, products and measures. If so required, the service supervisor can also take over the processing of particular customer inquiries.

Cross-Application Roles

Apart from the user specific roles there are also roles that are not assigned to any particular application. SAP examples of such cross-application roles are:

- ESS (Employee Self Service)
- Recording and processing of problem notification
- Creation and display of classifications for tasks of standardization within the company, for example in the setting of standards
- The creation, processing, display and search of documents

ESS makes it possible for employees to display and maintain the data stored on them in the system, for example, address, time management and compensation management, physical inventory data on devices used, and so on.

Integration of Office Functions

Right from the beginning, mySAP CRM has been designed for close integration with Microsoft Office products. These products come into operation in diverse mySAP CRM applications – for example for activity management – and can be called up directly from the particular mySAP CRM application.

Microsoft Project and Microsoft Excel are, for example, used in Marketing Management (compare chapter 7, "Marketing Planning and Campaign Management" on page 59). The marketing manager can plan marketing campaigns in mySAP CRM and reproduce them in a Microsoft Project project plan. Any possible changes or additions – for example the insertion of necessary activities – can subsequently be made in Microsoft Project and synchronized with mySAP CRM at a later time. The same principle applies for the integration of Microsoft Excel. The user can do budget planning for marketing initiatives in an Excel table. The budgets planned in this way are automatically available in mySAP CRM as projected figures and can at any time be compared against the accumulating actual costs in the finance system in the context of the execution of marketing initiatives.

The planned integration of mySAP CRM with Microsoft Outlook also follows the SAP principle of making working with the system as simple and intuitive as possible. mySAP CRM makes it possible for the user to exploit information necessary for his task – for example address details and company data on business partners, activities and tasks as well as schedule dates – in a working environment that he knows and is familiar with. Online, the data provided are at all times synchronized with information contained in mySAP CRM and allow the user a complete and up to date view of customer records.

In a further step, the integration of Microsoft Outlook with Microsoft Excel and Microsoft Project make it possible to process complete business procedures in a further step offline and to synchronize them with mySAP CRM at a later time. For example, as part of planning a campaign, a marketing manager can include the budgeting in the form of a Microsoft Project task in the project plan and afterwards forward it to the responsible employee using Microsoft Outlook. The employee in question will be informed by a task in his inbox and can work on the budget plan in Microsoft Excel. At the next online connection the data will be loaded into mySAP CRM from Microsoft Excel and the task receives the corresponding status. The marketing manager will automatically be informed of the conclusion of the budgeting by an entry to his inbox. At the same time the project plan is updated in Microsoft Project.

Overall, it can be said that the integration of Office products with mySAP CRM makes for significant improvements in productivity, thanks to the ease of use, the fact that there is no need for costly training and the high rate of acceptance by users because of the familiar and easy to use system environment.

7 mySAP CRM – Comprehensive Functions Through the Entire Customer Interaction Cycle

The Phases of the Customer Interaction Cycle

mySAP CRM brings employees, business partners, business processes and technologies together in an optimal customer relationship management – something which occurs through all four phases of the Customer Interaction Cycle [Siemers 2001]. These four phases are:

▶ **Customer Engagement**
Identification of potential customers and advancement of same to (first-time) buyers

▶ **Business Transaction**
Conclusion of business agreements

▶ **Order Fulfillment**
Sales order processing, that is, fulfillment of the supplier commitments arising from the business agreement (sales order) and invoicing of services

▶ **Customer Service**
Provision of after sales services

The following chapters present the individual functions of mySAP CRM for all phases of the Customer Interaction Cycle.

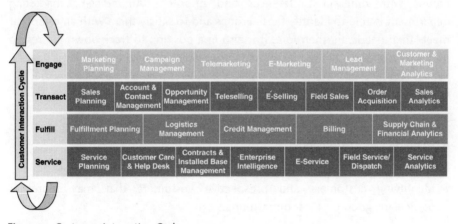

Figure 7.1 Customer Interaction Cycle

Customer Engagement

Overview

Nobody knows an enterprise's customers better than the marketing department. True or false?

Marketing managers who would tend, with convinced spontaneity, to answer *true* should ask themselves two questions. Firstly: Why is my competitor more successful? The market leader – and there can be only one – can of course skip this first question, but not the second: Do I know those who *could* be customers of my company?

A critical examination of the market situation gives rise to further questions: How can a company guarantee that their customers of today will still be customers tomorrow? How can they be quick to react to the changing needs of their customers? How can new customer groups be identified, won and maintained for the long term? None of these are fundamentally new questions in the business of marketing. However, the time left to companies to find a strategic, conclusive answer is dramatically shorter.

The consequence of this is: Either an enterprise *can* react quickly enough or the customer finds another supplier who can. *Off-the-peg* products or services are out – the demand is for goods and services that match the customer's requirement profile as closely as possible. It is a long time since the clientele could be considered as a homogeneous group. Rather they are made up of individual groups with different preferences and priorities. An efficient marketing department is able to identify these groups and to satisfy them with an offer that meets their needs. Furthermore: It is also in a position to track down interested potential customers in the market and in this way gain new customer groups.

Marketing in mySAP CRM

mySAP CRM Marketing supports three important objectives:

▶ Winning new customers
▶ The development and strengthening of existing customer relationships
▶ Identifying customers and prospective customers that may represent particularly good business opportunities

The fact that marketing always works on *the front line* emphasizes the importance of having a software solution that permits those responsible to react early, quickly, flexibly and efficiently to changes in the market and that will also allow those in charge to identify and personally address the target groups, within the clientele as a whole, that are of particular importance for the company. To achieve this, six main components are available. They will be explained in greater detail below:

▶ Marketing planning and campaign management

▶ Lead management

▶ Segmenting of business partners

▶ Allocation planning

▶ Product proposals

▶ Personalized communication

Marketing Planning and Campaign Management

With the help of these components, marketing activities can be planned and campaigns can be launched. The core tool for processing marketing plans and campaigns is the Marketing Planner. This makes for a smooth exchange of data, not only within the CRM system, but also with other SAP components and other applications.

Marketing plans can be structured hierarchically, for example, according to region or product, and be given a start date and end date in Marketing Planner. An important part of the solution is that it is compatible with standard Office products. Therefore, in an online/offline scenario, marketing projects could be exported to Microsoft Project for graphical schedule processing and then later re-imported into the CRM system. Finally, the campaign products are assigned a target group and conditions.

On saving, the campaign is automatically stored in the Business Information Warehouse so that key indicator planning (planned costs versus planned revenue) can be carried out. If cost control is needed, the campaign can be transferred to the SAP R/3 project system where it is available as an account assignment object. Actual costs and revenue can then be entered directly into mySAP Financials.

Finally the campaign is passed to the chosen communication channel and the target group is addressed via e-mail, fax, SMS (short message service), letter, mobile sales application or via the interaction center. All communications channels automatically consider the conditions set down for the campaign when giving out prices.

▶ **(E-)Mail**
The customer receives a personalized e-mail, an SMS, a fax or a letter with an (optional) link to a web store. The choice of products in the store can be determined by the product catalog assigned to the campaign. On making an

Figure 7.2 Planning a marketing campaign

order, an association is made between the order and the campaign via the link. This is useful for the later analysis of the campaign.

▶ **Mobile Sales**

The campaign is replicated on the field sales employees' laptops, which ensures that all the necessary information is available to them. A sales action is generated for each customer in the target group at the same time. Should an order come in as a result of an action, a reference to the campaign is automatically produced.

▶ **Interaction Center**

On passing the campaign on to the Interaction Center a calling list is produced, the items of which are distributed out among the agents. They carry out the calls assigned to them. On the entry of an order, once again, a reference is made to the campaign.

Trade Promotion Management

The customer is also approached directly within the context of campaigns or actions to promote sales, something which represents a cost-intensive mandatory exercise for all consumer goods producers. Within the context of such promotions, customers are approached right where they make their purchasing decision: at the Point of Sale (POS). What a consumer finds before him on a visit to a store – the washing detergent package with the special red bow, a cleverly arranged, eye-catching display, a gigantic chocolate bar or a stand with free food samples – is the result of an extremely complex process. The whole process starts out as an idea in the marketing department and if it actually reaches the customer in the store, then all links in a consumer-goods producer's value added chain have been involved along the way.

No other sector of industry offers a wider range of products than the consumer goods sector: It includes everything from food and drinks, to household goods, personal hygiene products and drug-store articles to shoes or electronic devices. Competition in these markets is intense and the battle for customers is also fought out at the point of sale. According to reliable estimates, the consumer goods industry invests between 130 and 160 billion dollars *every year* on cleverly devised measures to promote trade and sales. The customer can be approached in three different ways:

▶ Via the media (radio, TV, billboards, newspaper supplements, advertising on public transport)

▶ Personally, as a user (mailings, product presentations at home with friends or neighbors)

▶ In POS promotions (displays, demonstrations, sample tasting stands, special price events)

The SAP solution described below, which at the time of going to press was still being developed, will support the entire sales promotion process (*Trade Promotion Management*).

As is the case for other mySAP CRM components, Trade Promotion Management also displays a closed cycle. It supports:

▶ Strategic (overall) planning in the enterprise

▶ Field planning

▶ Customer sell-in and negotiation

▶ Campaign execution and validation

▶ Analytical evaluation of the campaign. The circle ends here and the planning cycle for a new campaign can begin.

Trade Promotion Management contains the following important process steps:

▶ **Strategic planning**
Setting all relevant parameters such as size of budget and trade volume of a sales promotion: The sale of which products should be promoted in which regions, in which stores and over what period? Offers to retailers include payment compensations and terms of payment.

▶ **Field Sales Planning**
On the basis of the existing objectives for trade volumes, budget limits and trade structure, the field sales team can produce a turnover forecast for each dealer, off-line, taking promoted and non-promoted products into account. The field sales team has access to supplier and consumer data to assist in setting optimal timing and appropriate volumes.

The costs arising from sales promotion activities are compared against the additional revenue achieved.

▶ **Volume Forecasting**
How will the promotion affect the sales figures of the product at the retail outlet? Does it influence the delivery time from manufacturer to dealer? Will the measures also have an effect on the manufacturer's products that are not on promotion? Answers to these questions make the inclusion of previously gained point-of-sale data necessary and they make it possible to compare the influence of different actions on consumption and profitability, before the relevant product budgets are assigned. The forecast for the overall volume gives an overview of monthly sales figures and plays a part in demand planning.

On the basis of forecast data the SAP system produces standard charts and graphics, which support the Key Account Manager for the sales promotion. In addition the system has access to models for analyzing the effects of sales promotion measures. In this way the best time for an activity can always be determined. This step towards *fact-based sales* contributes to optimizing the sales promotion.

▶ **Clear invoices**
Clearly presented invoices are often half the analysis. The transparent presentation of an invoice with "clean" billing documents and clearly presented discounts and invoice reductions is an important analysis tool for the salesperson.

▶ **Execution**
Activities for field sales employees are generated from planning and their schedules are updated. This schedule makes it possible for field sales employees to promote sales on the spot, for example by having the product better placed in the store or working towards having the dealer order increased

quantities of a product in time for a planned promotional activity. Once planning and validation have been agreed, the normal business process starts. Orders are accepted and executed. This includes logistic execution, that is, the customer is supplied, the goods issue is recorded and finally invoiced. After invoicing, the data is passed on to cost accounting, financial accounting and the SAP Business Information Warehouse.

Once data has been transferred to the SAP BW, they are made available for the planning of future campaigns.

▶ **Evaluation and Analysis**
So, at the end of the day, what has this sales promotion activity achieved? How do the current figures for the quantities sold and profitability look when compared with the planned figures? What figures or values could be calculated during the campaign? What conclusions can be drawn from this? Do they show a need for changes in the planning of the next campaign?

mySAP CRM Trade Promotion Management supports the entire life cycle of the promotion process. It makes for a shorter planning cycle, a well-directed delegating of tasks, more precise sales forecasts and helps avoid having stores lying vacant. To this end, Trade Promotion Management brings together all parties that play a role in a trade or sales promotion activity.

Lead Management

No customer is static. Over time customers change, imperceptibly but continuously. Their habits and preferences change with them, as do their income and their requirements. These changes are also significant to the life cycle of a customer relationship – they provide opportunities for an enterprise.

The business world is also in the grip of constant change: Bookshops ask publishers for audiobooks – something still relatively unknown just a few years ago – retail chains are opting strongly for organic products, insurance brokers offer combination policies for pension plans, drugstores discover detox products.

Such changes in the client structure, which crop up umpteen times every day, offer enterprises new trade opportunities – if they are able to recognize them. This objective – to track down market opportunities – is supported by Lead Management in mySAP CRM Marketing. With the help of Lead Management potentially valuable *existing* customers or *new* potential customers can be identified. Lead Management allows an enterprise to keep an eye on existing customers, to gain new customers and to qualify their interests in a product or service. Lead Management prepares the ground for sales.

Leads are tomorrow's potential customers or today's customers that one would like to interest in other types of products. As soon as a customer comes into contact with the enterprise via a channel of communication (dealers, telephone, fax or Internet), they can be identified as a lead. A lead is, for example:

▶ The owner of a compact car who makes arrangements with their dealer for a test drive in a medium-sized model

▶ A customer who already gets their electricity supply from a utility company, who makes a request via Internet for a quotation for water supply

▶ A sports equipment dealer who asks the manufacturer for information on new products

▶ A bank customer who seeks investment advice

▶ A medium sized enterprise that wishes to buy their company cars in future instead of leasing

Leads can be created at any time – every time a customer or interested party comes into contact with an enterprise. Leads can also be created for particular customers in a target group (considered *High Potential* regarding sales turnover) within the context of a marketing campaign. However a lead always gives the employees of an enterprise a message: An eye must be kept on these customers and they must be "looked after", because they offer a *potential* opportunity for additional sales

Before a Lead becomes an opportunity, a *concrete* sales prospect, a qualifying process is carried out, during which the lead is allocated different statuses: *lost*, *in progress* or *won*. This classification can be made on the basis of indices, by direct questioning or right at the creation of a lead. As soon as a lead that is 'in progress' reaches a particular classification step it can be converted into an opportunity and be passed on for further processing in sales. Using the Monitoring that is integrated into CRM Marketing, an eye can also be kept on potential customers in the future. With the help of strategic reports the success of leads can be appraised and this can be used to support medium and long-term decision making processes.

Segmenting of Business Partners (Segment Builder)

In this age of Internet and mobile telephony, marketing is provided with an incomparably large (and cost effective) apparatus for reaching customers: e-mail and SMS have also become new and widely used channels of communication, practically over night. Web forms and clickstream analysis (analysis of navigation behavior on Internet sites) give marketing additional and, to an extent, very precise information on customers. Marketing departments spare no efforts in acquiring as much customer related information as possible to then use it for personalized marketing activities. Because the *well directed* approach of a customer increases the probability of making a sale, increases customer satisfaction and strengthens a customer's relationship with the enterprise. It also reduces costs because it minimizes scattering losses.

Segment Builder in mySAP CRM Marketing offers extremely helpful support for selecting target groups suited to a campaign. With this application, target groups can be filtered out of the customer master, with characteristics (often shared) which make them destined, so to speak, for the purchase of a particular product.

An Example of Customer Segmenting

A fictitious, albeit practical example should help to explain the work with Segment Builder: A car manufacturer has established that drivers of their compact-class cars usually change to a medium-sized model when they are between the ages of 38 and 45. 85 percent of these drivers are male, 15 percent are female. In addition, when they change model, two-thirds of customers opt for automatic transmission and almost half for climate control – both features which are usually supplied at an extra cost. Surprisingly, the car upgrading mentality among customers in the south and west of California is significantly more pronounced than among those living in the north and east of the country. Therefore, the marketing department plans to address the customers who will potentially be willing to change models directly. With the otherwise freely configurable medium-sized car, the equipment features *Automatic transmission* and *Climate control* are offered as a package that represents a 15 percent reduction in the regular price for these extras.

Marketing employees can call Segment Builder directly from Marketing Planner. Once they have opened it, they set the characteristics and the characteristic values, on the basis of which the target group should be selected from the database. In principle, these characteristics can come from different sources:

▶ From customer master data (age, gender)
▶ From mySAP CRM Marketing itself, if they have specifically been put there for marketing purposes (for example, hobbies)
▶ From the SAP Business Information Warehouse, if they are changeable data (for example, amount of monthly car sales)

Because the marketing campaign – and therefore also the segment building – can be intended for both the end customer and also the dealer or business partner of an enterprise, they are all grouped under the term *business partner*.

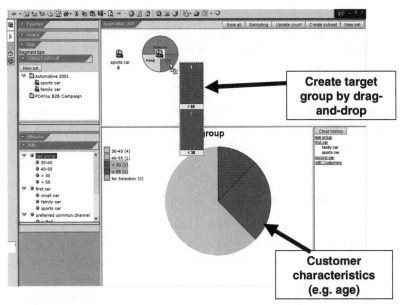

Figure 7.3 Graphic Interaction with Segment Builder

Molding a customer profile

A marketing or customer profile is molded from the characteristics or their characteristic values. This can be done very simply using Drag&Drop on the screen: You click on the relevant characteristics and drag them with the mouse into the profile-molding area. The characteristics combined in a profile then describe the business partner.

In our example *all* characteristics are included in the customer profile. It is also conceivable that there may be a longer list of characteristics which could be molded into various customer profiles in *any* meaningful combination. The marketing department could also decide to present the offer of a change of model just to women in the south of Germany: This second customer profile would thus be differentiated from the first with respect to the characteristic values *gender* and *zip code*. The target groups resulting from the database balancing, who finally become the addressees of the marketing campaign can be contacted via different communication channels: While men are personally contacted by the Interaction Center or the car manufacturer's business partners, women receive a well written letter from the head of sales together with a give-away.

Testing the size of customer segments with samples

The marketing department of the car manufacturer is undecided whether the target group *women* should be approached at all and – if so – in a comparatively costly way. Is this expenditure advisable in view of the expected size of the target group? Marketing therefore defines a sample for the female customer profile. mySAP CRM Marketing offers a whole range of sampling rules as standard, which can if necessary be expanded with enterprise-specific rules. Generally a sample is based on an absolute figure or a percentage value of the population.

Each sample is a selection of all the elements of the target group that are to be expected, based on the customer profile that has been molded. If the sample has 1,000 data records, 25 percent of which match the customer profile, then we can estimate that in the entire customer master data record a quarter of all customers correspond to the profile that has been molded. If a sample is taken with, for example, 2 percent as a predetermined value, then the target group for the campaign – in accordance with the percentage value of the samples – will be around fifty times bigger.

Working with samples, which is integrated into both Segment Builder and SAP Business Information Warehouse can, for example, answer the question as to whether the customer profile will correspond to enough customers at all, before the actual profile building – during which the characteristics are compared against the *entire* contents of the database. In a 2 percent sample (based on a population of 5,000,000 units) if only 25 percent of the sample data records (25,000 units) possess the set combination of characteristics, then the profile molded would correspond to around fifty times as many customers (1,250,000). Perhaps the marketing department considers this figure too low for a campaign. They can then decide to shape a different customer profile.

Forecasting the return quota with the RFM method

Using the well known RFM (Recency, Frequency, Monetary) analysis (see chapter 13, "Application Scenarios" on page 225) a forecast can be made on the expected return quota, but only if empirical values are available for a similar campaign. In this case the RFM analysis makes it possible to forecast the profitability and return on investment (ROI) of a marketing campaign (see figure 7.4). One restriction on the significance of RFM analyses is that it should be noted that they are derived from customer behavior gauged *in the past*, a-priori statements for a *present day* campaign. According to the business environment, this assumed context can be significant or may be practically non-existent. mySAP CRM therefore offers possibilities for checking the significance of RFM analyses.

In particular, for marketing in enterprises with numerically large customer databases – such as publishing houses or insurance companies, banks or utility companies, mail order firms or travel organizations – segmenting business partners makes it possible to track down profitable customer groups, to whom a well-directed, tailor-made offer can then be presented.

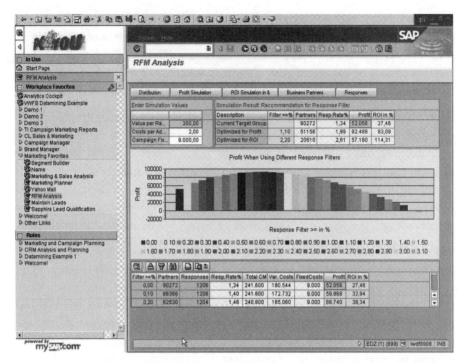

Figure 7.4 Forecasting the profitability of a marketing campaign with the RFM method

Allocation Planning

Allocation Planning is an application in mySAP CRM Marketing that has been specially developed for the Business-to-Business sector. It gives support for the allocation of limited quantities (products, for instance) to a particular number of business partners (such as retailers).

Allocation Planning is linked with Marketing Planner and Segment Builder, as well as with the Interaction Center, the Business Information Warehouse and mobile applications.

In general the beginning and end of a marketing campaign are established. In addition to the budget, the number of products necessary for the duration of the campaign is also available. Therefore, in the context of the campaign the products are prepared in a pre-determined quantity, for the first time or in addition to regular production – all the while keeping an eye on costs. In both cases however it will be a limited quantity which must be divided among the busiess partners of the target group – to the best possible advantage. There is little point in sending 50 of the latest generation TV sets to a dealer in a small town as part of a product promotion, when barely ten sets would sell in a month.

Allocation Planning divides the limited available product quantity on the basis of standard allocation methods:

▶ **Fixed Value**
The allocation quantity is established at a fixed value without taking other factors into account. If for a regional promotion there are 20,000 products available for 100 agents, then each sales agent receives 200 units. This method of procedure could be considered for testing the acceptance of a new product in general or in a particular region.

▶ **Attribute method**
The allocation quantity is decided based on an attribute in the business partner master data. These attributes could be the location, the size of the enterprise or the monthly turnover – that is to say *characteristics* of the business partner that would suggest a greater probability of sales. Therefore, a television manufacturer would allocate a much larger number of television sets to a city center dealer with over 5,000 square feet of sales floor area than to a store measuring just over 1,000 square feet in an outlying location. The calculation of this additional allocation is carried out – on the total quantity available – on the basis of certain attributes.

▶ **Visibility method**
With the help of this method it can be guaranteed that with constant replenishing of diminishing product quantities throughout the duration of the campaign, a specific quantity of the product is always available – that is to say *visible*. The visibility method is based on available sales figures, to which an extra percentage rate is added: This *lift factor* makes allowances for an expected increase in sales as a result of the campaign. The application of this method could be considered for a product that has just been introduced and for which a campaign has been launched, to increase turnover or in an effort to halt falling sales figures.

Using what are referred to as Business Add-Ins, enterprises can also define their own allocation methods

With the optional extra *Ranking* function, business partners can be allocated a priority. Therefore, it can be ensured that for example, important customers receive more consideration – and customers with low turnover can possibly go without if quantities are limited.

Both Allocation Planning and Ranking are based on methods and rules which are determined practically in the standard functions of mySAP CRM Marketing. Both applications can, however, be adapted to the specific requirements of an enterprise with a whole range of Business Add-Ins. The results of Allocation Planning and of Ranking can be changed manually at any time.

Product Proposals

For marketing experts the world of e-commerce is an Aladdin's cave. The geographical area of web stores is always global, the number of potential customers can be measured in millions. Companies that are in the position to give their target groups a clear profile can make direct and personal contact with their customers and make them tailor-made offers. This does not mean however, that the customer's potential for the company has been exhausted until the next order.

On the contrary: Now the customer has to be retained, satisfied, bound long term to the company and turnover potential has to be sounded out. These goals are – simultanaeously – supported by the *Product Proposals* application in mySAP CRM Marketing, and also via the communication channels of telesales, interaction center and mobile services. It automates not only cross-selling scenarios and up- and down-selling activities but also puts together a specific number (*n*) of products in *Top-n-Product lists*.

Product Association Rules

How does this automatic product proposal function – which has proved to be a highly effective tool particularly in online scenarios and in the interaction center – work? The relationship between different products can be defined with the help of what are known as *product association rules*. The rules contain, on the one hand, those products, *for which* one or more others should be recommended, and on the other hand they contain *those dependent products* that should be recommended. Using this invisible association, further product recommendations can be made for purchase with a chosen product.

▶ **Cross-selling**
A customer orders a computer. He is also offered a printer or a useful software package: Perhaps he happens to need a new printer at that moment in time.

▶ **Up- or down-selling**
A customer orders a fax machine. A more expensive fax machine with a scanner function is suggested. Perhaps he is not aware that this type of multi-functional fax machine exists or perhaps the fax machine is too expensive for him. So as not to lose the customer, he can be recommended a simpler (and less expensive) machine: It is better to have a customer with a lower sales volume than for that customer to be lost to a competitor.

Product association rules can be freely defined but are compelling in their application. The most commonly used rule is probably: If A is selected then B is also proposed. But more ambitious variations are also possible: If A and B are selected, but C is not selected at the same time, then only product F is suggested.

For the automatic generation of cross-selling suggestions several product association rules can be combined in a method schema. They are then automatically read and analyzed and evaluated with the resulting products being combined in a special procedure. The cross-selling suggestions are automatically shown on a web store as soon as a customer has selected a product, they could of course also appear on the screen of a telesales agent or on the hand-held display of a sales employee.

Lists of Products

A further possibility for suggesting additional products for a customer to buy involves the use of product lists.

Due to the fact that they belong to a characteristic group (for example: *Age 20 to 30 years old*) business partners can be assigned to one or more target groups, which show this characteristic (among others). By evaluating the sales data from the Business Information Warehouse a list of the best selling products (bestseller lists) can be compiled for each target group and be shown for all customers in the particular target group.

The compilation of a top-product list – whether it is a Top Ten or a Top Fifty – may seem arbitrary, but is actually based on real sales figures. It reflects the product preferences of all customers of a target group who present a particular characteristic. It is true that it may at first seem erroneous that some men who buy diapers also bring a six-pack of beer to the supermarket checkout, but in fact measured sales figures do indeed imply such a probability. Ultimately the product combination in a best-selling-product list is as random as the contents of a shopping cart. But because they reflect the product preferences of a very large number of customers with at least one identical characteristic, they can at least be considered useful for recognizing trends.

Apart from Top-n-product lists, the compilation of which can be changed relatively quickly, *permanent* product lists can also be maintained. They can contain products for which no sales data is available, or warehouse stocks that should be sold at a reduced price (*special offer*).

Personalized Communication

"Dear Sir or Madam" – such an impersonal, antiquated greeting should make the hair on the back of any marketing professional's neck stand on end. There is practically nothing worse in their business than to give customers the impression that they are an anonymous variable in the sale of industrial mass production. No: The customer deserves the undivided – personal – attention and esteem of an enterprise. In deregulated industry sectors and globalized markets a whole new status is attached to the customer: He stands in the center, bar none. Marketing professionals know: The customer *is* number one, and wants to be treated as such.

As the last functional link in the process chain of marketing or campaign planning, personalization is of the utmost importance. After careful cost and schedule planning, painstaking segmentation of business partners, optimal allocation planning and finely perfected product proposals, the well structured campaign is launched and the customer is addressed directly and personally. The most suitable communication channel with which to reach the customer is determined in Marketing Planner. Telephone or fax, letter, SMS or e-mail.

The functional scope of personalized communication is of considerable application to the user. The latter can:

▶ **Produce mailing presentations**
With the help of different tools such presentations – compiled in plain text or HTML format – can be configured in almost any way, both regarding content and visually, and can be sent as an e-mail, fax, letter or SMS. Mailings support a visually attractive message design.

▶ **Produce mail forms (personalized standard letters)**
The contents of the message can be tailored to fit the customer profile of the recipient. To do so, place holders that represent the characteristics of the customer profile are added to the text blocks that make up the message. The data behind the characteristics are first replaced by the most suitable versions of the form for this particular point in time ("Best wishes on your 40th birthday"). Typical personalization can for example mean that each customer is addressed in his language of correspondence – a very important feature for pan-European marketing.

▶ **Preview and test mailings**
With the aid of the preview function a mailing can be checked before it is finally sent, to ensure that it meets the content and visual requirements. With the test-mail function you can check to see if e-mails are sent out correctly.

▶ **Monitor mailings**

With the help of mailing lists it can be ascertained whether mails have been transferred without any problems, whether links to other web sites integrated into e-mails have been clicked on or if there were any errors in mails.

▶ **"Track" e-mails**

With the integration of some links (such as to a web store) in an e-mail a *Tracking Identity* can be inserted which can help to establish whether or not the recipient has visited the website associated with the link. Then on visiting the site the recipient can, for example, be greeted by name.

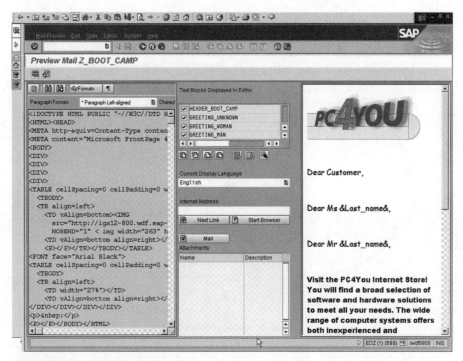

Figure 7.5 Personalizing e-mails

Business Transaction

Overview

The *Transact* Phase, the second step of the Customer Interaction Cycle, is devoted to sales management and the actual selling process. In this phase, which is closely related with the *Engage*, *Fulfill* and *Service* phases, sales processes run with the objective of reaching transaction agreements with customers.

Apart from the organization tools

▶ Territory management

▶ Activity management

the mySAP CRM sales management solution offers support for all planning, execution and control activities in Sales and Distribution:

▶ Sales planning

▶ Account and contact management

▶ Opportunity management

▶ Order acquisition

▶ Sales analytics

Figure 7.6 Transact phase in the Customer Interaction Cycle

Figure 7.6 demonstrates how the transact phase presents its own, closed cycle within the Customer Interaction Cycle. Information and data on potential customers and orders as well as on sales organizations, teams and areas are entered directly to the planning phase. Here – with support from the marketing department if necessary – strategies are developed to provide sales personnel with all the instruments and information needed for a successful sales process.

In day-to-day practice the steps of a selling process rarely run in linear fashion. Often, complex requirements with disruptions and dependencies have to be taken into account in individual phases. In addition, each phase has its own cycles which are also the result of planning, action and analysis. Interfaces between sales management and other business areas and also with external partners and competitors must also be taken into account.

After the conclusion of a contract all details are recorded and are then available for analysis and evaluation. On this basis planners and decision makers can, for example, determine which products have been successful in which areas, how often opportunities are converted into orders and in which segments additional sales resources or initiatives are needed.

Territory Management

Territory management refers to the planning and structuring of sales organizations according to individual sales areas (*Territories*). A territory is not necessarily a geographical area, but can also be used to describe an area of responsibility which may also depend on, for example, customers, products or services.

Territory management supports the shaping of functional organization structures, for example to depict the hierarchy of departments, the report structure and the responsibilities in a sales organization. Employees can be assigned to different regions, groups or offices. Workflow management uses the data from territory management for the automatic forwarding of transaction activities.

Example In a particular business territory a lead is generated. mySAP CRM uses the rules defined in territory management to find out the corresponding telesales agents, based on the enterprise's zip code. Because this is an important customer an automatically generated workflow sends the information directly to a premium telesales agent who can then call the lead to categorize it, that is to find out if there is a genuine chance of sale here.

If there seems to be, mySAP CRM automatically assigns an appropriate Key Account Manager for this customer. The Key Account Manager receives the lead in his in-box and knows that this sale must be given priority. He can see when the last contact with this customer took place, what was discussed and what information has already been sent to the customer.

Activity Management

Activity management is a general component of mySAP CRM and supports (sales) employees in the organization of their daily work. For example, it supplies answers to questions such as:

▶ What appointments do I have next week?

▶ For when should I plan the visit to Ms. Miller?

▶ Who can stand in for the sick colleague in the export department?

For example, a sales employee has the possibility of having a look at the result of a telephone call after the first visit to a customer. Activity management offers the head of sales a fast and clear-cut overview of all activities that have taken place in his department over a particular period of time.

Activity management includes the following elements:

▶ **Calendar**
Activities are recorded as appointments in the calendars of all those people for whom this is deemed necessary regarding the business transaction.

▶ **Documents for transaction activities**
Documents include information on business partner addresses, times and dates and any related documents such as product information, letters to the customer, marketing brochures, and so on.

▶ **Activity results and the reasons for them**
For analytical purposes it is important to record what has happened with an activity and why. Therefore, together with an activity, it can be recorded and evaluated why the activity was carried out, its status, and whether or not it was successful and why.

In transaction activities, details are kept on numerous interactions between the enterprise and customers. On the other hand, employees can organize both tasks waiting to be dealt with and private appointments. All activities of the employees in a department can be administered quickly and easily with just one operation.

Activities can be listed as subsequent documents for a large number of other business procedures which concern opportunities, leads, customer orders or contracts for example. Each activity also offers a quick link to the business partner cockpit (see "Account and Contact Management" on page 79) with customer information and the history of interactions with each customer.

Working With Activities

Activities are related to all aspects of the daily selling processes. Activities can be entered at any time to document an interaction with a customer. The activities appear automatically in the calendar of all employees listed as partners in the activity. In this way all partners involved are informed at all times of conversations, customer visits and events in their department. Apart from the information sheet that is available in every activity, it can also be established which employee has been in contact with a particular business partner when and what status has been assigned to these activities.

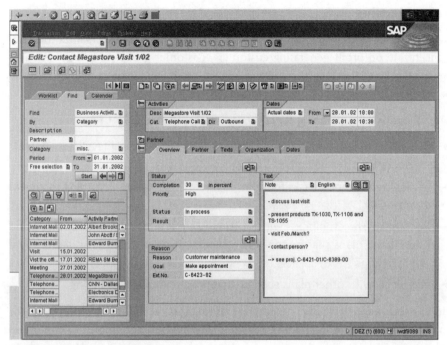

Figure 7.7 Example of a typical activity

Monitoring Activities

In addition to further documents, activities offer a reliable history of the results obtained by employees and a prognosis possibility for future tasks. mySAP CRM has reporting tools with which individual activities can be followed closely. Two types of report are available:

▶ **Operative**

This type of report offers, for example, all open transaction activities for a particular business partner, or all business partners with whom no contact has been had during the last month. The employee in question can call up these reports on the system directly and view them in his portal. In this way he can find out what has to be planned for next week or where there is a need for action.

▶ **Analytical**

Reports on this level give information on how much time has been spent on engaging a customer and what results have been achieved. Therefore, it can be established if the efforts of following this lead have been worthwhile. This type of evaluation is possible using SAP Business Information Warehouse.

Sales Planning

With effective sales planning, simulation and forecasting sales organizations can concentrate on profit generating customers, customer groups and products. This helps sales to convert existing customers into profitable customers and to decide which leads could possibly become profit generating customers.

The following sales planning functions are available in mySAP CRM:

▶ Multi-dimensional planning with flexibly designed planning levels for strategic and operative sales objectives

▶ Personalized planning tasks for individual sales employees, according to area of responsibility

▶ Comprehensive toolbox with planning methods for modifying and restructuring plans such as top-down allocation, assessments, simulations and copy functions

▶ Integration with other plans such as strategy and financial planning

Bottom-up and top-down planning completed with special planning for individual customer contacts and activities give the best conditions for continued sales success. With top-down planning, guidelines are specified downwards to the smallest sales unit. Bottom-up planning, on the other hand, condenses the plan figures upwards along the sales organization hierarchy. To do this, structure information from territory management is used.

Sales planning is supported by the figures in sales analyses. For example, it can be seen which products were successful in which regions and which customers made the biggest contribution to profits. On the basis of this information, future turnover figures can be forecast and decisions can be made on whether or not to use individual sales employees.

With the aim of making sales planning as uncomplicated as possible mySAP CRM user interfaces offer different views according to each task area. These include a Microsoft Office front-end, which is tailored to meet the needs of sales, a web front-end and a special planning screen. Particular attention should also be paid to occasional users working locally with the planning function. Microsoft Excel has been integrated into the user interfaces especially for this user group.

Sales planning is integrated with both SAP Business Information Warehouse (SAP BW) and with SAP Strategic Enterprise Management (SAP SEM). SAP BW ensures consistency of data and high performance data evaluation while SAP SEM supports top management with planning and monitoring.

Integrated Sales Planning for Key Accounts

To deal with the special needs of Key Account Management, SAP delivers *Integrated Sales Planning for Key Accounts*

Key account managers have a good overview of the sales prospects of their company's products with their key customers. Frequently the key account manager and the customer – for example, a purchaser for a chain of warehouses – consider together how revenue and sales will develop.

Planned figures, past data, market and customer data as well as product hierarchies, prices and campaigns form the basis for this planning, which is carried out offline. The key account manager can call up current figures on his laptop to discuss planning for the coming year with his customer at the customer's premises. The results (planned figures, campaigns and price conditions) are subsequently uploaded again.

Account and Contact Management

mySAP CRM Account and Contact Management administers all relevant information on business partners and supports cross-enterprise cooperation. All employees have access to the information and thus know about all customers relevant to them at all times.

In Account and Contact Management information can be administered by people other than those involved in the sales process, including:

▶ Customers
▶ Leads
▶ Suppliers
▶ Component suppliers
▶ Employees

The data is stored centrally as business partner master data. Duplicate tests ensure that each business partner is in the system only once for a particular role. The information in the master data contains address information, contact people, relationships between different people and credit, payment and delivery information.

All employees have direct access to all master data information when interacting with customers. When a customer calls the interaction center, for example, the agent can check the customer's telephone and address data and if necessary update them. To do so the agent neither has to leave his personal working environment on screen nor inform any other employees of changes made.

Account and Contact Management is also capable of storing information on individual employees and can therefore always provide an overview of the qualifications, expertise and experience of employees. With the help of organization management suitable employees can then be assigned to particular customers, projects of interaction centers.

To make it easier for all employees involved to access the data on business partners that is relevant to them, mySAP CRM offers a Business Partner Cockpit.

Business Partner Cockpit

The business partner cockpit gives sales managers and employees easy access to the vast amount of information stored on business partners. The following channels are available for this:

▶ List of the most important business partners

▶ Quick links to related transactions, for example the creation of activities

▶ Information sheet with master and transaction data on each business partner. Examples of transaction data in the information sheet are:

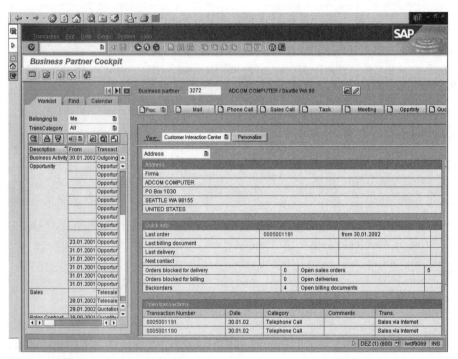

Figure 7.8 The Business Partner Cockpit

- The latest activities recorded for this customer, such as telephone calls or e-mails
- Open customer orders or contracts
- Possible problems, for example, delivery delays

With this information an employee has immediate entry to all past operations such as deliveries or payments. Before calling a customer to offer a new product he knows, for example, that delivery problems have occurred in the past with relation to this customer and he can prepare the conversation accordingly.

The information recorded in the business partner cockpit can be adapted for different groups of employees according to their information requirements. Therefore, for example agents in the interaction center receive information that is important for processing of any questions or problems from a customer that is on the line, whereas a sales manager would use the business partner cockpit more for analytical purposes. In this way all employees, no matter how or where they work, are informed of the entire interaction history of the customer in question at all times.

Opportunity Management – Structured Sales Methodology

An opportunity is a *qualified sales prospect*, that is to say a validated possibility for a company to sell products or services. Opportunities can come from leads or be directly created by a sales employee, for example as a result of a conversation at a trade fair, of an advertising action or a bid invitation.

Example Via his Personal Digital Assistant (PDA), a member of the sales team is informed of a new and very interesting opportunity that must be worked on immediately. He checks the business partner cockpit of the interested party and in this way finds out what customer service, marketing and sales activities have already taken place. He quickly checks the Internet to find out about the most important competitors. Via e-mail he requests more precise information from the marketing department and informs them of the opportunity.

Opportunities are fully documented in mySAP CRM, including:

- A description of the party interested in buying
- A description of the product or service enquired about
- The prospective customer's budget
- The potential sale volume
- An estimated probability of getting an order

Over the continuing course of the sales cycle, this information can be adapted, confirmed, completed and finally passed on to mySAP Business Intelligence for evaluation.

According to analysis by the Swiss Infoteam, Sales Process Consulting AG, in eight out of ten cases where a sales project is rejected, the real reasons for rejection lie in the sales process itself. Common key problems are:

▶ The real decision makers are identified and contacted too late.

▶ Efforts are concentrated on the wrong person

▶ Resources are wasted because of inadequate project evaluation and qualification

▶ The sales team is not coordinated

▶ The solution offered lacks a convincing, personalized argument of the benefits and the costs of same are not justified

▶ Rather than learning from mistakes, excuses are offered

To avoid such problems of quality in the sales process, mySAP CRM implements a structured sales methodology. With the aid of this methodology, sales projects can be controlled and documented right from the start and their success can be monitored. The individual steps of the sales process are organized by the mySAP CRM component *Sales Assistant*

Sales Assistant

Sales Assistant leads the sales employee through a structured sales process and supports him in the planning of activities, while at the same time, not limiting his decision making freedom. It offers an activity plan including a checklist with recommended activities and tasks that the employee should perform in each phase.

The Sales Assistant can be adapted to fit in with the specific sales processes of each enterprise. If for example different sales cycles are implemented, one for regular and one for new customers, then special activity plans for each cycle can be deposited in the system with mySAP CRM.

The sales team member has the possibility of displaying the recommended activities for each phase and of copying them in his personal activity plan. Of course he can also include his own ideas in the plan.

Tips and background information on each activity – which are supported by tried and tested sales practices – are available to the employee. A tip for the activity *first visit to a potential customer* could, for example, contain key questions and topics that should be discussed during the visit. Things that could be recorded in the activity plan include; a deadline by which an activity should be carried out, which employee is responsible for doing so or whether a task has already been dealt with. If an activity is overdue or has not yet been dealt with, a reminder icon will automatically be displayed.

Figure 7.9 A sales process supported by Sales Assistant

Integration with mySAP CRM Activity Management

The personal activity plan prepared by Sales Assistant is closely linked with mySAP CRM Activity Management. All activities in the personal activity plan (such as customer visits, telephone calls, e-mails or meetings) can be called up from Activity Management at any time and edited. Partner data (such as customer, customer contact person or employee responsible), remarks or texts and notes are automatically transferred from the opportunity to the activity.

The mySAP CRM Sales Methodology

The most important elements of the mySAP CRM sales methodology are:

▶ Description of project objectives

▶ Project organization structure (buying center)

▶ Analysis of competition

▶ Opportunity assessment

▶ Opportunity plan

▶ Analysis and reporting

All of the above-mentioned elements are described below.

Describing project objectives

In order to find out if and how a customer can benefit from a sales offer, it is important to understand what the customer's requirements are and what results they expect. In addition, the sales employee must clearly define his short- and long-term objectives regarding this customer. Both objective settings – from the point of view of the customer and of the enterprise – can be drawn up and can then be accessed by all employees involved in the sales process.

Buying Center

In order to be able to sell successfully the organization structure and all important decision makers in the customer's enterprise must be identified from an early stage. Many sales projects fail because this factor is underestimated. The project organization structure function in mySAP CRM Opportunity Management offers support for answering questions such as:

▶ Who at the customer's enterprise makes the final decision?

▶ On whom does the approval of the project depend? What does the relationship network look like?

▶ Who will benefit from the solution offered?

▶ Key attributes for each individual player, such as their opinion on the solution offered and a personal argument of the benefits

mySAP CRM offers as standard a range of predefined categories of buyers who play a role in the sales process:

▶ **Approver**
This person gives final approval and can raise or lower the budget.

▶ **Decision maker**
Advises the approver on which of the alternative solutions offered should be bought. This person is responsible for the success of the project and for sticking to the budget.

▶ **User**
This person will benefit from the purchase decision. He assesses the solutions offered with regard to their use for his work processes.

▶ **Tester**
This person evaluates alternative solutions from a technical point of view.

► **Coach**

He gives support and guidance throughout the sales process. He makes suggestions and gives information important to the success of the sale, such as whether or not important people have been overlooked.

Individual, customer-specific categories can of course also be defined.

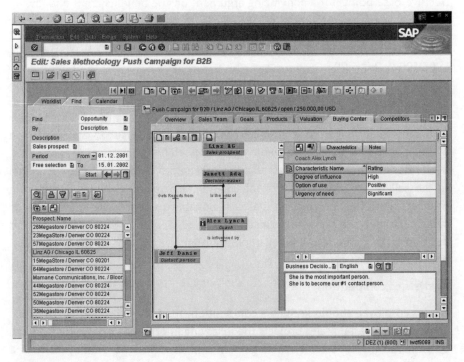

Figure 7.10 An example of a typical project organization structure

Apart from the people involved in the sales process, the relationship between these people is also of great importance. In order to be able to sell successfully, this relationship set – which can go well beyond the official hierarchy – must be understood. The following relationship types can be defined for the individual persons in the project organization structure:

► Formal relationship, based on the enterprise structure (person A informs person B)

► Informal relationship, based on personal relationships and influences (person A influences person B)

In customizing, relationship types can be defined in accordance with individual company requirements.

As soon as the principal decision maker and their influence on the purchase decision are known, the next step must be to highlight the advantages of the offered solution for the customer. A common mistake that can be made here is to put functionality in the spotlight, rather than shaping a personalized argument of the benefits.

Decisive base points for a convincing argument on the benefits are the following facts:

▶ The importance and urgency of the project from the point of view of the person in question
▶ Personal and business objectives and decision making criteria of all persons
▶ Knowledge about how individual people assess the solution

All the information mentioned can be recorded for each person in the description of the opportunity, in order to identify gaps or need for action as early as possible. In addition, further important assessment criteria can be defined that are central to the selling process. Risks and information deficits can be highlighted with warning signs. This information makes it possible to adapt sales campaigns to meet customer requirements exactly. Knowledge of business objectives and decision making criteria are, for example, extremely important for the preparation of customer specific presentations.

Analysis of competition

A sales employee should know his competition, their strengths and weaknesses. For support in certain sales projects the following information on competitors can be gathered in Opportunity Management and used for the development of a counter-strategy:

▶ Solutions offered by the competitor
▶ Competitor's strategy
▶ Coach at the customer's company who can answer direct questions about competitors

Opportunity assessment

Before an enterprise pours greater sales expenses into a particular project it must be clear if the expected sales and chances of success are in a justifiable proportion to the investment required. If this issue is clarified as early as possible in the sales process, risks can be identified from the outset and, if appropriate, they can be excluded before a lot of money has been spent on a costly sales project. Figure 7.11 shows an example of how an opportunity is assessed.

Figure 7.11 Assessing an opportunity

For calculating a project's chances of success a computer aided questionnaire tool – *Survey Tool* – is integrated into mySAP CRM. With the help of this tool the opportunity valuation questions and answers are evaluated and, based on the sales employee's answers, the chances of success and a forecast are produced. Alternatively, the employee also has the possibility of giving their own forecast, based on their personal appraisal of the project.

Opportunity plan

An Opportunity Plan can be compiled for every opportunity. This brings together all the key information on an opportunity.

▶ **Project overview**
   Expected sales turnover, customer's budget, chances of success, current phase in the sales cycle, contract date, sales team, customer's project objectives, sales objectives

▶ **Product overview**
   Products, quantities, expected product value

- **Buying center**
Organization structure of the customer or prospective customer, key people with descriptive attributes such as influence, opinion, decision making criteria, personalized argument of benefits

- **Analysis of competition**
Competitors' strengths, weaknesses, strategies

- **Opportunity assessment**
Sales employee's estimation of chances of success, system's calculation of chances of success

- **Activity plan**
Overview of all activities, employees responsible, level of completion

The opportunity plan offers a comprehensive overview of the current status of a project. It serves as a base for presentations and discussions during internal project meetings and can be displayed, printed or sent in an e-mail at any time.

Analysis and reporting

Opportunity management uses SAP Business Information Warehouse for analytical tasks. Ready made *queries* are available there, which make it possible to have a comprehensive overview of all opportunities and thus they act as a basis for detailed sales planning and simulation. The opportunity pipeline offers, for example, information on the current status of all opportunities and makes it possible to monitor long and short term sales possibilities.

Order Acquisition

This phase of the sales process concerns the exchange of sales documents between provider and customer as soon as the customer has decided to go ahead with concrete sales negotiations. Normally this phase comes after a successful opportunity management phase.

If an opportunity has not already been structured, the starting point of order acquisition can be an inquiry or an offer to buy products or services. Once the conditions have been agreed upon, the offer can be copied into a sales order or contract and thereby conclude the sales process.

Inquiries, offers and orders are grouped under the term *sales documents* and can be registerded via any channel of communication, either by agent in an interaction center, a sales employee at the customer's premises or by the customer himself via the Internet. Once a customer has decided to buy a product, all data on the customer can readily be inserted into the relevant documents.

Because all documents are linked in the course of a single transaction it is possible to automatically transfer information from one document to another. It is possible to determine what data is to be transferred in each case, whether organizational and partner data or product and price information.

Integration with backend systems means that it is possible to check credit and product availability in real time and ensures the forwarding of relevant information to the employees responsible. Prices, taxes and product availability are automatically calculated from the data entered and displayed and stored in the business transaction.

> **Example** Customer X places an order for Y quantity of a particular product over the telephone. In *SAP Internet Pricing and Configurator (SAP IPC)* it is recorded that customer X should receive a discount of 10 %. As soon as the order is entered in the interaction center the system receives data from IPC and automatically calculates the reduction on the goods ordered by the customer.

Content of a Sales Document

A sales document is arranged in the following two sections, each of which can be further sub-divided into tab pages:

▶ **Header**
This section contains all important data that concern the entire document, for example, type (offer, sales order or service contract), number and status of the process. It can also contain information on the campaign which originally gave rise to the business transaction. This makes it possible to calculate how many sales orders were received as a result of a particular campaign. The header also contains information on shipping conditions, terms of payment and delivery, tax data, organizational and administrative data, partner information and texts.

▶ **Items**
This section contains details on each individual item including schedule plans, prices, conditions, descriptive text, order information as well as partner, supplier, payment and organizational data. Products can be configured on item level with the help of *SAP Internet Pricing and Configurator (IPC)*. The item details offer a comprehensive overview of all products ordered, their prices and terms of delivery.

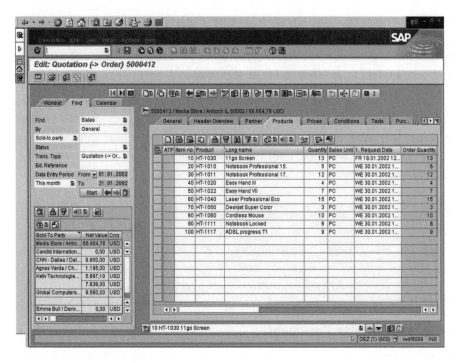

Figure 7.12 Example of a sales document

General Functions for Documents

A range of general functions are available for sales documents (business transactions). These are listed below in the order of their usage in the sales process:

▶ **Determination of organizational data**

If the organization structure of the selling company is stored in the system and rules have been defined for the determination of the relevant organizational unit, this information can be used for completing sales documents. If, for example, a sales order is recorded and the name of the customer is entered, mySAP CRM can automatically determine the corresponding sales office for this customer.

▶ **Partner determination**

In partner processing it is established which partner roles are important for which processes and what the tasks of each individual role are (for example, ship-to party, payer or contact person). It can be defined which partner roles should appear in a document and whether these are obligatory or optional. As soon as these settings have been made, mySAP CRM automatically inputs the necessary partner into the document. A sales order can, for example, contain an ordering party, a contact person and a ship-to party. The fields for entering these people automatically appear on the screen as soon as a sales document is started. When the name of a contact person is entered, mySAP CRM determines the names of the ordering party and the ship-to party. If necessary, these can be changed manually.

▶ **Partner/Product selection**
A partner/product selection is a combination of business partners and products that is applicable in a predefined scenario for a particular period of time. Therefore, there can be a list containing products and services that are important for a particular customer, or with products that should not be sold to a particular customer, perhaps because the price is not appropriate for that customer. A partner/product selection can be assigned to individual business partners, business partner hierarchies or marketing segments and can be based on products, product categories or product hierarchies.

▶ **Product determination**
For the time-saving determination of products, product keys can be stored in the system. As soon as these keys are entered into the business transaction, mySAP CRM automatically determines the desired product and fills out relevant fields such as product number, description and partner/product selection.

▶ **Pricing**
The pricing function automatically calculates all relevant price conditions in a business transaction. Different types of pricing elements are available such as material price, surcharges or discounts. If required, information on gross and net price, taxes, currency and exchange rates are available. Pricing is implemented centrally in the CRM system by SAP IPC and sent to the relevant business transactions so that constant and reliable pricing information is available for the entire sales process.

▶ **Availability check**
The availability check offers the following service in the sales process:

  ▶ Checking the availability of a product

  ▶ Reservation of products in the desired quantity

  ▶ Forwarding requirements to the production or purchasing department

The availability check runs in *SAP Advanced Planner and Optimizer* (SAP APO). Further details on the availability check will be given in this chapter under "Availability Check" on page 100.

▶ **Date definition**
With the help of date definition any number of dates can be included in the documents, for example, planned and actual dates of activities or the

beginning, end and validity period of a contract. Dates can also be set according to rules such as "the validity period for a contract is always 12 months from the beginning of the period".

▶ **Credit check**
With the credit check, financial risks can be reduced from early on, during the processing of the sales procedure. This check is not actually done in mySAP CRM itself, rather it is triggered by a function call up in the backend system.

▶ **Administration of texts**
In the administration of texts, processes or objectives can be described in detail and separate notes or documents can be generated and linked to the actual business transaction. These texts refer either to the entire business transaction – in which case the document will be linked to the header – or only to a particular item.

▶ **Attachments**
Additional documents – even if they are in special formats such as presentations, product descriptions, information brochures or hyperlinks on the Internet – can be added to a transaction as attachments, at either header or item level. Each business transaction can have a list of attachments.

▶ **Output**
The output format for documents via different output channels (printing, fax, e-mail) can be selected at will. Each document contains selected information from the business transaction such as address, ship-to party, company related data, sales texts and order items.

Sales Documents in the Process Run

Sales processes are managed with the help of the following functions:

▶ Create actions
▶ Copy sales documents
▶ Display document flow
▶ Oversee status

If required, these functions can automatically set off entire event chains and make effective customer care easier for sales employees.

Actions

Actions support the scheduling and triggering of follow-up steps in the process of the transaction as a reaction to certain conditions and aid the automation of sales and service processes. They are started automatically once the corresponding conditions have been fulfilled. Therefore, for example, automatic subsequent documents can be generated or documents that have already been processed can be changed, printed or sent by fax or e-mail. The type and schedule of actions can be designed in accordance with the needs of customers or with company processes.

Actions can be planned manually in the document related to a business transaction. Each document (business transaction) has an *Actions* tab page, on which the user can view what actions are planned, have been started or completed.

Action planning can also be done automatically with the implementation of a method. In the *create an offer* method, for example, it can be arranged that two weeks later the system will automatically generate an activity for the sales team member responsible, to remind the customer in question of the offer by telephone and to answer any questions that may have arisen.

For more complex processes, such as the creation of subsequent documents that require approval, actions can also start off *workflows*. It is possible to arrange that four weeks before the expiry of a contract the system will automatically send a customer an offer for a new contract that corresponds to the current one. Beforehand the contract should be forwarded to the credit representative responsible, with the help of *WebFlow* – the workflow component of mySAP Technology – so that the latter can check if the customer's credit status is satisfactory.

Copying documents and document flow

Both users and the mySAP CRM system can copy business transactions – for example, the related documents – or create subsequent documents for certain operations. This ensures that certain information is always consistently passed on to other documents, so that data only have to be entered into the system once. This saves working time and minimizes the probability of errors.

Copying documents means that during work on a business transaction a new transaction of the same type and with the same header and item details can be created, such as creating a new sales order from the original order. When this is done the system creates no link between the two documents.

With the help of *subsequent business transactions* data can be copied from one or several transaction documents. After selecting the transaction type for the subsequent document, the system copies the header data. Then items to be used can be selected or new items can be added. The new document is linked with the original via a *document flow*, which makes it possible to display the connection between the business transactions. If, for example, an opportunity has two activities and one concluded sales order attached, then all four documents are listed in the document flow.

As mentioned above in *Actions*, the mySAP CRM system can also copy documents itself or create subsequent documents. This helps sales employees in the creation of automatic workflows which make the necessary documents available to them at the right point in time.

Status administration

mySAP CRM differentiates between system status and user status.

A *system status* is assigned to a business transaction internally and automatically by the system. It gives information on whether particular business processes are completed, for example, if a new document has been created or if a document has errors.

A *user status*, however, is assigned to a document manually by the user and it offers certain additional information such as *to be released*, *released*, *rejected* or *delivered*.

Workflows or actions can be triggered by the status. If, for example, a contract is given the status *canceled*, automatically an activity in the form of an e-mail can be instigated that informs the sales manager of this occurrence.

Contract Administration

Contracts are long term agreements which allow a customer to acquire products or services at special previously negotiated conditions, for instance, at a particular price. Contracts are an important means of securing customers because they help to increase customer satisfaction and customer loyalty. Moreover, with the help of contracts, greater knowledge on the customer's desires and behavior can be gained. Such long-term agreements are also advantageous for customers because they can acquire goods or services at the most favorable conditions.

E-business has heightened competition between suppliers. Contract Management in mySAP CRM helps enterprises to adjust to these changes by offering a flexible and intuitive solution for creating and updating customer-specific agreements. The following contract types are available:

▶ Sales contracts

▶ Service contracts

▶ Leasing contracts (planned)

Sales contracts are based on the same documents as sales orders and are therefore very similar in function and structure. Three types of sales contract are supported:

▶ **Quantity contracts**
Agreement that a customer will acquire a particular quantity of a product over a certain period of time

▶ **Value contracts**
Agreement that a customer will order products up to a particular value over a particular period of time

▶ **Combination of quantity and value contracts**

Working with contracts

Contracts with conditions of price and duration are generally negotiated between the sales team and the customer over a certain period. During negotiations the items in the contract, even if they are already created in mySAP CRM as a document (business transaction), are given the status of *open* or *in progress* and as such cannot be released from the contract.

The contract can only be released when the final contract conditions have been agreed and set. Release means that the customer can now call products from the contract. Authorized employees then create customer orders for the products as subsequent documents to the contract. As a result, all relevant documents are always linked with each other. Employees can at all times call up the document flow in the system and thereby get an overview of the number of products or the value that has already been released from the contract.

If a customer gives an order, via whatever communication channel he should choose, mySAP CRM automatically checks to see if any contract exists for this business partner. If such a contract exists, the conditions agreed in the contract are taken as the basis for this new order and the quantity ordered or the value are automatically entered in the contract. It can be individually stated whether or not a customer may go over the target quantity or target value set and if the system should automatically set the contract status at *completed*, as soon as a target quantity or target value are reached.

Special functions and their use in sales contracts

The sales contract is the same as a sales order in structure and function. However, sales contracts have additional characteristics that are important for working with contracts:

► **Schedule profile and rules**

mySAP CRM offers schedule profile and rules with which validity periods in contracts can be defined and controlled. The most important dates in a contract are:

- ► Start of contract
- ► End of contract
- ► Contract validity period

In addition, it is possible to set different schedule rules, for instance, default parameters for start date and length of contract so that all contracts start on January 1 and run for at least two years. In this way it is assured that all employees pass on consistent information to customers. When an employee enters a new contract, if this data is already set as default, the system automatically calculates the date on which the contract will finish. Where necessary the employee can – if authorized – change the default data manually.

► **Action profile**

The status of currently running contracts can be followed with the help of action profiles. There is the possibility of automatically generating an activity for a particular employee to remind him or her to get in contact with a customer whose contract will soon expire. Also, if a customer will probably not call forward the agreed quantity of products in time, an automatically generated activity can inform the employee responsible of this fact. This warning function helps to increase customer satisfaction and ensures that customer relationships are developed more actively.

► **Cancelation rules**

In the event of a customer wishing to cancel a contract, mySAP CRM offers a cancelation procedure with which the different rules and reasons for a cancelation can be defined and evaluated.

► **Products that can be released**

When a contract of quantity or value is being drawn up, the products related to the same can be entered manually. However, mySAP CRM also offers a predefined product selection, product categories or a combination of both. This function sees to it that all employees can easily determine which products can be released by which customer.

► **Agreements**

Specific terms of delivery and terms of payment and special prices and discounts can be agreed in contracts. These agreements are automatically ascertained when part of the contract is released.

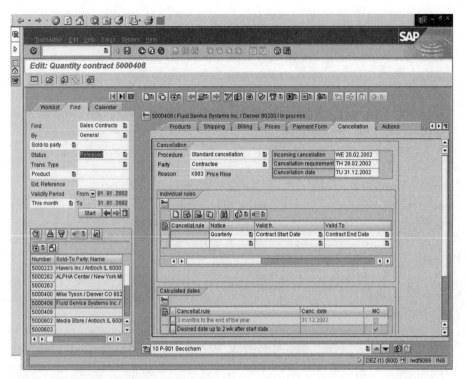

Figure 7.13 Example of a sales contract

Sales Performance Analysis

All data from activity management, opportunity management and order acquisition is gathered and stored and can later be analyzed. mySAP Business Intelligence offers flexible data warehouse functions, with which it can be set exactly how and when which data should be evaluated. The evaluation can be done from different perspectives:

▶ Operative

▶ Analytical

With the help of *operative* reports the status of current sales operations is checked. It can be determined how many sales orders are open, which contracts will expire soon, or if there is any delay in delivery. In addition, information from previous sales operations can be used for product recommendations.

> **Example** From a report a sales manager finds out which customers buy which products. Depending on how much money a customer has spent or what type of products they have bought, the sales manager may decide to offer them an additional product (*Cross-Selling*) or a more expensive product (*Up-Selling*). The sales manager can enter this information in a partner/product selection as a product recommendation. When the customer next makes contact with a sales employee, the latter automatically receives a note that he should recommend the selected product to the customer.

With the help of *analytical* reports, the sales team's services and the success of the sales strategy can be measured. For this the Sales Performance Analysis element in mySAP Business Intelligence offers many diverse sales-specific analyses, such as pipeline and profit/loss analyses as well as evaluations of the efficiency of the sales cycle.

Sales Performance Analysis is divided into four areas, as follows:

▶ **Finances**
  Pipeline analyses for opportunities and open contracts give an overview of current and expected developments. With the help of sales order analysis, open and incoming sales order values – and with them potential turnover – can be evaluated.

▶ **Customers**
  With the help of an ABC analysis different customers can be compared to each other and categorized according to their importance. Analysis of customer value and profitability are also available.

▶ **Internal sales processes**
  Here the business transactions initiated by the sales team can be monitored, such as opportunity-quantities, success rates, profit/loss comparisons, offer analysis and the correlation between offers and contracts or orders that were actually won.

▶ **Employee development**
  Here processes that affect employees and their satisfaction and productivity are examined. Among other things, it is possible to analyze personnel turnover, number and cost of training courses and number of participants, analyses of illness and overtime ratios and degree of employee satisfaction (gauged with the help of surveys).

Most of the analyses mentioned can be presented in detail for individual sales regions with the help of a web-based geographical information system (GIS) that facilitates a clear-cut visual account of information and figures for individual regions.

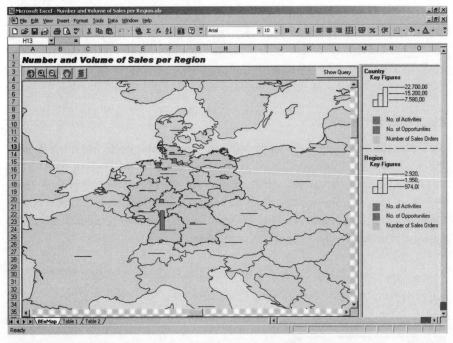

Figure 7.14 Data analysis in GIS format: Number of activities vs turnover

Most of the data used in the sales performance analysis come from the mySAP CRM system. It is also possible to extract data from an SCM or HR solution which can be passed on to mySAP Business Intelligence.

Order Fulfillment

Overview

After an order or a contract have been signed, the next phase is order fulfillment, which includes the following steps:

▶ Availability check

▶ Payment processing and credit management

▶ Shipping

▶ Transport

▶ Invoicing

▶ Monitoring and analysis of the processing of the sales order

Information on products, supplier data and payment details are essential for processing a sales order. mySAP CRM collects all necessary product availability data, processes payment information and checks the customer's credit status. As soon as the order is confirmed and saved, mySAP CRM sends all information to the backend system where, if necessary, material planning, shipping and invoicing are initiated. Both customers and employees can inquire about the current status of the order at any time. In addition, sales management can evaluate and analyze sales order data to get an overview of the efficiency of the fulfillment process.

Availability Check

Before a sales transaction can be confirmed, vendor and customer must know if the product in question will be available for delivery by the desired date. To do this mySAP CRM offers an availability check: the *ATP (Available to Promise)* check. With this tool, warehouse stock can be released and goods can be reserved for incoming customer orders. Furthermore, production or purchasing can, if necessary, be flexible and adapt to the request.

Example In figure 7.15 a customer has given an order for 100 pieces of product 4711; delivery should be effected on October 10th.

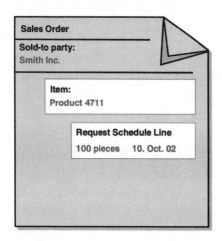

Figure 7.15 Sales order with desired delivery date

In this example the availability check for this order may give the following result:

60 pieces by October 10th
40 pieces by October 15th.

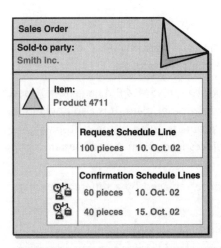

Figure 7.16 Sales order with confirmation schedule

The information in the above example is displayed as a *confirmation schedule*. As soon as the order has been confirmed definitively, which means that the customer has accepted the quantities and dates concerned, the products in question are reserved. Reserving here means that these products are temporarily assigned to the order in question and are as such no longer available for other orders. However, production, purchasing and material planning have not started yet. Only when the sales order has been checked for errors by an employee and saved is the temporary allocation started and the final product allocation carried out. Material planning can now start; the business transaction is now of relevance to supplies and shipping.

Simulated Availability Check (Information on Availability)

In some cases it is useful, for information purposes, to do a simulated availability check. This can be done for offers, for instance, for which a certain delivery date has already been agreed for certain products, but the customer has not yet made a binding order confirmation. In this case it is possible to get availability information for the products in the offer to see if they would be available for the desired date. There is no reservation of products here, and the check has no influence on material planning. The follow-up processes mentioned above will only be triggered when the offer has been converted into a sales order. Availability checks are also possible for probable, but as yet unconfirmed sales. Here the system checks the availability of a percentage rate of the quantity in the sales transaction. This is calculated by multiplying the total quantity inquired about by the sales order probability. The quantity actually needed later is then represented more accurately.

If Products are not Available

In the event of a requested product not being available, mySAP CRM offers the possibility of automating the ensuing decision making process:

▶ If a product is not available at a particular plant, mySAP CRM can check to see if the product in question is still in stock in another plant. It is also possible to complete a delivery to a customer with products going to the customer from different warehouses, for example 100 pieces from plant A and the remaining 50 pieces from plant B (*Order Split*).

▶ If a product is no longer in stock it can be replaced by a different, perhaps similar or better product.

This type of check can also be used for optimizing advertising campaigns, season sales or up-selling and cross-selling. If for example, if there is to be an advertising action with something like "Buy a PC and get a free CD burner", then on receipt of an order for a PC mySAP CRM not only checks to see if the PC is available, but also if the PC plus CD burner combination is available.

Summary of Deliveries

As we saw in the example above, the availability check can produce the following results:

▶ Different delivery dates are given for the individual items on a sales order

▶ There are several delivery dates for a single item

Sometimes it is necessary to ensure that all items in a sales order are delivered at the same time, or that all units in an item are delivered together. This may be necessary to meet a customer's wishes or because products that are linked to each other, perhaps as a result of an advertising campaign, must be delivered together. To ensure that they are delivered together, these items can be put together in a *delivery group*. All items in such a group would then be delivered on the date on which the item with the latest availability date is available.

Backorder Processing

If customer demand exceeds supply or if a more important customer is given preference and is to receive delivery first, it may be necessary to reallocate already confirmed quantities among the existing sales orders. This can be done with the help of backorder processing. This means that all quantities that have already been confirmed but are still open – that is, they have not yet been delivered – are recalculated with respect to the quantities available. Then a new availability check is carried out and the results of same are sent to mySAP CRM. Sales orders are automatically adapted so that employees and customers can at all times have access to the modified, up-to-date availability information.

Payment Processing and Credit Management

Methods of Payment

Independent of the scenario in which the business transaction has occurred – business-to-consumer or business-to-business – payment is normally effected by

▶ Payment card

▶ Cash on delivery

▶ Invoice

In the first two cases payment is direct and as a result the risk for the supplying company is minimized. In the third case the main risk lies with the executing company on accepting a sales order. A credit management process can reduce this risk.

mySAP CRM supports all of the abovementioned methods of payment. The following solutions are currently available:

Payment Card Processing

Most one-off customers, especially if they order via the Internet, pay with a card, whether it is a credit card, a customer card or procurement card. From a dealer's point of view the use of payment cards reduces the risk of transactions with unknown partners, because payment is guaranteed – once the card has been authorized.

Authorization of payment card transactions

By authorization we refer to a process in which a clearing house guarantees payment of a transaction amount. When a sales order is saved, mySAP CRM establishes contact with the corresponding authorization module in the clearing house. The clearing house checks the following details:

▶ Card number

▶ Name and address of the card holder

▶ Card verification code
  A three-to-four-figure number in the signature field or in the magnetic strip, with the help of which it can be verified that the card and card account do belong to a particular customer

▶ Address verification system
  Checks that the address given in the sales transaction matches the data

recorded in the clearing house and whether or not the customer is the holder of the card used

The answer from the clearing house – authorization approved or authorization denied – is noted in the sales order. If authorization has been approved the sales transaction can be processed further. Otherwise the transaction is stopped.

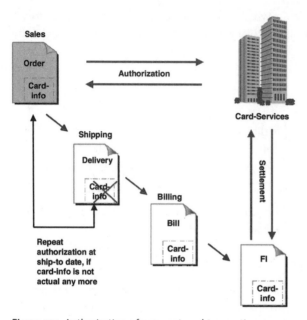

Figure 7.17 Authorization of payment card transactions

Sales orders with payment card

If a customer or employee creates a sales order, the payment card details are included in the order, for example, card number and name of card holder. If necessary, a pre-authorization check can be carried out in which it is checked to see if the card details are correct. In addition, the name, address and card number are sent to the clearing house and a verification is received. In this way the risk of problems at a later stage with the actual authorization can be reduced. It can be decided immediately if the payment card in question is accepted or not.

As soon as a customer order is confirmed, the following occurs within mySAP CRM:

▶ Authorization of the transaction by the clearing house, including verification of address and payment card and entry of the results in the sales order

▶ Encryption of the card data (if they are still not encoded), so that they do not appear in the database as legible text

▶ The transaction is sent on for further processing

Authorization interval

If goods are not available until several weeks or months after the entry of the corresponding sales order, it is not sufficient that the payment card was valid on the day on which the order was made. Instead, it must be checked that the card authorization is still valid on the agreed delivery date, which is when the goods ordered will pass into the possession of the customer. In mySAP CRM it is possible to set how many days before an agreed delivery date the authorization check should be carried out. The number of days between the authorization date and the delivery date are what is known as the authorization interval. In this way it is ensured that an up-to-date and valid credit check is carried out immediately before the delivery of the goods (see also figure 7.17).

Cash on Delivery

Cash on delivery is another method of payment available to customers. It is particularly recommendable when the goods ordered are to be forwarded by a shipping company such as the postal service or a courier service. The customer receives the product together with a bill which must be paid on delivery.

It must of course first be checked that the COD customer can pay cash. In the business partner master data, business partners can be marked as cash-on-delivery (COD) customers. In addition, a particular dispatch firm can be entered as the regular dispatcher for a particular customer. When a sales transaction is created for a business partner who normally pays cash on delivery, this method of payment is automatically given as default for the sales transaction.

Credit Management

Since customers can acquire products or take up services via so many different channels and can, as a result, remain to a large extent unidentified, credit management has become a critical feature. mySAP CRM makes it possible to display all credit information in customer records as well as do a credit check in real time when the sales order is made. The integration of this data into customer relationship management makes it possible both to monitor a customer's credit history and also enable the use of what are known as *Early Warning Lists* or *Alerts*, which are warnings that the system gives when a customer sends in an order but the credit limit for that customer has already been exceeded. Non-creditworthy customers can thus be identified and blocked. With analyses, payment history and credit risk can also be tested and as a result payment security is guaranteed for the company and the customer.

Credit check

A credit check is possible as soon as a sales transaction has been entered. The credit check verifies the customer's credit standing, that is, their ability to pay. The appraisal establishes, among other things, the credit control area (setting who is responsible for the allocation and monitoring of credit), the credit account of the payer and the risk classification of the account. Then the credit standing of the payer can be established and the credit status can be put in at header level accordingly, both for individual items and also as a general credit status for the entire document. If the credit status is OK when the transaction is finally confirmed then the transaction can be released for delivery and invoicing.

Informing employees about credit problems

In order to guarantee a trouble-free running of credit management, employees can be informed of potential problems in different ways.

Many enterprises set up a workflow process that forwards all sales transactions for which the credit status has not been deemed satisfactory directly to the appropriate employee in credit management. The employee can then consider each transaction individually and decide whether it should be released for further processing or whether it should be refused.

Credit information can also be sent to the information data on business partners (see "Account and Contact Management" on page 79) so that an employee who is currently working on an order from the partner in question is immediately made aware of credit problems.

Shipping

Shipping includes all procedures that are necessary for the customer to receive the ordered goods. All relevant sales data is sent from mySAP CRM to the logistics system responsible for shipping.

If mySAP SCM is installed as the logistics system, an efficient and automated shipping process is initiated, with the following functions:

▶ Monitoring deadlines for sales documents to be delivered
▶ Planning and monitoring of worklists for shipping activities
▶ Monitoring availability of material and processing open re-stocking orders
▶ Monitoring warehouse capacity
▶ Delivery

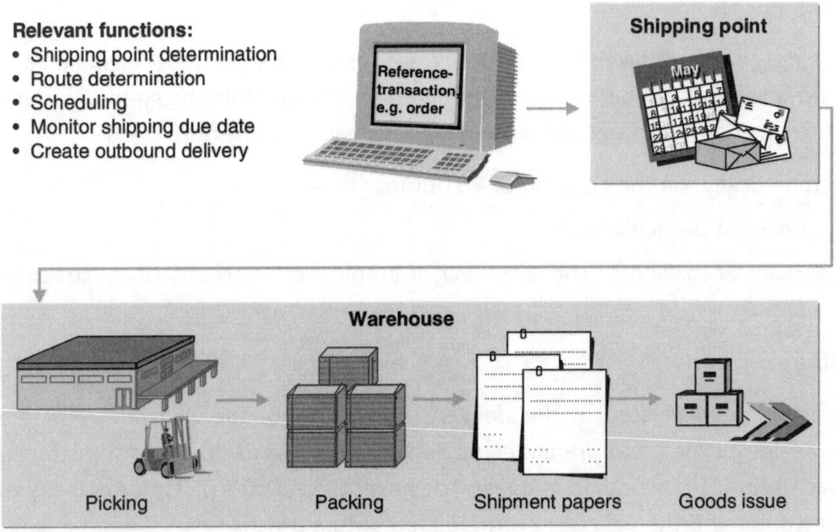

Relevant functions:
- Shipping point determination
- Route determination
- Scheduling
- Monitor shipping due date
- Create outbound delivery

Reference-transaction, e.g. order

Shipping point

Warehouse

Picking   Packing   Shipment papers   Goods issue

Figure 7.18 The shipping process

The activities linked with delivery as a part of shipping are described in more detail below.

Delivery

The following activities are part of the outbound delivery process:

▶ Creation and processing of outbound deliveries

▶ Goods picking

▶ Packing of deliveries

▶ Printing and transmission of shipping documents

▶ Processing goods issue

▶ Considering foreign trade requirements

During the delivery process, information on shipping plans is recorded, the status of delivery activities is monitored and data collected during the shipping process is documented. When a delivery is created, shipping activities such as goods picking or delivery planning are initiated: data generated during the shipping process are included in the delivery.

If required, deliveries can be created automatically, by worklists, or manually. Agreements can be made with customers about total or partial deliveries or a combination of the two forms of delivery. Outbound deliveries can be grouped together in a single delivery group.

Picking

In picking, goods are taken from a storage area and forwarded to a picking area in the correct quantity, where they are prepared for shipment. In the system, picking can also be adapted to suit the customary processes in each firm:

▶ Automatically, on the creation of an outbound delivery

▶ Routinely, at particular times

▶ Manually, according to the overview of employees' worklists on a particular day

Packing

Packing is the next step in the delivery process. Here the delivery items are selected for packing and are allocated specific *Handling Units*. So, for example, delivery items can be packed in boxes, the boxes placed on a pallet for delivery to the customer and the pallets, in turn, loaded onto a truck.

Goods issue

As soon as the goods leave the enterprise, the business transaction is complete as far as shipping is concerned. In mySAP CRM this is recorded by the posting of the goods issue. The data necessary for this are copied from the delivery document into the goods issue document. On the posting of a goods issue for a delivery the following functions are carried out on the basis of the goods issue document:

▶ The warehouse stock of the material is reduced by the delivery quantity

▶ The change in value is recorded on the balance sheet of materials accounting

▶ Requirements are reduced by the quantity delivered

Transport

Effective and reasonably priced transportation planning and shipment completion are of great importance to customer satisfaction – one only has to think of on-time delivery and transport costs, which have a significant influence on product pricing.

Incoming and outgoing transport is planned, executed and monitored. The costs arising are billed and settled with the transportation service agents. It is also possible to pass on shipment costs directly to the customer.

Outbound transport is arranged and planned on the basis of outbound deliveries (see "Shipping" on page 106). In the corresponding transport documents the following transport planning and completion functions can be executed:

- ▶ Grouping together of different deliveries that should be transported together
- ▶ Assigning and entrusting services
- ▶ Organization of means of transport
- ▶ Determination of transport route and shipment stages
- ▶ Registration of means of transport
- ▶ Loading, weighing and posting goods issue
- ▶ Printing the necessary transport papers

To facilitate an overview of the planned transport activities and any shipments currently underway at any time, lists, a graphic information system and Gantt charts are available.

Shipment Costing and Settlement

Shipment costing and settlement includes the calculation of all costs arising from transport, the forwarding of these costs to accounting and settlement with service providers and/or passing these costs on to the customer invoice.

To calculate costs automatically, different outgoing values and account determination keys can be referred to, for example distance, weight or transport zone.

Invoicing

Today, invoices can contain much more than the regular notice of payment due. They are often used as an effective opportunity for communicating with the customer, as they can contain, for example, further product information or notification relevant to customers. In general, modern invoicing solutions have to cope with increasing demands of cost, flexibility, system openness and customer orientation, brought about by strong competitive pressure. *CRM Billing*, the mySAP CRM invoicing solution is prepared for both sales and contract related invoicing. It has the following outstanding features:

- ▶ Support for the entire invoicing process
- ▶ Can be integrated with different SAP and non-SAP systems as a source or follow-up application
- ▶ Invoicing not only for orders from mySAP CRM, but also from other solutions such as mySAP Telecommunications and mySAP Media.

In invoicing with CRM Billing, data from different contributing source applications can be merged together, with prices calculated and combined in one common invoice. All transactions that do not involve shipping, such as credit and debit memo requests, are transferred directly to invoicing, whereas transactions involving shipping are only passed on to invoicing when the delivery in question has taken place.

Invoicing Sub-Processes

Creation of invoices with CRM Billing involves the following three sub-processes:

▶ Processing of input data

▶ Billing

▶ Processing of output data

Cancelation is also possible. Figure 7.19 illustrates the procedure for the creation and processing of invoices with CRM Billing.

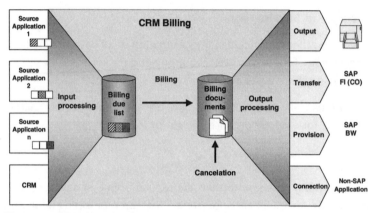

Figure 7.19 Invoicing procedure

Processing of input data

During the processing of input data, data related to invoicing are transferred to the billing due list. CRM Billing adds additional data (for example, master data) and starts a processing check.

Billing

In the creation of invoices, CRM Billing draws up complete invoices from individual billing due list items. Therefore, *billing documents* (for example, invoices, debit memos, credit memos) are created with items that may come from different CRM business transactions. In the creation of an invoice the system can bring together many different billing due list items in a single billing document. Such a merging is not possible if this is prevented by one or several split criteria. For example, the system cannot merge two billing due list items that have the same sold-to party but different payers in a single invoice, because each invoice must be prepared for one particular payer. Payer is therefore defined as a split criterion.

With the help of data from the billing due list the entire billing process can also be simulated. This makes it possible, for example, to test a particular invoicing run.

Processing of output data

CRM Billing supports a range of output media including printer, fax, e-mail or external output management systems. The following functions are available:

▶ Creation of invoices by printing, fax or e-mail

▶ Optical archiving with the help of *ArchiveLink*, the interface between mySAP.com solutions and archiving systems

▶ Preparation of billing data for Internet (electronic invoice creation)

▶ XML interface to external output management systems

With the help of *Smart Forms*, a SAP tool for processing the graphical structure of forms and documents, various different layouts can be defined for different types of billing documents – such as invoices, credit memos and debit memos. The adaption of these forms to enterprise or industry specific needs is also supported. So, for instance, different layouts can be stored for different customer categories or different fonts and logos can be incorporated into the forms.

With the aid of CRM Billing it is possible to select whether the invoice output is triggered automatically or done manually. Automatic output occurs immediately after invoicing or after a specified period of time, such as after one week or one month. In addition, it is possible to send copies of invoices – also delayed – to another recipient via any channel.

Cancelation

With CRM Billing, one or several billing documents can be canceled. You can choose between full cancelation (which cancels the entire billing document) or partial cancelation (this cancels a particular part of the billing document, such as a particular item). CRM Billing transfers the cancelation data to the corresponding accounting application, such as to contract accounting in mySAP Financials.

Transfer of the Billing Data to Downstream Applications

CRM Billing provides interfaces for transferring billing data to downstream applications:

▶ Accounts receivable accounting

▶ Contract accounting

- ▶ Controlling
- ▶ Analysis applications (mySAP BI)

Monitoring and Analysis of Sales Order Fulfillment

To distribute all information needed for the trouble-free flow of the fulfillment process to the sales manager and other authorized employees, mySAP CRM offers many different reports and analyses, covering the entire sales order processing, incorporating shipping, payment processing (including credit management) and invoicing. As is the case with sales performance analyses, these reports can be used for both operative and analytical purposes. All reports can be provided with different warning functions that indicate different problems.

Operative reporting makes it possible for specialized employees to monitor current business processes, as demonstrated in the following examples:

- ▶ A credit representative can see all customers whose credit status is so poor that they are blocked from further sales orders.
- ▶ A service employee can view delivery hold-ups or warehouse problems that make it necessary to change a delivery date.
- ▶ A transactional user working on invoice processing can track incoming invoices, credit or debit memos.

Analytical reporting offers comprehensive possibilities for evaluating sales order processing in the enterprise. The sales manager gets a complete overview of all fulfillment processes with, for example, answers to the following questions:

- ▶ How reliable are our deliveries?
- ▶ How often do backlogs have to be dealt with?
- ▶ How often and for what reasons do we get returns?
- ▶ What is the comparison between the planned sales figures and the revenues actually invoiced?

With the help of these analyses problem areas can be easily identified and suitable solutions can be worked out.

Customer Service

Overview

Customer service plays a key role in efforts to build a long term relationship with the customer. No other area in the enterprise is in direct contact with the customer more often than the agents in an interaction center or the members of the external sales force. SAP has incorporated the importance of customer service into the general solution mySAP CRM with a wide range of functions. The service components of mySAP CRM support the entire service cycle – from initial contact, to the execution of services or the shipping of replacement parts, right through to billing.

As an integral part of the CRM general solution, the service element of mySAP CRM offers:

▶ All tools necessary for efficient customer care (Customer Care and Helpdesk)
▶ Access to a database that can "learn" for problem solving (Enterprise Intelligence)
▶ Central management of the existing installations (Installed Base Management) with data pertaining to customers
▶ Customer service control and resource planning (Field Service & Dispatch), taking mobile terminals into account
▶ Planning of service offers with respect to target groups (Service Planning)
▶ Easy analysis of services (Service Analytics)

The customer service functions of mySAP CRM are closely linked with other application components in the enterprise:

▶ The integration of SAP Business Information Warehouse (SAP BW) in the mySAP CRM solution means that it is possible always to have up-to-date analysis of serivce processes with regard to volumes, (for example, number of orders), quality (for example, number of complaints) and cost efficiency. Additional key figures can be defined by the user.
▶ Links with financial applications such as mySAP FI ensure a smooth transfer of financial control related data between both systems. In this way, the entire value flow of a service process, including costs and revenue, can be analyzed.
▶ mySAP CRM also works efficiently with human resources components such as mySAP HR. Data relating to employees, such as working time or activity reports, which can also be passed on to the CRM system via mobile terminals, are stored in the ERP system and processed further. The latter, on the other hand, provides information on holiday time or, for example, time lost due to illness for the CRM system so that the controller of resource planning can have an up-to-date overview of the availability of all field sales employees at all times. Therefore, all data only has to be recorded once and is then available to all integrated applications without any time delay.

▶ If mySAP CRM is linked with the materials management element of an ERP system, it can report the use of replacement parts, equipment and resources by technical field service directly to the ERP system – which in turn generates replacement orders within the context of a workflow – and controls stock.

Customer Care

In large enterprises it can happen several times a day: A customer gets in contact. Whether the customer calls in in person, calls the interaction center, sends a fax or an e-mail, selects Self Service on the Internet or requests a call back on the Internet, is ultimately of little importance. The enterprise is there for the customer – via all communication channels and right around the clock. Using the Unified Messaging system that combines different communication channels (fax, telephone, SMS, e-mail) in a common input channel under a common user interface, customers can even call the interaction center via their computer or the Internet (*Voice-over-IP*, that is, an Internet-based call).

Essentially, the following are the four main reasons that prompt a customer's decision to contact the manufacturer of a product or the provider of a service:

▶ He has a question

▶ He has a problem

▶ He has a request

▶ He wants to complain

All four scenarios and the possible reactions that an agent can have with *mySAP CRM Interaction Center* are presented below with the help of examples.

Answering Customer Questions

Let us assume that a customer calls his utility company because he does not fully understand an item in his last electricity bill. The agent can register the customer's name or contract number in the interaction center application. *mySAP CRM Interaction Center* offers a working interface for this that is functionally linked to all necessary system components – rather similar to a control panel that triggers follow-up activities when used.

The agent can now see the complete history of the customer on the line at a glance: when the customer has called with a question, problem or service wish; when contracts have been amended or newly concluded; what goods or appliances have been obtained and when; who were the contract partners involved in a business transaction – for example in the installation of appliances –

and what deliveries and invoices the customer has received. The history of this customer is visible to the agent at a single glance, and he or she can communicate knowledgeably with the customer about transactions on which the agent has not worked at all.

As a result the agent is in a position to answer the customer's questions promptly. The customer may well be amazed, given that the last time he spoke to somebody at the company he spoke to a man and not a woman, yet will certainly appreciate the fact that he does not have to repeat the entire story – perhaps about a technical problem or a complaint – in this call. The agent knows about it and can immediately and conclusively answer the customer's question about the electricity bill.

Alert Modeler

During the conversation the agent can retrieve additional information in a text field, for example: "Customer is also a commercial electricity consumer". This information is provided by an assisting function of the mySAP CRM Interaction Center – the *Alert Modeler*. The agent now knows that the person on the other end of the line does not only consume electricity for private residential use and can thus draw his attention to current offers for commercial customers.

The Alert Modeler is an invisible background observer that warns, prompts or reminds the agent of particular things in particular cases. If a customer's data coincides with certain pre-set criteria, a note appears on the agent's screen with a message. For example, in a large car manufacturer, Alert Modeler could send employees a message for all customers that drive a certain type of car to bring the winter tyre action to customers' attention. An agent at an airline company could receive a message reading "offer frequent-flyer program" for all customers who have flown more than 100,000 miles in one year but who do not yet participate in the frequent flyer bonus program.

Solving Customer Problems

Customer questions about a bill can usually be answered quickly, the solution of technical problems, on the other hand, normally takes up more time. In some cases it is even necessary to get technical customer service involved. In any case, the agent at the interaction center acts as the problem solver – even for customers whose recently installed heating system will not start.

The agent sees the details of the customer's installation with just one glance at his interaction center application. Also, with the help of the customer-specific, definable service-level agreement in the service contract, which is displayed automatically, the agent can see that the customer has concluded a service contract with 24 hour reaction time for the installation. Further information about the on-site installation and the contract terms are made available to the agent from the central database of Installations Management (*Installed Base Management*, see "Installed Base Management" on page 122). In this Installed Base database, not only are the customer's physical installations (devices) displayed – such as in a computer manufacturing concern, but also – for example if the CRM user is an insurance company – policies can be displayed. In general, in the installed base database anything from contracts to accounts, machines to vehicles, buildings or fittings and furnishings can be displayed.

The agent learns as much as possible about the problem with the heating before looking for a solution. In the search for a solution the entire knowledge in the company (*Enterprise Intelligence*, see "Managing Enterprise Intelligence" on page 120) is at his disposal. The customer informs the agent that "off 8" is shown in the display of the heating installation, while to the left, a red light has come on. The agent then consults the list of frequently asked questions (*FAQs*) which does provide an answer as to why the red light is shining (for example, "water level too low"), but does not find anything about the "off 8" message.

Solution databases and Interactive Intelligent Agent

Then the agent consults the *Solution Database*, in which all known error descriptions and their solutions are stored. The *Interactive Intelligent Agent* helps the agent to find a solution. At the same time it minimizes unnecessary or repeated searches, because it notes problem descriptions and the solutions that have been found and considered by the user as helpful. In this way Interactive Intelligent Agent makes a useful contribution to the permanent optimizing of the solution database.

Of course, it also knows about the "off 8" warning message, although it does not occur very frequently, and identifies it as an error in the control electronics. The agent in the Interaction Center will enter a service order in the mySAP CRM system that will automatically be passed on to resource planning in technical field service. The department manager there will immediately arrange an appointment with the customer – within 24 hours as agreed in the contract.

Fulfilling Customer Wishes

A company has leased a building with large offices and divided the space on the three stories into several separate units, which it wishes to sublet. Because the electricity and water consumption of the rental units has to be billed separately, it is necessary to install additional meters. An employee of the company contacts the utility company via Internet to convey this wish.

On the utility company's home page he not only finds up-to-date information on products, but also various electronic forms for communicating change of address, concluding new supply contracts, placing an order for maintenance work or even requesting the installation of additional meters. The Internet, as a communication channel, is as easy to use as any other for this utility company's customers. This is precisely the intention of the utility supplier, who would like to offer customers (and potential customers) a comprehensive, easy to use service via the Internet that is also cost effective for them.

What the site visitor does not see are all the complex functions that lie behind the Internet pages. All of the electronic forms are produced with the mySAP CRM tool *Web Requests*. First of all the individual fields are specially set with the help of an XML scheme, and finally a complete HTML form can be generated. When forms are filled out they automatically put a service process in motion in the CRM system, for example reserving a vehicle at a car hire company, requesting a catalog from a mail order company or renewing a library card at the local library.

In the abovementioned example of the sublet office spaces the customer enters 14 water meters and several electricity meters in the *request appliances* field and in the *preferred appointment* field, for example, selects "weekday afternoons" or "within one week". The form is then passed on to an agent in the utility company's interaction center who confirms the order and preferred appointment time with the customer by telephone or e-mail, for instance, and gets the next steps of the process underway in good time.

Yet the *e-Service (Internet Self Service)* integrated into the mySAP CRM solution can do a lot more than just change contract details or take in orders and see to it that they are carried out automatically. Self-service on the Internet means that a company's customers can not only view bills or enter orders, it also allows them access to the networked business intelligence. In the event of problems, customers can refer to a catalog of frequently asked questions (FAQs) at any time of the day or night or can consult the solution database with the support of the interactive intelligent agent

Processing Customer Complaints

After the installation of two new servers for their CAD (Computer Aided Design) application a construction company experiences problems if more than three work stations try to access the application at the same time.

The agent enters the name of the customer and immediately receives an overview of all the equipment installed at their company from the Interaction Center application. He can see when and, if appropriate, by which business partner the two new servers were set up, and also that since installation the construction company has already had two different problems dealt with over the previous four months. Most of the appliances are still under guarantee and the service level agreement in the contract provides for problem solving within six hours on weekdays.

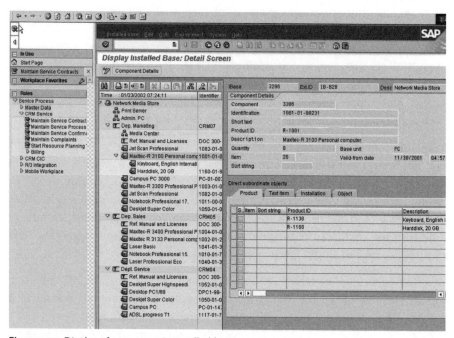

Figure 7.20 Display of a customer's installed base

Because the customer is now rather annoyed, the agent creates a complaint process with the help of the mySAP CRM function *Complaints*. In the corresponding entry fields the agent enters, among other things, the object of the complaint (the two servers) and the reason for the complaint (server performance inadequate). In addition, the agent takes steps to see that the customer is satisfied as soon as possible. To this end, the mySAP CRM interaction center offers the agent a range of different possible actions. For example, the agent can give instructions for a credit memo to be issued to the customer, can arrange for the return of a product and the provision of a replacement at the same time, or – as in our example – see to it that a service technician deals with the problem by creating a service order. Having received the order from resource planning, a few hours later the service technician sends a message from his laptop to the CRM system to say that the order has been dealt with.

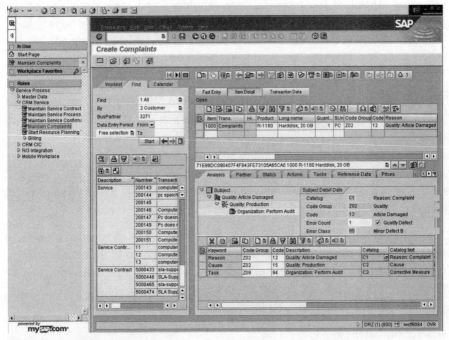

Figure 7.21 Creating a complaint

With this, the complaint has now been dealt with as far as the customer is concerned, but not for the server manufacturer. Their CRM system records both the object of the complaint and the reason for the complaint, which the service center agent usually chooses from a pre-set catalog and can mark, for example, *unfriendly employee, late delivery* or *problems with product xy.* In this way weak points can be easily identified in the context of a subsequent service analysis and they can be remedied with appropriate measures. Such measures could be employee training, the introduction of additional delivery vehicles, or an order to quality control. No company is happy to receive complaints, but a customer-oriented company will use them to optimize their processes. This optimizing is supported by mySAP CRM *Service analysis* (see "Service Analysis" on page 129).

Managing Enterprise Intelligence

Not so long ago, in the support centers of manufacturers there were specialists working exclusively with demanding software programs or complex technical installations, who were responsible for a particular product range. They were in complete control of the technical inner workings and the functioning of the products assigned to them. Any customer that had a problem would be very lucky to be able to talk to this specialist – if he or she was available at the time.

Enterprise Intelligence

Today, every service center agent is a specialist for all questions, assuming that their enterprise works with sophisticated Customer Relationship Management. mySAP CRM makes it possible for agents – and also customers via the Internet – to have authorized access to the entire enterprise intelligence. These functions are grouped under the term *Enterprise Intelligence*, a powerful element of mySAP CRM that not only manages knowledge, but also increases it with well-directed collection and classification.

The searching for specialists in the enterprise who can give competent answers to tricky questions is over. No single employee has access to more *problem solving* knowledge than the enterprise intelligence component integrated into mySAP CRM, which offers precise, consistent and tried and tested solutions for complex problems. With the help of tools like

▶ Solution Database

▶ Interactive Intelligent Agent (IIA)

▶ List of frequently asked questions (FAQs)

a central information pool for all employees, customers and business partners can be easily and cost effectively set up.

Solution Database

The long term memory in the service area is known as the *Solution Database*. All known problem descriptions are stored in it. They are entered as user-defined text with attributes (such as description of type) and/or with defined codes which describe a problem or any defects that have arisen. One or more solutions are assigned to each problem description, which may contain user-defined text, codes, detail display, video clips or even websites. Ultimately the solution database – supported by Interactive Intelligent Agent – uses a number of different sources of information to document, record and link a problem and its possible solutions.

Interactive Intelligent Agent

The *Interactive Intelligent Agent (IIA)* is an interactive search engine that knows its way around the many and varied paths in the solution database and always finds the quickest and shortest way to the solution. It optimizes the search by minimizing redundant or repeated search operations. In addition it notes problem descriptions (symptoms) and the solutions found for them that have been rated as helpful by the user. This learning process (*Adaptive Learning*) means that not only is it in a position to contribute to the permanent optimizing of the solution database with statistical reports (for example, the solution to a problem that is most frequently deemed useful), but it is also equipped to make concrete solution recommendations for a whole range of problem descriptions.

In the Interactive Intelligent Agent entry field a user can use any combination of user-defined text, attributes or problem-specific codes to enter a problem description. Then – if it has not already found the solution – the IIA suggests terms or codes to the user that are suitable for narrowing down the solution search. The solution that is finally found can be printed or sent by e-mail. In the latter case the customer's e-mail address, if it is recorded in the customer master data, is automatically displayed. In addition, the IIA offers the user access to a list with solutions that have been recently or frequently found for a particular problem. In this way, similar or repeated search operations can be avoided.

On entering user-defined text, the Interactive Intelligent Agent also offers the possibility of searching for the stem of a word, for a word contained in another term or for phonetic agreement. It also works closely with two further components that help make it particularly straightforward and user friendly: with the *Learning Engine* and the *Optimization Engine*.

▶ **The Learning Engine**
The Learning Engine analyzes the accuracy of a search result and immediately improves the quality and precision of subsequent search operations by evaluating the significance of information in relation to a solution. This information ("better than previous solutions") is then passed on from the learning engine to the optimization engine.

▶ **The Optimization Engine**
The Optimization Engine assists the specialists responsible for the content of the solution database by providing statistical data processing with the help of user responses, supplying reports from different points of view and automatically generating suggestions. In this way the content of the solution database and the quality of searches can be continuously improved. The list of frequently asked questions (FAQs) is a concentrated version of all the enterprise intelligence stored in the solution database and represents an

important source of information for customers and also for the employees of a company.

Installed Base Management

Installed Base Management refers to the maintenance and administration of all relevant information. The following example will serve to illustrate the details of installed base management.

Example: Overview of an Installed Base

A machine tool manufacturer, together with several cooperation partners, provides a large part of the technical installations for a car component manufacturer's new workshop. Because the component parts are delivered to the car manufacturer 'just in time', the component supplier has a service contract ensuring very quick reaction times with the machine tool manufacturer for installations that are important to production.

As the main contractor, the machine tool company guarantees customer service for the technical equipment supplied by them and their partners. In mySAP CRM this equipment is graphically displayed in Installations Management.

An agent in the interaction center, or any field service employee with access to the CRM system via mobile devices, can see at a glance in Installations Management that this car component supplier has, for example, three CNC lathes, two four-axle milling centers, a laser cutting tool and four hand-operated machines installed. From the general tree structure it can also be seen whether or not the three lathes are of the same type or if they have different equipment characteristics. From the installation displayed the agent can also tell which installations are supplied by which of the company's partners.

Because Installation Management is integrated into the service process, contracts can also be accessed from there. Field service employees can thus quickly get information on the terms of the agreed service contract before a visit to a customer or on the spot.

Example: Individual Objects

A building administration firm offers their commercial and private customers maintenance and repair services. This also includes the replacement of meters and defective thermostats on heaters. The building administration firm has created a description of the installations (*Installed Base*) for each customer in their CRM system. The installed base for a legal firm's two story office building has the following structure:

Installed Base
- – Building
- – 1st floor
  - – Room 1
    - ■ Heater
    - ■ Heater
  - – Room 2
    - ■ Heater
    - ■ Heater
  - – Room 3
    - □ CENTRAL INSTALLATION
- – 2nd floor
  - – Room 1
    - ■ Heater
    - ■ Heater
    - ■ Heater
  - – Room 2
    - ■ Heater
    - ■ Heater

This installed base description means that it can immediately be seen how many heaters are on each floor and in each room. The same information is displayed for each heater: identification number, thermostat type and meter type. The component in room 3 catches the eye. The central installation with integrated hot water supply, specially made for the office building is displayed in the installation management as an *Individual Object* and for which further additional information is displayed, for example device type, year of construction, service data, maintenance interval. In the event of a malfunction in the central installation the building administration firm will not entrust a fitter with the task of repairing it, rather they will get one of their heating specialists and provide him with the installation specific data.

Every enterprise can adapt the installation management in the CRM system to meet their own requirements. Therefore, for example, it is possible to display all installed bases in a single installation description, to combine several installed bases of the same type in a single description, or to have a separate installed base in the system for every customer and their installations.

Field Service and Resource Planning

The functions provided by the service component in mySAP CRM for field service and resource planning (Field Service & Dispatch) support the entire service cycle from the customer inquiry, to order execution right through to billing.

In Field Service and Dispatch, *Service* should not, however, be understood only in the sense of the classical task spectrum of technical customer service – that is to say maintenance, repair, replacement or re-installation of a device. A *Service* task is also carried out by an insurance company field service employee, for example, when they investigate a claim. A customer of a health insurance company also makes demands on *service* when they request personal advice on a rehabilitation program. And the field service team of a security company also offers *service* when they introduce a customer, at the request of the latter, to new technologies for safeguarding objects. Whether or not these services are provided as part of an existing service contract, are offered free of charge, or are billed separately is of no consequence for the automated service process in mySAP CRM.

Nevertheless, the easy functioning of the service component *Field Service & Dispatch* can be best explained with the help of a request for technical field service:

Example: Technical Field Service

The air-conditioning system in a customer's house has broken down. At 8:30 in the morning the customer rings the manufacturer's service center hotline number from his office. The manufacturer is based a few hundred miles away, but they have an extensive network of combined sales and service support points. The provisioning of replacement parts is carried out centrally at the company headquarters.

The customer gives the interaction center agent the serial number of the appliance and a description of the problem. The possible defect causes (power supply, level of coolant) that the agent has asked the customer to check have already been ruled out. "It would be best if you could send a technician round" requests the customer.

Resource Planning and Order Execution

The agent creates the service request with the necessary customer data (name, address, type of air-conditioning system, description of problem) in the interaction center application and explains to the customer that another employee will soon be in contact to arrange a time for the service visit. mySAP CRM checks the customer's place of residence or zip code and automatically transfers the service order to the corresponding regional manager responsible for *resource planning*. The latter gets an overview of the field service employees available in that region.

The resource planner can see on the screen that there are potentially eight technicians available. However, two of them are currently on holidays, one is off for the rest of the week due to illness, four technicians are already fully occupied with orders for that day; only the fifth available employee still has some free time. The manager can see that the technician is free from 1 pm that afternoon, so he calls the customer and suggests that the technician call between 1 and 4 pm (see figure 7.22).

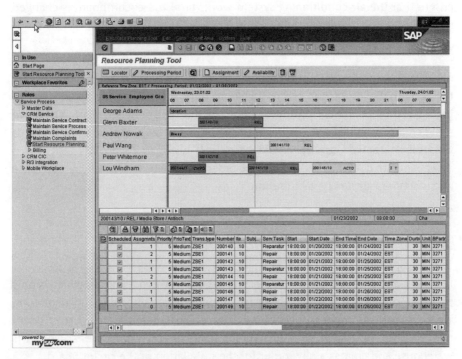

Figure 7.22 Employee scheduling with the resource planning tool

With a simple mouse click, the manager can allocate the order to the technician who is still available for today, chosen manually, and the CRM system automatically conveys the order to the field service employee's mobile terminal (a laptop, WAP phone or hand held computer). The manager knows that some technicians only enter their service confirmations in their mobile devices offline in the evenings, to send them to the CRM system the next morning while at the same time they pick up the current day's orders. That would be too late for the customer with the broken down air-conditioning system. For this reason, the manager also informs the technician by sending an SMS message or by paging him. A short time later the service employee confirms the new, high priority order.

Around 1 p.m. the technician arrives at the customer's home and immediately gets to work. He quickly locates the problem in the central controls of the air-conditioning system with the help of his diagnosis device. However he does not have this older type of circuit board with him, but he can bridge the defective circuit by putting in an additional switch – an emergency solution which will ensure that the air-conditioning system works until the circuit board is changed shortly.

Automatic order fulfillment

mySAP CRM service also supports fully automated order fulfillment. In this case the agent in the interaction center suggests a time to the customer for completing the request (*Appointment Offering*) – Thursday morning between eight and twelve – and creates a service order with a description of the fault. mySAP CRM forwards the order to a field service employee who is qualified to do this task and is available at that time. This method of order fulfillment is favored by appliance manufacturers with mass distribution.

Service Confirmation

Service confirmation can be done via different channels of communication and, when necessary, start off various different automatic workflows.

In his handheld device the service technician enters the data order, which is only partially completed, quoting the order number, times of arrival and departure, working time, and material used (switch). He also orders the new circuit board needed for controlling the air conditioning system from the spare parts warehouse and creates a new order for the installation of the circuit board.

The technician could also transfer all of this data to the CRM system in a telephone conversation with a service center agent, online via the Internet or offline on his laptop with subsequent data transfer. The CRM system in turn forwards it to the corresponding components of the ERP system (personnel planning, materials management). The process steps resulting run automatically in the ERP system:

▶ The materials management component registers the withdrawal of the switch and the circuit board, checks the target stock and if necessary arranges a (replacement) purchase order. It also registers the material used in the service order placed for the customer.

▶ The CRM system reports the technician's travel and working time to the *Cross-Application Time Sheet (CATS)*. This application records the confirmation times, both on the technician's time account *(mySAP HR Payroll)* and on the customer's single or collective service order. For subsequent invoicing all items in the bill (material, time) are automatically changed into amounts of money and clearly detailed. The customer receives a bill for the whole amount due, the individual items of which are easily understood.

mySAP CRM service also offers the possibility of giving several confirmations for one service job, such as if a field service employee, as in our example of the broken air-conditioning system, needs more than one day to complete an order or if more than one employee works on the same service job. It is also possible to send confirmations for several service orders at the same time, for example, if they are entered offline in a laptop or hand-held application and are later transferred to the CRM system all together during the next online connection.

Integrated Service Concept

The mySAP CRM integrated concept behind all this means that it is possible for all service employees also to have access to the functions of the field sales team. If the customer in the example of the broken air-conditioning system had decided to extend or upgrade his home system, the service technician could have given concrete and forthcoming recommendations. In this case it was not the field *sales* team, rather it was a member of the *technical service* team – with the customer's situation right before his eyes – who generated additional revenue for the enterprise.

Invoicing

Invoicing (*CRM Billing*, see also "Invoicing" on page 109) provides all necessary functions for displaying time, material and services rendered in a bill for a customer. Service contracts can be billed periodically, in which case it can be set in the billing plan what amount or percentage should be billed at that time. The invoicing of *individual* orders or service tasks is also possible, independent of one order confirmation that was perhaps not necessary, after each confirmation or after the full completion of the job.

Service Planning

mySAP CRM *Service Planning* is a flexible tool, with the help of which services can be defined as *products* and can be aggressively marketed, even including a view of previously defined customer target groups and in the context of a widely structured campaign. Service planning basically supports all types of services: Customer service and technical installations, training and advice.

A telecommunications enterprise could, for example, plan the following services and offer them via the Internet, their interaction center or field service employees:

▶ Exchanging fixed telephones in the home for cordless telephones for a set price. This offer runs for six months and is only valid if the exchange of telephones is done on a Tuesday or Thursday, because normally the technical field service employees work at less than 70 % of capacity on these days.

▶ Technical service offers all customers with an ISDN Internet connection a change to a broadband connection, faster net access, at a flat rate if they decide to make the change during the next six months. The telecommunications company informs their customers of this offer via the Internet, in the monthly bill and with nation-wide television advertising.

The following example demonstrates that service products like this are conceivable for almost all enterprises, who see customer service not merely as an obligatory service that accompanies the sale of products, but as a value-added instrument with which relationships with customers can be strengthened and extended.

▶ A heating system manufacturer has ascertained that over 85 % of their customers request an inspection of their heating system in the months of November and December. So that their technical service team have their work more evenly distributed, the company offers a cheaper inspection in the months April through June, together with a "Winter Guarantee" which ensures a breakdown service within six hours.

▶ Via their subsidiaries and appointed dealers, a car manufacturer offers customers a specially priced pre-holiday inspection of their vehicles, offer valid only on Tuesdays. On Tuesdays the work load in all workshops is significantly lower than on other days.

Service Processing

There are normally special agreements in service contracts, known as *Service Level Agreements* or *SLA Parameters*. In mySAP CRM the SLA Parameters *Service window* and *Reaction time* are integrated as standard; however, additional enterprise specific parameters can be defined by the user to support specific business processes.

These parameters serve not only to give descriptions of special agreements, they can also be turned into controls for the administering of a service process, with which the CRM system compares confirmations with the time targets stipulated in the contract. Where it can be foreseen that these time targets cannot be met, pre-determined internal escalation steps will automatically be started to avoid the scenario where the customer might lodge a complaint. An example of such escalation measures might be to punctually inform the customer that a service employee will be delayed or to inform them if replacement parts will not be available in time or that they will not be billed for worktime to make up for the inconvenience.

Service Contracts With Special Agreements

Basically, service contracts are long-term agreements between an enterprise and its customers. The classic case is the legally proscribed guarantee period for a product, which normally includes service too. On the purchase of the product a standardized guarantee and service contract with the same conditions for all purchasers comes into effect.

For many customers, however, the standard offer is not sufficient and they request service contracts tailor-made to meet their personal requirements. They may, for instance, want a two year service contract for their air-conditioning system including clauses that assure that a technician will do periodical maintenance work – always after 5 p.m. – and a special agreement that any functional problems will be dealt with within 24 hours.

In mySAP CRM Service, both standard and personal contracts can be administered and drawn up with SLA Parameters. Where a contract refers to an appliance or a technical installation, the technical equipment will be indicated in association with the contract. Any time a service process that is based on a service contract is created, the CRM system automatically compares the services to be executed with the terms of the contract. If for example in a computer user's special contract there is an agreement guaranteeing an on-site service within 24 hours, but because of an urgent order the customer now requests a technician within six hours, then this faster reaction time can be billed separately. Services like this that are not covered in the contract are priced and entered in the CRM system under *Conditions*. Similarly, it can be noted in a maintenance contract that all service work for an installed base will be carried out free of charge during a certain time period.

Service Analysis

Service and field-service employees, together with their colleagues in sales, are closest to the customer. From the customer's point of view *they* represent the company – people with whom one can talk, who can answer questions and help with problems. The opinion that the customers have of an enterprise is largely formed by these employees, with whom they are in direct contact. When the quality of a product or a service is little more than a distinguishing characteristic, the satisfaction of the customer with customer service gains greater competitive significance as a deciding factor.

Customer oriented companies do not only bear the satisfaction of their clientele strongly in mind, they also gauge it. mySAP CRM makes the necessary data available. *Service Analytics* looks after the evaluation and the graphic presentation of same.

The main feature is the possibility of monitoring and analysing all service processes (planning, prognosis, execution). On the basis of the results of the analysis, new customer relationships can be build up and existing ones strengthened with well-directed measures. Key indicators can be defined for analyzing a service process that makes it possible to assess the following points, for example:

▶ Volumes (number of orders)

▶ Quality (number of complaints)

▶ Cost efficiency (expenses compared to revenue)

On the basis of such fundamental key figures, which the CRM system makes available to the SAP Business Information Warehouse, the enterprise can also define additional key figures in line with its information requirements. The service analysis can, for example, supply answers to the following questions:

▶ Which Service Level Agreements (SLAs) are most frequently requested by customers?

▶ In what percentage of cases could the agreed SLA times *not* be adhered to by the company? What were the reasons for this?

▶ Which products cause the most problems?

▶ What percentage of all complaints come via the Interaction Center, the Internet Self Service and the field service employees?

▶ In which customer segment (categorized, for example, according to age, service contract or private/commercial) is the level or complaints the lowest?

▶ What customer group takes up new product or service offers most often, which group takes them up the least?

▶ Can any regional differences be seen in customer satisfaction levels?

There are hardly any service-related questions that cannot be answered in a service analysis with the help of the dataset in mySAP CRM, and if necessary in connection with other internal sources. The results of the analyses put an enterprise in a position to identify ineffective developments early on and to react with adequate measures. Ultimately all analysis serves to optimize the service process and to shape it continuously to meet customers' wishes, and in this way ensure that satisfied customers will become loyal customers too.

8 mySAP CRM – Key Capabilities and Business Scenarios

Apart from the integrated view of the Customer Interaction Cycle with the phases of Engage, Transact, Fulfill and Service, as was presented in the previous chapter, mySAP CRM is geared towards concrete business scenarios that are derived from customer requirements. These business scenarios are brought together to form functional key areas and act as a basis for both product development and for the sales process and customer implementation projects. More specifically this means:

▶ mySAP CRM Product Developer and Product Manager identify and analyze key capabilities and business areas in collaboration with customers. Then come design, development, test and delivery, each under the general responsibility of a person in charge of the scenario. This process serves to portray the business flow optimally, as it actually occurs for the customer, in the mySAP.com software.

▶ mySAP CRM sales employees discuss concrete business scenarios with their customers and, with the help of *e-Business Case Builders*, can establish profit potential for the customer from an early stage.

▶ mySAP CRM consultants support customers in the swift implementation of mySAP CRM with the help of CRM business scenarios, pre-configured in *Best Practices*.

The following overview lists important key capabilities which are generally supported by Development, Sales and Consulting:

▶ Marketing Management
▶ Sales
▶ E-selling
▶ Field Sales
▶ Interaction Center
▶ Customer Service
▶ Field Service & Dispatch
▶ Integrated Sales Planning
▶ Leasing & Asset Management (planned)

The most important business scenarios belonging to these key capabilities are outlined below.

Marketing Management

Marketing Management supports the planning, target group selection, execution and analysis of marketing activities and campaigns through all interaction channels. The main scenarios are:

▶ **Campaign management**
Campaign development, from market analysis through campaign execution to analysis of results

▶ **Lead management**
Automation of the steps preceding the sales process, to enable the sales department to concentrate on the potential customers and opportunities that show the greatest chances of success

▶ **Modeling target groups**
Determination and establishment of target groups for particular marketing initiatives

▶ **Analysis of customer behavior**
Analysis of customer purchasing and straying behavior

▶ **Analysis of customer profitability**
Determining the profitability of individual customers, either as a difference between revenue and expenses per customer or as a detailed customer profit margin analysis taking into account different forms of revenue, product and sales expenses

▶ **Analysis of customer lifetime value**
Customer Lifetime Values (CLTV) can be used to determine how customer stock and profitability have evolved per customer segment and per lifetime period

▶ **Trade promotion management**
Solutions for the planning and development of sales promotion measures, available with the 3.0 follow-up releases.

Further details on the subject of *Marketing Management* can be found in chapter 7, "Customer Engagement" on page 58.

Sales

Sales embraces all steps in the sales process – from initial customer contact to the closing of a contract – via all interaction channels. The main scenarios are:

▶ **Opportunity management**
Business processes from the identification of a sales opportunity to a sales agreement (or earlier termination)

- ▶ **Opportunity management and mobile sales**
  Support for field sales employees with automatic data reconciliation between their personal laptops and the CRM server
- ▶ **Sales order processing**
  Order processing incl. availability check and delivery scheduling. Invoicing is carried out with the billing function in mySAP CRM or with the SAP R/3 Supply Chain Execution System.
- ▶ **Value contract processing**
  Creation and processing of value contracts. Each time a customer releases products from a value contract, sales processing is set in motion and the value remaining is adjusted.

Further information on the subject of *Sales* is presented in chapter 7, "Business Transaction" on page 73.

E-Selling

E-Selling is the comprehensive SAP solution for the sale of products over the Internet. All phases of the sales cycle from marketing, to catalog browsing to placing an order, payment, order fulfillment and customer support are included. The principle scenarios in E-Selling are:

- ▶ **Business-to-Business (B2B) sales ordering transaction**
  With this scenario, business partners can order products and services via the Internet. Marketing aspects play only a small role.
- ▶ **Business-to-Consumer (B2C) sales ordering transaction**
  With this scenario, consumers can order products and services via the Internet. Marketing aspects play a very important role.
- ▶ **Product catalog management and product recommendations**
  Here it is determined which products are to be offered in the web store, the make-up of the web catalog, what personalized or current product recommendations will be used for catching the customers' attention, and which cross-selling or up-selling products will be offered to the customer.
- ▶ **Web analysis**
  Analysis of customer behavior on individual web pages and evaluation of technical aspects such as availability and performance of web servers and web pages with the help of SAP BW.

More detailed information on the subject of *E-Selling* can be found in chapters 9 and 13.

Field Sales

Field Sales permits traveling field sales employees, who work both at customers' premises and in the office, to use the entire range of possibilities offered by modern customer relationship management. The main scenarios in Field Sales are:

▶ **Customer visit with order entry**
Support of field sales employees in the successful planning and execution of customer visits including order entry

▶ **Execution of campaigns**
With this scenario providers are in a position, within the context of a campaign, to generate the mass creation of activities for field sales employees.

▶ **Visit planning**
The drawing up of efficient itinerary plans for customer visits on the part of the field sales employee

▶ **Handheld sales**
Sales employees can consult current sales data or enter orders using their handheld equipment at any time.

▶ **Mobile sales**
Field sales employees can download customer data, product information, and so on, from the CRM server to their personal laptop and send back orders or updated data

Please refer to chapter 7, "Business Transaction" on page 73, and especially chapter 11 for more detailed information on the subject of *Field Sales*.

Interaction Center

The Interaction Center for communication with clients via extremely varied channels of interaction is a key component of the mySAP CRM solution. The principal scenarios in the interaction center are:

▶ **Qualifying leads and opportunities**
Planning and execution of call actions to evaluate the interest level of leads and opportunities

▶ **Inbound telesales**
Processing of customer or potential customer inquiries in the interaction center

▶ **Outbound telesales**
Sales campaigns or periodical calls from the interaction center, administered with call lists

► **Information help desk**

Offering guidance to customers in response to their questions about products and services. Support for employees in the interaction center in the form of the Interactive Intelligent Agent (IIA).

► **Interaction center service**

Processing of service inquiries and orders incorporating the Installed Base database and Interactive Intelligent Agent (IIA).

► **Processing complaints**

Dealing with complaints on products and services. Complaints can be made in relation to a product or may perhaps have no connection to any particular product.

Further information on the subject of *Interaction Center* can be found in chapter 10.

Customer Service

This key capability of mySAP CRM covers the central processes in the service organization, beginning with the creation of service contracts, to the execution of services through to confirmation. The main scenarios are:

► **Complaint processing**

Processing the complete complaints procedure from the receipt of a complaint, to technical analysis through the follow-up steps to be taken in customer service and sales, for example the creation of credit memos

► **E-service (Internet customer self service)**

Internet based self-service functions for customers and internal users such as access to Frequently Asked Questions (FAQs), as well as inquiring about the status of service orders

► **Service confirmation**

Confirmation from service employees (activities, materials, travel and work times, expenses) via different interaction channels

► **Service contract processing for installations**

Agreement about particular services (for example, maintenance, hotline) for an installed base, specified in a Service Level Agreement if required.

► **Processing returns**

Return and exchange, for example, because the wrong product has been bought or the product is faulty

► **Service processing with a contractual Service Level Agreement**

Execution of service procedures on the basis of a Service Level Agreement reached with the customer

Further details on the topic of *Customer Service* can be found in chapter 7, "Customer Service" on page 112.

Field Service & Dispatch

Field Service & Dispatch covers various activities in the context of service processing. The main scenarios are:

▶ **Service processing with resource planning**
Resource planner plans and monitors service procedures with the help of a graphic plan table

▶ **Handheld service**
Service employees on duty can call up important information related to their work and send in service order confirmations via their handheld equipment (PDAs, mobile phones, and so on).

▶ **Mobile service**
Field service employees can download information on planned service jobs from the CRM server to their personal laptops or can upload updated data.

Please refer to chapter 7, "Customer Service" on page 112, and to chapter 11 for more detailed information on the subject of *Field Service & Dispatch*.

Integrated Sales Planning

Integrated sales planning has the task of creating the prerequisites for a long-term business success by planning sales measures for key customers. Putting plans together in collaboration with the customer at their premises can be done with offline planning using Microsoft Excel (see chapter 7, "Sales Planning" on page 78).

Leasing & Asset Management

CRM business scenarios are continuously being developed and expanded. One function that is planned for the next versions of mySAP CRM is *Leasing & Asset Management*, a solution for leasing enterprises that lease appliances and assets. All core processes needed by leasing companies will be supported:

▶ Quotations

▶ Contract management

▶ Changing existing leasing agreements

▶ End-of-lease transactions (return, extension, purchase, and so on)

▶ Finance quotations

9 E-Selling With mySAP CRM – The Internet as a Strategic Sales Channel

When products are sold over the Internet, this is always connected with customer relationship management. In this respect e-selling forms an integral part of customer relationship management – on operational, collaborative and analytical levels.

Electronic Selling Beyond the Shopping Basket

With the advent of e-commerce many enterprises readily believed that the Internet would open up new markets, increase sales potential, cut sales costs drastically and bind customers closely to a company long-term. Companies of all sizes and from very different sectors have high expections of the Internet as a new distribution channel. Often huge budgets are set aside so as not to miss the link to the Internet age.

However, e-commerce projects that are only technology driven, focused only on the web store, run the risk of wasting the new medium presented. E-business should be treated as an opportunity to redefine business processes and to tailor processes to fulfill the desires of customers. Apart from convenience and simplicity in making a purchase, customers also expect efficient and reliable sales processing and customer service from an e-business solution. Many e-commerce solutions show serious deficits in this area – and the number of unsatisfied Internet customers grows. Reasons for this include, for example:

▶ Elaborate ordering procedures
▶ Inaccurate or erroneous data on product availability
▶ Goods delivered too late or not at all
▶ Invoices that do not coincide with what was delivered

Usually the problem lies in the fact that the web store is not sufficiently integrated with the company's existing IT environment. In practice, there is often a wide gap between the claims made and the reality of e-commerce. The advantages of the Internet as a distribution channel are obvious:

▶ Unlimited market presence, worldwide and right around the clock
▶ Speeding up the sales process with automatic procedures
▶ Reducing transaction costs thanks to cross-enterprise automation of the sales process

- ▶ Cutting personnel costs by reducing the number of telephone orders and inquiries
- ▶ Specific, direct contact with customers thanks to comprehensive information on the customer
- ▶ High rates of customer satisfaction and strengthened ties with customers thanks to optimized customer service.
- ▶ Increased turnover thanks to the opening up of new customer groups and fully exploiting the potential of cross-selling and up-selling

However, e-business solutions only really offer advantages to suppliers if a customer receives real added value. It is not enough to present products on the Internet with colorful pictures and an electronic shopping basket. More often than not, competitive advantages occur beyond the shopping basket. Relevant advantages for the customer, which is how the efficiency of an e-business solution must be measured, could be derived from the buyer's requirements and desires in the purchasing or procurement process. These include:

- ▶ Quick searches and easy navigation
- ▶ Comprehensive product information
- ▶ Customer specific offers, in accordance with their needs
- ▶ Tailor-made products
- ▶ Up-to-date and accurate price information
- ▶ Precise data on availability
- ▶ Simple and convenient ordering procedure
- ▶ Fast sales order processing
- ▶ Transparent queries on order status
- ▶ Reliable, punctual delivery
- ▶ Correct invoicing
- ▶ Value added after-sales service

For suppliers who wish to use the Internet as a strategic interaction channel for customers, certain factors of success, which may sometimes appear trivial yet are absolutely critical, can immediately be derived from this: In the world of e-business the companies that achieve lasting competitive advantages over their rivals are those that can record and process the needs and desires of their customers more personally, more effectively, quicker and cheaper.

Strategic Competitive Advantages With Electronic Selling

The starting point for attaining strategic competitive advantages in the area of e-selling can be assigned to four core areas:

▶ Full integration of the sales process in the value processes of vendor and purchaser

▶ Incorporation of the Internet into the enterprise's CRM strategy

▶ Personalizing interaction with customers

▶ Acquiring *Business Intelligence*, to find out more about the needs and behavior of customers and to be able to offer them a better service

The four areas mentioned will be presented in detail below.

Integration of the Sales Process in the Value Added Process

The aim of a successful e-selling solution is to bring about beneficial value both for the vendor and for the buyer. Such a mutual advantage can only be achieved if the two parties are linked so closely together in the sales process that a common added value can be achieved. Automation must go so far as to practically eliminate the boundaries between the supplying enterprise and the customer. This requires the full integration of the sales transaction in the customer's procurement process and in the sales and logistics processes of the vendor.

An e-selling solution for Internet based purchasing/sales processes is therefore oriented both to the needs and wishes of the customer and to the sales requirements of the vendor, and can ideally be subdivided into the following steps:

▶ Product search

▶ Product selection

▶ Ordering

▶ Order processing/delivery

▶ Payment

Product Search

The main priorities for the customer regarding the search process are: simple navigation through the product offer (*product catalog*); easy-to-use search functions for finding the desired product quickly; and the presentation of customer-specific offers. As far as the vendor is concerned, this requires flexible

Vendor **Customer**

Catalog Management	Multimedia Catalog	Search Products
Personali-sation	Customer Specific Offers	Select/Configure
Marketing	Cross Selling	ATP Check Order
Order Processing	Logistic Execution	Order Tracking
Billing	Electronic Bill Presn.	Invoice/Payment
Customer Services	Call Center	Services/Returns

Figure 9.1 The sales process from the point of view of the customer and of the vendor

catalog management, powerful search engines and well developed one-to-one marketing functions.

Product Selection and Configuration

To offer customers optimal support during the selection of individual products they should be offered options that are specifically suited to them. Apart from catalog selection, product selection is possible from customer specific offers, user-defined order forms as well as from offers accepted and previous orders. Or perhaps a customer would like to configure the product according to their own ideas. In each case reliable price information is important. Pricing and configuration should be based on the conditions and rules applicable in the backend system. Only in this way is it guaranteed that the customer-configured variant can in fact be produced in the required way and that the price shown on the Internet coincides with the amount subsequently invoiced.

Purchase Order

When a customer wants to order a particular product on the Internet, this is generally done using a (virtual) shopping basket. The selected product is placed in the shopping basket and can then be ordered. The use of purchase order forms or the direct entry of purchase order numbers makes purchasing easier. Before submitting the order the customer often requests a reliable delivery date. The availability check in the backend system can supply this information online. An order confirmation is expected immediately after the purchase order has been sent.

Order Fulfillment

The problem-free processing of an order made over the Internet, right up to the delivery of the goods ordered, is of prime importance for customer satisfaction. To guarantee this, the fundamental requirement is an efficient backend system. The seamless process integration of the web store with the backend applications is a prerequisite for fast and reliable order processing. However, in practice many e-commerce solutions lack this general automation. This results in unnecessary delays, erroneous deliveries and high handling costs. A useful service, that fosters customer satisfaction on the one hand and shows greater cost-cutting potential on the other, is offered in the form of online queries on order status, allowing the customer to find out about the status of the order processing at any time. Without backend integration this service is not possible.

Payment Transaction

When placing an order the customer can choose between the various different methods of payment offered by the vendor – for example, credit cards, invoice, cash on delivery. In the processing of the payment transaction, it is once more of vital importance to have integration with the backend system to ensure that any applicable discounts are taken into account, invoice amounts are correctly calculated, receipt of payment is correctly posted and, when necessary, that reminders are sent at the appropriate time. *Electronic Bill Presentment & Payment* systems go one step further by digitalizing the process of invoicing and invoice payment completely. They permit customers to check on bills and their status at any time via the Internet and to effect payment immediately.

After-Sales Services

In the area of after-sales there is a range of possibilities for offering the customer useful self-service after the purchase has been completed. This includes, for example, a returns process for goods that have been delivered by mistake or damaged, or for goods that the customer simply decides they do not want. The possibility for customers to give maintenance and repair orders via the Internet is also part of this area, as are FAQ (Frequently Asked Question) sections or knowledge databases with information on the setting up or use of the product, and so on.

Incorporation of the Internet Into the Enterprise's CRM Strategy

The Internet presents an important channel of interaction which allows for a high degree of personalization in interactions with customers, despite automation.

A good e-selling strategy focuses not only on the Internet as a mere distribution channel, but in some cases includes other channels of interaction with the customer (such as field service, retailing, and so on) and in others also pursues a general strategy with regard to a systematic pre-sales, sales and after-sales cycle. Therefore, in many cases, e-selling implies a multi-channel strategy and essentially includes the areas of marketing, sales and customer service.

For this it is important that the different contact channels are synchronized, that is to say, no matter what medium the customer uses to make contact with the enterprise it is guaranteed that the information gained in the process will not contradict information received during other contacts with the vendor (see also chapter 3, "Multi-Channel Interaction Between Business Partners" on page 30).

Personalizing Interaction With Customers

The possibility of using the Internet as an instrument of one-to-one marketing by personalizing the content of product offers is therefore an important starting point for achieving strategic competitive advantage. Direct interaction with the customer is in line with the basic ideas of personalized, dialog-oriented marketing and allows customer-specific contact which goes far beyond the possibilities of conventional marketing and classical media advertising. Customer-specific communication enables enterprises to carry out more effective marketing. Personalization can take different forms (see also chapter 3, "Individual Customer Contact by Personalization" on page 22):

▶ Customer-specific catalogs

▶ Individual pricing and conditions for customers

▶ Customer-specific product configuration (*Mass Customization*)

▶ Specific product recommendations

▶ Personalized user interfaces

Many innovative enterprises already install systems with which they can combine different types of information together to produce personalized offers. In the analyses, for example, there may be data from clickstream analysis as well as from examinations of the effects of marketing activities. Furthermore, the analyses may include variables on demography, buyer behavior and on the preferences of customer input.

The drawing up of meaningful customer profiles containing customer characteristics that may be relevant to buyer behavior (for example, gender, age, income, hobbies, product preferences, habits of use), represents a fundamental prerequisite for successful one-to-one marketing. The definition of target groups can be done on the basis of customer profiles (for example, "men between the ages of 30 and 40 who earn more than $5000 net per month and who enjoy practicing sport in their leisure time"). Tailored to match the personal needs and requirements of individual users, very specific marketing measures can be executed, for example, recommending particular products.

Acquiring Business Intelligence

Customer Relationship Management is planned less and less on the basis of general market research information and more on the basis of personal customer data. Only when vendors analyze the wishes and needs of *their* customers in detail can they serve *their* customers better. This is of particular importance in e-selling, because on the Internet the competition is often just a mouse-click away.

For this reason, vendors must monitor their web store systematically, both regarding the technical condition and also from a business point of view. This includes, in particular, the recording of information on purchasing and interaction behavior over the course of a business relationship, in order to compare these with other customer characteristics that may be relevant to buyer behavior, for example, from other distribution channels, and in doing so, obtain a more comprehensive view of the customer.

For this one can use simple clickstream-analyses (*hits and visits*) and classical sales statistics (including channel comparison), and also the specific evaluation of complex questions with the help of a data warehouse, for example, regarding the appeal of product offers and web-contents, customer retention or the creation of what are known as conversion rates (for example, look-and-buy ratio).

Selected E-Selling Business Scenarios

mySAP CRM E-Selling supports different business scenarios for describing cross-enterprise business processes. It is possible to integrate the Internet solution into business processes for both single-step and multi-step sales processes. The following sections describe the basic features of the five most important business scenarios.

Business-to-Consumer (B2C)

Direct selling to the end-consumer stands at the center of the Business-to-Consumer (B2C) sector. In this context the procurement and sales processes of one vendor to a large number of diverse buyers is of significance. The Internet complements conventional, existing distribution channels or, in some circumstances, is a distribution tool in its own right. In B2C, transactions are characterized by being spontaneous, often of low to medium volume and having no strong links between the transaction partners.

A deciding factor for the success of individual enterprises is knowledge of the user or customer structure. Only those vendors who present their activity program on the net in a manner that is appropriate for the target group will be able to make convincing offers. For example, in conventional channels of distribution the atmosphere (type and decoration) of a store and customer orientation have considerable effect on customers' willingness to buy and their subjective quality appraisal. Given that with online shopping it is not possible to produce a physical store environment to stimulate buyer behavior, it is necessary to give consumers a similarly vivid shopping experience.

To produce a sensory shopping atmosphere and to build long-term relationships between vendor and purchaser, some features of design take on particular significance in B2C. This includes the design of multimedia product catalogs, the layout of the web pages, one-to-one marketing – that is, personalized product proposals – cross-selling and up-selling offers, bestseller lists, special offers and the support and secure processing of various different payment transactions (invoice, cash on delivery, credit cards, and so on). For consolidating customer relationships in the Business-to-Consumer sector, the reliability of sales order processing and distribution logistics is of considerable importance. From a strategic point of view it should, if appropriate, be considered how best to arrange the interplay with conventional channels of distribution (subsidiaries, dealers and field sales team).

Business-to-Business (B2B)

The electronic processing of business transactions between enterprises (component suppliers, manufacturers and dealers) forms the object of the Business-to-Business (B2B) sector.

Unlike in B2C, the transaction partners in B2B usually maintain long-term business relationships, so that a link between vendor and buyer is built up. Transactions are usually characterized by being of medium to large volumes. As a result the negotiation of conditions and contracts is of greater consequence than in B2C.

Whereas customer behavior in B2C is mainly characterized by searches in product catalogs, business purchasers generally have a clear idea of what products they wish to acquire. Therefore, the type and method of navigation is different from one transaction partner to another.

In consideration of the particular requirements specific to relationships with business patrons, the following design parameters, among others, are prominent in B2B:

▶ Possibility of customer-specific product and price creation

▶ Masks for fast order creation, availability checks and order status checks

▶ Links to the purchaser's procurement system

Integration, consistency and transparency in business processes take on particular importance in B2B – from selecting the product, to availability check and pricing, right through to order processing, production and finally delivery to various different ship-to addresses and invoicing.

With respect to the linking of dealers on the Internet in the B2B scenario, some special features should be taken into consideration. These are, on the one hand, attributable to the go-between function of dealers and also to the often close relationship between manufacturers and dealers. Sometimes dealers put quite high demands on catalog content and status information on order and invoice items. It should be possible to change or even to cancel orders that have already been created via the Internet. In addition it is advisable to support web-based handling of returns too. Outline agreements, annual arrangements and price protection clauses, which are quite frequently referred to in purchase orders, also play an important role.

In particular, if the business processes, on both the side of the vendor and of the purchaser, are supported by the technical systems, the possibility of one-step business materializes (see chapter 2, "Purchasing and Sales Processes Grow Together" on page 18). With this the possibilities of linking a store-solution with the e-procurement software used come fully into play.

Business-to-Marketplaces (B2M)

Internet-based electronic marketplaces (exchanges) use the infrastructure, technologies and standards of the Internet to support or execute market transactions. They act, on one hand, as mediators that enable several vendors and buyers to come together in a common place on the Internet. Technologically speaking, on the other hand, they serve as connectors between procurement systems – on the side of the buyers – and store solutions – on the side of the vendors. In this way, they also create the technological basis for one-step business. The objective of these Internet marketplaces is to bring together the biggest possible share of business volume in a certain market and to process electronically via this exchange.

If the B2C and B2B scenarios were the first manifestations of electronic commerce, many enterprises since then have transferred their purchases and/or sales to the Internet and together started joint ventures for the operation of electronic exchanges. In practice, the actual arrangement of electronic marketplaces can vary considerably. Nevertheless, they are ultimately based on the same key concept: Electronic exchanges present a market system of suppliers, dealers, service providers, infrastructure providers and customers who use the Internet for the communication and execution of specific business transactions.

Basically, exchanges can be designed as *open* or *closed*. Open electronic marketplaces (*Public Exchanges*) present market platforms that can be accessed by all vendors and purchasers. In contrast, with the closed varieties (*Private Exchanges*) there are regional, personal or institution-related restrictions to access. Usually a private exchange is started by a single larger vendor or buyer.

Web Store solutions can be securely implanted in the execution of cross-enterprise business processes via private or public exchanges. Regarding the conversion, different groupings can be distinguished, independent of systems already existing on the part of the selling enterprise:

▶ The vendor already has an e-selling solution, this can be linked to the exchange as what is known as an *On-Ramp*, that is, the enterprise can sell their products via the exchange with the help of their e-selling solution. For this they use no services on the exchange. Because the e-selling solution operates on the vendor's systems, they also have the possibility of linking their solution to various different exchanges.

▶ Vendors who have so far not implemented any web store solutions can engage the relevant functions on the exchange in the form of a *Hosting solution*.

▶ If the vending enterprise has an ERP system installed but no e-selling software, it can use the special functions for preparation of content (information on product, price, availability and configuration) on the exchange. By means of a link with the vending enterprise's ERP system the latter can receive purchase orders or send confirmations and shipping notifications.

▶ If enterprises have no e-business software installed, yet still wish to sell their products via an exchange, this is possible with the help of a simple browser access. In this case the enterprise leases a web store solution and an order processing system on the exchange as a complete solution.

Business-to-Business Mall (B2B Mall)

The Business-to-Business Mall (B2B Mall) sector can be seen as a further development of the classical B2B scenario, in which several vendors offer their products via a shared *Storefront*. This can represent the different sectors of one diversified enterprise or several different enterprises, which, with the idea of *One Face to the Customers*, offer consumers the possibility of convenient *One-Step Buying*.

The participating vendors offer their products to their customers on the web, where they provide a product catalog, the appeal of which can be further enhanced by the inclusion of multimedia elements (picture, sound, video). With this, companies have the possibility of presenting their offer in a company-specific product catalog (*Corporate Branding*) or as part of a shared product catalog (*Multi Supplier Catalog*).

The special features of a B2B Mall include:

▶ Easy, cross-catalog search functions
▶ Centralized availability check and status queries (order and invoice status)
▶ Customer-specific pricing and product configuration among all vendors
▶ Centralized shopping basket which brings together products selected from all catalogs and calculates and displays their total price.

For individual vendors within the mall, however, it is necessary that the procurement order items relevant to them are filtered out of the shopping basket. For this it is necessary to split the collective order into several vendor-specific suborders (*Order Split*). The sub-orders are posted in the backend systems of the corresponding enterprises and are thus available there for further logistic processing. It is absolutely necessary to enable integration with backend infrastructures to ensure the problem-free linking of existing IT environments with the sales process. Connections to the customers' procurement systems complete the buying process and make the execution of *one-step business* possible.

This type of solution is particularly suitable for vendors who have a large number of customers with relatively low sales volume. In conventional business processes, customers run up enormous expenses in making contact with companies participating in the mall via conventional channels of communication – for example, fax, telephone and e-mail. Both the manufacturer and the customer benefit mutually from this scenario – orders can be processed and dealt with more quickly, more efficiently and more precisely while at the same time service calls and transaction costs are significantly reduced. By offering complementary products in a mall the customer potential for all vendors is increased.

Distributor & Reseller Networks (B2R2B, B2R2C)

If the scenarios described up to now were one-step business processes, the *Distributor & Reseller Network* presents multi-step business processes. In this case the vendor takes on the function of *Channel Master*; by controlling both direct and indirect distribution channels via the Internet. The vendor or purchaser roles can thus be taken on by different market participants. Generally the vendors are large enterprises. The purchaser can be the end-user, or may be a reseller (for example, wholesalers and retailers).

An example for a distributor & reseller network can be seen in a computer manufacturer who sells products both directly to end-users and also indirectly through the linking of dealers to their *Internet* distribution channel. In such a network, the manufacturer – as channel master – can undertake the centralized maintenance of the multimedia product catalog. Individual dealers then have the possibility of extending the product catalog with services that they offer their end-users, and with any other complementary products that can only be obtained via that dealer. The ideas of the *Store within a Store concept* are thus transferred to the Internet world. In this way the manufacturer and their dealers present the end-customer (whether consumer or business customer) with a common *Storefront*.

Synergy effects in this network lead to considerable cost reduction. Firstly, products only have to be created once with product description and multimedia data. Furthermore, it guarantees that the customer will have access to a uniform and up-to-date product program in the catalog at all times. In addition, the purchaser has the possibility of executing product configuration and availability checks directly at the manufacturer's site. Problems with obsolete product lists, configuration possibilities and availability, as they occur in conventional, multi-step business processes are thus a thing of the past. The possibility of cross-enterprise one-to-one marketing, with personalized product proposals and cross-selling and up-selling, further enhances business relationships.

The distributor & reseller network has to cover a broad spectrum of functions, because not only the special features of the Business-to-Consumer sector have to be taken into account, but also those of the Business-to-Business sector. Moreover, it is necessary to support both purchase orders for the dealer's or reseller's warehouse, and purchase orders from customers with direct or indirect delivery (*Sell-Through-Scenario*).

Regarding reselling to enterprises that do not have their own order processing system for reasons of capacity or costs, for instance, it may be necessary to make an order processing system available to these business partners on the private or public exchange in a hosting operation. In this case, such a procedure would also provide for the integration of manufacturers' and dealers' logistics chains.

E-Selling With mySAP CRM

mySAP CRM offers a comprehensive e-selling solution which covers the following subject areas:

▶ One-to-one marketing

▶ Catalog management and product selection

▶ Purchase orders and sales order processing

▶ Web auctions

▶ Interactive customer support

▶ Web analyses

▶ Web store design

Figure 9.2 shows the individual modules of the mySAP CRM E-Selling solution.

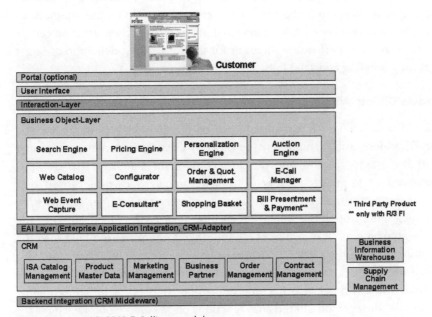

Figure 9.2 mySAP CRM E-Selling: modules

One-to-one Marketing

With its marketing functions, mySAP CRM E-Selling offers the possibility of using the Internet as a powerful marketing tool. According to Peppers and Rogers [Peppers 1993] one-to-one marketing is based on four principles:

▶ **Identify**
Identify customers

▶ **Differentiate**
Differentiate between customers on the basis of their value and their requirements

▶ **Interact**
Dialog with customers

▶ **Customize**
Tailor the dialog content to fit the customer

These principles are outlined below.

Identify and Differentiate: Define Customer Profiles and Target Groups

The basis for successful one-to-one marketing is meaningful customer profiles, which can be created and maintained in mySAP CRM. They are made up of purchase-relevant customer characteristics and statistics (for example, areas of interest, age, income, product preferences, behavior patterns on the Internet). By means of an online questionnaire, individual preferences and information can be recorded. Customer profiles are the basis for the subsequent definition of target groups for marketing and sales initiatives.

Interact: Dialog With Customers

mySAP CRM E-Selling offers many and varied possibilities for interaction and dialog. Therefore, for example, on the basis of existing customer profiles and with the assistance of the mySAP CRM component *Campaign Management*, personalized or target-group specific e-mail campaigns can be carried out. E-mails can be personalized for individual customers or customer groups from the subject line through the salutation and the text itself, right through to the possible attachments. It is also possible to integrate personalized links into the web store: if customers click on them, they are greeted by name and, for instance the product proposals established for them or their target group are displayed. The customer also has different opportunities for initiating dialog. For example, they can be offered chat functions on the web store, which means that they can use their keyboard to communicate with a service center employee, or there may also be a button with which the customer can express the wish to have an employee call them (*Call Me Back*). With the e-selling solution from SAP, customers can even interactively configure products according to their own ideas.

Customize: Personalized Product Proposals and Target-Group-Specific Best Seller Lists

The most outstanding application of one-to-one marketing must be the possibility of proactively recommending certain products or services to customers. With this mySAP CRM E-Selling supports both personalized product recommendations and best seller lists and also cross-selling and up-selling proposals.

By personalized product recommendations we refer to lists of products that have been compiled for particular customer profiles. They contain, for instance, new products which, on the basis of observations or analyses (for example, cross-selling analyses), may be of interest to customers of a particular profile.

Target group-specific best seller lists are an important special case. They are based on the evaluation of the products sold in a target group. The underlying idea is that products that are frequently bought by customers of a particular profile may be of particular interest to customers of similar profile who up to now may not have bought the same products. In addition, the best seller lists can also be used to offer business customers the service of displaying the products they buy most often in a separate list in the web store.

Personalized cross-selling suggestions make it possible to recommend customers products that are potentially useful in association with products already selected, such as image processing software in combination with a scanner. On the other hand, personalized up-selling suggestions highlight products that promise greater benefits for the individual customer than the product selected, for example, a scanner with higher resolution. The objective of both measures is to generate greater sales volume for the vendor.

Catalog Management and Product Selection

The search for and selection of products is normally done with the help of a product catalog. In addition, in mySAP CRM E-Selling products can be selected from personalized product recommendations, best seller lists, order forms and earlier orders or offers taken up or – in the B2B scenario – items can also be added to the shopping basket directly by entering the article number. It is of no significance how the products are selected, the product information always comes originally from the product catalog.

Functions of the Product Catalog

To provide customers and potential customers with information on products, prices and availability via the Internet, mySAP CRM E-Selling offers a web store solution with electronic product catalog. The advantages of this product catalog in comparison to conventional printed catalogs are lower production costs, simple and cost effective distribution, attractive product presentation, and powerful searches. Furthermore, the information contained therein is more up-to-date.

With mySAP CRM E-Selling, attractive web catalogs can be created, offering simple and fast search capabilities, quick access to desired information and effective presentations with multimedia information content. The Business-to-Business scenario also supports the *SAPMarkets Enterprise Buyer Professional (EBP)* catalog interface, an electronic procurement solution from which direct access to the web catalog is also possible.

There is also the possibility of, for example, sending the catalog content to customers or making it available to other applications by XML-export. It Is possible to export the entire catalog, or to export certain catalog views adapted for individual customers in different formats. By defining a business partner as the export recipient, various exports with different content can be generated from a single product catalog and treated as a common data basis.

Catalog and Content Management

The compilation of the product catalog and the definition of the content take place in the catalog management module of the CRM system. According to the user scenario or target group it is possible to put the catalog together from a functional or a marketing point of view.

The catalog structure can be created with user-defined catalog sections, which can in turn be arranged hierarchically at will, to meet specific enterprise requirements. Products and/or other catalog sub-sections can be assigned to a catalog section. The corresponding products are selected from the product master data in the CRM system, which receives data automatically from the material master data in the R/3 system or from another backend system. In addition, product masters can be created or modified in the CRM system directly. Changes in the material master data in the R/3 system are immediately synchronized with the data in the CRM system – in this way the catalog is always kept up-to-date. List prices, scale prices and customer-specific prices can be displayed in the product catalog. These are determined by *SAP Internet Pricing and Configurator (SAP IPC)*.

Apart from displaying master data in the product catalog, it is also possible – and from a marketing point of view, essential – to present additional information relating to sections and products in the form of texts, images, documents and multimedia files (audio and video files, and so on). Therefore, the contents of the product catalog are enriched with all the information and data that an enterprise would like to put at the disposal of its customers. For the active administration of additional information or documents the *Knowledge Provider* of the SAP Web Application Server can be accessed in catalog administration. It is also possible to link external content servers in this way.

Attributes can be defined for each product which should make it easier for the customer to find the desired product or which present useful product information. One or several catalogs or different versions of the same catalog (for example, for different languages, currencies, sales organizations, and so on) can finally be published on the Internet as the web catalog. By defining catalog views, an enterprise can present customer-specific catalogs which only permit viewing of the areas of the product catalog relevant to that particular customer. Using this possibility the enterprise can present a customer-specific product offer on the web with no need for any additional maintenance work.

Attractive Catalog Presentation on the Internet

Via a browser, customers have access to the web catalog published on the Internet and the contents of same. With the help of the catalog structure displayed the user can navigate very easily through the web catalog to find the desired product. The visual design of the web catalog – and the entire web store – can be freely defined. There are no special restrictions to web design. The HTML templates delivered with mySAP CRM can be easily adapted to individual design ideas. The sequence of web pages during interaction can also be freely defined.

Search Functions in the Web Catalog

Apart from browsing through the catalog and searching hierarchically, the customer can also use a powerful search engine that will lead him directly to the desired product. Various different search criteria can be combined and price brackets can also be set. In this way the search for products is particularly fast and effective and boosts customer satisfaction.

The specification of product characteristics using checkboxes, in which attributes are displayed, is especially convenient. These attributes are freely defined by the vendor. The customer chooses the characteristic value that matches his requirements from the options offered and is then shown all products that correspond to his wishes.

It is also easy to integrate solutions from third party suppliers such as intelligent product consultant (for example, eConsultant), avatars (virtual, personal representative) and so on in the web catalog, which make the search for certain products easier for the customer or identify the customer's preferences and can be helpful in product selection.

In the B2B scenario there is also the additional possibility for an enterprise to use contracts to display contract-specific data and prices for products on the web catalog for their customers. When the customer logs on to the web store the system determines the corresponding contract. The customer can also call up contracts directly in the web store and select and order products from these and the system will automatically generate a release order.

Purchase Orders and Order Processing

The ordering of products is processed by mySAP CRM E-Selling with the use of a virtual shopping basket. The shopping basket is the central administration tool for the ordering procedure and has a range of important functions. First of all, by means of a simple mouse click the desired products are selected by the customer and then automatically placed in the shopping basket. This is not only possible directly in the product catalog, but also in all pages of the web store on which the product appears (product detail view, product configuration, best seller lists, product proposals, order forms, offers, orders). Finally, the articles can be ordered immediately from the shopping basket. In addition, prices and price components (for example, shipping costs, taxes) are indicated in the shopping basket, accessories, cross-selling and up-selling articles are merged and delivery dates are also displayed. In the shopping basket, customers can enter extra quantities, configure products, set a desired delivery date, add comments on the order and, if required, change ship-to addresses. Furthermore, the shopping basket can be completely or partially emptied and, of course changed or deleted. mySAP CRM E-Selling also enables customers to temporarily save the contents of their shopping basket. Therefore, there are no problems if the shopping procedure is interrupted; the shopping basket can be saved under any name and can be called up again when the ordering process is continued at a later point in time. It is also possible to enter the article number directly in the shopping basket; it is even possible to order in this way using article numbers used only by this particular customer. The system looks after the correct allocation in the background.

The most important ordering functions are described below.

Ordering With Order Forms

With mySAP CRM E-Selling, customers can create their own order forms. Products that are ordered regularly can be put in a fixed shopping list in which, if required, it is only necessary to enter the desired quantity. Such order forms can be called up from a list of templates at any time. Regardless of these, existing offers and orders can also be used as source order forms.

Efficient Fast Ordering

In addition to catalog selection, business customers can be offered fast order creation: The direct input of product number and desired quantity in the shopping basket is enough to fill it and create an order. Apart from the manufacturer's product numbers, customer-specific article numbers can also be used for fast order creation. The system looks after the correct allocation of manufacturer and customer product numbers. Professional purchasers, who often know commonly used article numbers by heart, can deal with orders more efficiently in this way.

Orders With Reference to Contracts

The agreement of contracts is common practice in trade between business customers. These contain the quantity and/or the price at which a product will be sold to the business partner during a set period of time. Products for which contracts have been agreed are specially marked in the catalog by mySAP CRM e-selling. Customers can select these products and create an order with reference to the contract, that is, execute a contract release at the agreed conditions. Information on the quantity remaining is updated and is available on the web store.

Increased Turnover With Cross-Selling and Up-Selling

A particularly interesting function of mySAP CRM E-Selling from the point of view of marketing and sales is automatic product proposal. As soon as a customer selects a product, alternative products of higher value (up-selling) are displayed in the shopping basket, or additional products such as accessories or other complementary services (cross-selling) are listed. The associated links between products are maintained in the product master data. By clicking on a product proposal, this is actively transferred to the shopping basket and in the case of up-selling, the product previously selected is replaced. The objective of this is to encourage the customer to select products of a higher value or additional products and so generate higher sales figures.

Accurate and Consistent Pricing

The determination and display of the correct prices on the Internet is often a big problem. Far too often the price invoiced on the bill does not coincide with the offer price listed on the web store pages.

To avoid this, mySAP CRM E-Selling uses *SAP Internet Pricing and Configurator* (SAP IPC) for pricing. This uses the same conditions and pricing rules as the SAP R/3 backend system or the CRM system. The efficient pricing in the R/3 or CRM system is therefore available on the Internet and it can be ensured that prices are always the same at the frontend and backend. The fact that the pricing and conditions model is maintained centrally and exclusively in the R/3 or CRM system eliminates the need to repeat this work.

The standard, familiar SAP R/3 condition types such as exclusive prices, discounts or scale conditions are automatically taken into consideration when prices are determined on-line in the shopping basket. In the B2B scenario customer-specific product prices are displayed with the support of SAP IPC. Net price, gross price, shipping costs and taxes are indicated separately. This occurs for both the individual items in the order and for the total order price. SAP IPC supports different currencies and quantity units.

Configuration of Custom-Made Products (Configure-to-Order)

The Internet represents a special challenge for enterprises that produce configurable products. Therefore, when a customer makes an inquiry it must be possible to identify the different product variations, dependencies and restrictions and to determine the correct offer price related to the components and options selected by the customer.

The interactive configuration of products in the context of mySAP CRM E-Selling is also made possible with the help of SAP IPC. When the customer selects a configurable product, they are lead through the configuration process by SAP IPC. The permitted options are displayed – if appropriate, with the corresponding increase or decrease in relation to the base price – and can simply be selected by the customer. To help in the decision making the options can be completed with detailed descriptions and image documents. The consistency of the configuration is continuously checked by SAP IPC and the price is updated online.

SAP IPC can use the configuration model in SAP R/3. In this way the effectiveness of the R/3 variant configurator is also available on the Internet. There is no need for separate product modeling. When a customer orders a product configured to meet his wishes, the configuration data of the order is sent to the backend system for further processing.

With SAP IPC, mySAP CRM E-Selling offers a powerful Configure-to-Order scenario that involves the customer and their specific wishes in the value added process from an early stage and with a determining influence.

Accurate Availability Checks and Binding Delivery Dates

With mySAP CRM E-Selling customers can get reliable information on availability and delivery dates in real time. For each order item in the shopping basket – also for configured products – SAP R/3 or *SAP Advanced Planner & Optimizer (SAP APO)* does an availability check, known as an *ATP (Available to Promise) Check*. To determine the delivery date, not only are average delivery times referred to, but a more precise date is calculated on the basis of current warehouse stock and production capacity in all plants and taking into account the time needed for commissioning and shipping. Customers also have the possibility of expressing desired delivery dates – in the B2B scenario it is also possible to request dates for individual order items. These are taken into account in the availability check and the determination of delivery date.

Furthermore a rules-based availability check *(Rule-Based ATP Check)* can be carried out with mySAP CRM E-Selling and SAP APO, which makes it possible to check the availability of products at different locations and to suggest alternative products if availability is insufficient.

The importance of a precise availability check and reliable delivery date setting should not be underestimated. These pieces of information play a decisive role in improving customer satisfaction. This is particularly true for the Business-to-Business area, because whether or not an order is placed often depends on the assurance of and presupposed adherence to a certain delivery date.

Flexible and Secure Methods of Payment

With mySAP CRM E-Selling, enterprises can benefit from automation of the payment process on the Internet. Different methods of payment are available to customers. Payment can, for instance, be effected using a credit card and immediately authorized online. In other cases, payment can be arranged cash-on-delivery or with an invoice, in which case – if available – invoicing can automatically take place in the SAP R/3 backend. The linking to the backend system also ensures that discounts are taken into account, invoice amounts are correctly calculated, payments received are correctly posted and reminders are sent at the appropriate time. In the event that no R/3 backend system is used, or that several R/3 systems come into play, invoicing can also be carried out centrally using CRM Billing in mySAP CRM (see chapter 7, "Invoicing" on page 109). The most up-to-date security mechanisms guarantee the highest level of security in the transfer of sensitive data.

Electronic Invoicing

The integration of mySAP Financials *Electronic Bill Presentment and Payment* (EBPP) means that it is possible to transfer, present and pay bills on the web store. The vendor is saved the expense of printing and mailing invoices, reminders and dunning notices and can also maintain customer relationships with electronic invoicing. The customer has the advantage of being able to view not only bills but also the current state of their account, including credit memos. To effect payment customers select the bill, any credit memos that can be offset and the desired method of payment. Once the payment has been authorized, a payment run is started in the backend system.

Ordering at the Click of a Mouse

As soon as the products have been selected, the desired quantities and the method of payment have been entered and price and delivery date have been specified by the system, the contents of the shopping basket can be ordered with a click of the mouse, that is, submitted as a sales order. If required the customer can enter a special ship-to address – in the B2B scenario this can also be done for individual items – and select the delivery type. In addition the customer can attach written remarks to their order (comments, instructions, and so on). In the B2B scenario it is even possible to enter an order text for each individual item. In this way even orders that deviate from the norm can be processed without any problems.

In principle, with mySAP CRM E-Selling, instead of giving an order, a customer quotation can first be requested. With reference to a particular quotation, the customer can easily place an order or transfer individual items into an order at a later stage.

Automatic Order Confirmation

As soon as an order is submitted as a sales order, the order number that has been generated is displayed to the customer on the Internet and they also receive an order confirmation by e-mail. This is also true for offers that customers have created themselves on the Internet.

Problem-Free Order Processing

With the integration of mySAP CRM E-Selling with other CRM functions and the backend system, the automatic processing of orders received via the Internet, right through to shipping and invoicing, is guaranteed. This ensures reliable processing of all orders and brings about a high level of customer satisfaction and strong customer ties. Complete automation, from order acquisition on the Internet frontend to order execution, results in an acceleration of the entire sales process and reduces transaction costs.

Transparency With Online Status Queries

mySAP CRM E-Selling puts customers in a position to view secure order forms, quotations and orders on the Internet, on their own at all times and to retrieve detailed information on the status of a quotation or the processing of individual items in an order. The customer receives a quick overview of all completed and opened quotations or offers and can, if necessary, use hyperlinks to follow the shipping of goods with the tracking systems of transport and logistics providers. Depending on the progress of the order processing the customer has the possibility to cancel or change orders completely or in part (individual items). With these self-service options the number of customer queries over the telephone can be significantly reduced; something which eases the workload of office-based personnel and also contributes to cost-cutting.

Additional Sales With Web Auctions

mySAP CRM E-Selling can be extended with a comprehensive solution for auctions on the Internet – *SAPMarkets Web Auctions* – with which all processes involved in the auctioning of goods and services can be developed. SAPMarkets Web Auctions is the perfect application for enterprises that want to obtain an optimal price for excess goods, remaining stock or goods with a short lifespan, or if they want to test the market for new products. It is a flexible, rules-based solution for creating auctions and bids, negotiating prices and the automatic reconciliation of bids.

SAPMarkets Web Auctions covers all phases of an auction: from putting together and publishing an auction posting to processing the incoming bids, reconciling bids and determining the winner, right through to order fulfillment. Products to be auctioned can be presented in the web product catalog in a special section – such as an *auction catalog* – or it is possible to mark auction objects as such in the regular catalog.

One of the functions available to customers is the monitoring of auctions in which they are participating or have participated. They can also inquire about the current status of an auction or view all auctions that have already been won. Among the functions available to the enterprise or vendor are the creation of sales auctions, the display of current auction status and the progress of auctions, the changing of auction status and one-to-one marketing functionality in the selection of particular target groups for auctions.

Interactive Customer Support

Not least of all, enterprises create web stores to cut down on sales expenses. Nevertheless, there is a lot to be said for not completely renouncing personal contact between customers and vendors. Perhaps customers have questions to which the answers cannot be found in the web store, cannot find their way around the web store or want to use the *Internet* distribution channel to request services after the purchase of a product. Therefore, interaction channels exist to facilitate communication between the Internet customer and a service employee. For example contact between the customer and the service employee can be established via the web store. Should questions occur to the customer during a visit to the web store, it is not only advantageous, rather essential, to supply an answer – otherwise he may just find that a competitor has the answers.

mySAP CRM E-Selling offers Internet customers three possibilities for requesting help directly via the web store:

▶ **E-mail**
The customer can address the enterprise via e-mail in the conventional way. Alternatively, a mail form can be made available on the web store so that customers do not have to use their own mail program.

▶ **Call Me Back**
If the customer has questions or problems that must be answered immediately – for example, they cannot find their way around the product catalog, or have a question about price or the order processing – interaction via e-mail is not the only method available. To initiate immediate communication with the vendor, the customer can make a *Call Me Back* request using the corresponding button on the website. This request is immediately transferred to a service employee in the call center, who then calls the customer. For establishing contact between Internet customers and service employees, exact rules can be set in the web store, such as subject to the status of the customer or the specialist knowledge of the service employee. In the call me back request the customer can even specify if they would prefer to be called via the telephone

or what is known as the *Voice Over IP procedure*. Because the customer is still in the web store at the same time, questions can be answered immediately.

▶ **Chat**
Alternatively the customer can also express a wish to 'Chat', especially if they do not have the necessary hardware for Voice Over IP or do not have a second telephone connection available. Within the chat, for example, URLs or files can also be sent to a customer.

Business Intelligence With Powerful Web-Analysis

The decision to set up a web store includes not only the design of the Internet pages and the hope that they will be visited every day by lots of customers, but the personalization and optimization of web stores is also becoming increasingly important. In this way, visitors can find their way around web stores quickly and can be received in a way that fulfills customer wishes.

How can the success of such measures be established? Direct customer contact is difficult on the web and customers rarely give feedback when requested. By displaying customer activity on the web store and the subsequent analysis of this data, however, it can be ascertained how visitors behave in a web store. Using this knowledge the web store can be optimized continuously and the shopping experience can be improved for each individual customer.

With the help of standard tools, web-server *Log Files* can be analyzed. These contain technical information such as browser versions, number of hits or page views and visitor sessions. The utilization of server capacity can also be gauged and evaluated. However, these tools reach their limits with the analysis of dynamically-created web pages, as often happens on web stores. Yet it is precisely this ability that is needed in order to analyze customer actions in a web store not only from a technical but also from a commercial point of view.

In mySAP CRM E-Selling customer actions, known as *events*, can be recorded in the web store. With this, for example, it can be established for each visitor session in the web store which articles each visitor has looked at, which articles were placed in the shopping basket or deleted from the basket, how much the quantity of articles in the shopping basket was changed and whether or not an order was placed. This data can be studied further with a special analysis tool.

Data recorded in the web store can be loaded directly into the SAP Business Information Warehouse (SAP BW) and immediately evaluated there with the help of pre-defined analysis applications. Moreover, with the seamless integration of components it is also possible to analyze data related to the visitor session in combination with data from mySAP CRM, SAP R/3 and other systems, such as business partner or product information and sales history. The results of the studies give web store operators a complete picture of customers, products and the situation of the web store so that upgrading actions can immediately be taken if necessary.

Apart from the usual evaluations on the technical status of the website (*Site Statistics*) – for example, analysis of links that give problems, download volumes, page loading speed, error status, and so on – mySAP CRM E-Selling also offers evaluation possibilities in the following areas:

▶ **Customer behavior**

  ▶ User data (analysis according to user-specific characteristics)

  ▶ Clickstream (evaluation of pages accessed by a user in chronological order)

  ▶ Top N external referrers (evaluation of sites from which the web store is most often accessed)

  ▶ Event statistics (overview of events triggered in the web store)

  ▶ Visitor session (evaluation of all information on one visitor session in the web store)

  ▶ Frequency of visits (evaluation of the visit frequency of individual visitors)

▶ **Sales statistics**

  ▶ Conversion rate (percentage of visitors who become ordering customers)

  ▶ Articles viewed, selected and finally bought by customers on the web store

  ▶ Top 10 articles (analysis of the 10 objects most frequently viewed, placed in the shopping basket, deleted from shopping basket or purchased)

  ▶ Value of shopping basket (for example, per customer or average and total values of shopping baskets at particular point in time)

  ▶ Overview of the articles in shopping baskets at a particular point in time

Using the data collected, aggregated and then analyzed, for instance, the marketing and sales departments of the web store operator can easily find out the make-up of customer groups, or what products are requested by certain customer groups most frequently. Based on this, well-directed marketing strategies can be developed and marketing campaigns can be executed in the best possible way.

Product management, on the other hand, is more interested in information on the products themselves. With configurable products, for example, direct conclusions can be drawn from the analyses of the product combinations ordered most or least frequently, which will affect the new or continued development of product groups. Finally, the analysis of the navigation and search behavior of visitors to the web store also means that any existing weak points in the web design or preparation of information (*Content*) can be identified quickly and remedied.

With the combination of recording customer and product related data in the web store and subsequent data analysis in the Data Warehouse, mySAP CRM E-Selling ensures that the large quantities of meaningful data obtained every day in a web store do not have to simply go to waste. In mySAP CRM E-Selling the different data is first structured and then analyzed to get a precise view of the buying habits of customers and their preferences regarding products, services and content. This information enables decision makers to execute sales analyses, foresee demand trends, optimize marketing initiatives and tailor an enterprise's web access to meet customer wishes.

Creative Web Store Design

The appearance of a web store must be attractively arranged and navigation must be optimally tailored to the target group if products are to be offered on the Internet successfully. This means that particular aspects of the web store should vary according to target group. The variations are based both on the demands and needs of the vendor, who sets up the web store, and also those of the user, who will visit the store to shop.

Web store solutions are displayed to users by means of a browser. Early on it is decided whether to enter the web store at all, whether purchases will take place and whether or not subsequent purchases will be considered. In this connection the structure of the user interface, that is, the design of the web store is of crucial importance. It cannot be assumed that potential users will all have the same prerequisites. They come from completely different demographic areas, with different prior knowledge, different objectives and requirements. If customers cannot find their way around the web store and if functions are not evident, confidence and acceptance diminish and purchasing will be restricted, if it occurs at all.

In addition to customer satisfaction, well designed web store solutions that are simple to understand and get to know have the crucial advantage of increased productivity. If customers make fewer mistakes, for example, execute fewer incomplete or erroneous orders, costs are reduced for the operator of the store.

For the reasons cited above, mySAP CRM E-Selling offers the possiblity of arranging the appearance of the store to comply with the operator's ideas. By choosing J2EE technology (Java 2 Platform, Enterprise Edition) a separation is made between program logic and user interface. The adjustment possibilities for both components are based on the use of Java as the programming language and

HTML as layout language. Adjustments to the design of the web store can affect the general layout, the colors and graphics used and the choice of font, and so on, without changing the application logic at the same time (see figure 9.3).

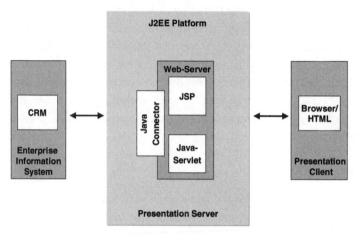

Figure 9.3 mySAP CRM E-Selling: architecture

mySAP CRM E-Selling supplies an outline design that can be shaped according to the needs of the customer. The *Ready-to-Run Templates* already contain attractive graphics, well defined colors and fonts that can be inserted relatively easily. This design was created by design experts and fulfills the criteria mentioned above. Notwithstanding, these templates can be adapted by web agents or in-house designers to meet any specific requirements, with no underlying design restrictions.

Multimedia additions such as Shockwave Flash for animated presentations or the inclusion of solutions from a third supplier can be done on the basis of the open standard HTML and JSP (Java Server Pages) with calculable effort.

Practical Examples of Successful E-Selling Projects With mySAP CRM

Integrated Customer and Supply Chain Management: E-Selling at Sony PlayStation

The two companies belonging to the Sony group, Sony Computer Entertainment Australia and PlayStation.com Australia work under *www.au.playstation.com*, a website with integrated electronic trade solution and based on mySAP CRM E-Selling.

PlayStation.com Australia must generate the same level of enthusiasm among the over 1.7 million Australian customers as the various different offline offers. Moreover, the online solution should contribute to increasing the PlayStation brand value.

In particular, the media company realizes its project with a target group oriented performance program, a multimedia product catalog, carrying out one-to-one marketing and ensuring high security for payment transactions. Sony also puts particular emphasis on a realtime availability check with reservation functions in production planning, on fast response time (performance) from the website regarding the order process and the integration of a call center as a service add-on. PlayStation.com Australia uses a highly integrated SAP e-business solution for its Internet access, to meet all the requirements of integrated customer relationship and supply chain management.

Customers can buy all Sony products (PlayStations, CDs, DVDs, and so on) online on the website and have them delivered to their homes free of charge. Shopping at PlayStation.com takes place as follows: First of all customers search for the desired goods in the multimedia product catalog and find out if the goods are in stock or when they will be available. With the help of the integrated solution both current warehouse stock and production planning, including the supply chain, are taken into account and temporary reservations are made. If they wish to buy the goods they place them in a virtual shopping cart. Then they send their order and their credit card data via secure connections to the ANZ e-gate service provider. This offers the first bank-operated payment solution for the Internet which guarantees the security of the transaction. If the customers have any questions they can contact the call center on the telephone, by fax or e-mail. The employees work with powerful SAP Interaction Center Software, integrated into the e-business solution, which immediately provides them with all the relevant customer data that is available. They are therefore in a position to offer customers excellent service.

With the mySAP CRM E-Selling solution, PlayStation.com Australia achieves a completely integrated frontend and backend. The integrated solution helps to ensure that products reach the customer quickly and cost-effectively. Sony therefore ensures that customers are satisfied with the electronic commerce solution throughout the entire business process – from ordering to delivery, all the way through to support or after-sales service. In addition, there is an improvement in profitability for Sony Computer Entertainment Australia and PlayStation.com Australia thanks to tighter management and reporting processes.

Personalization in Business-to-Business: Osram Sylvania Sheds Light on the Dense Undergrowth of Information

Osram Sylvania, the North American subsidiary of Osram GmbH, part of the Siemens group, is one of the three biggest lighting manufacturers in the world.

With the implementation of the mySAP CRM E-Selling solution, Osram Sylvania links all backend data on suppliers, customers and business partners with the front-office applications to which all those involved can have access via the Internet. All Osram Sylvania business partners can send in orders directly, process payment transactions and call up the status of order processing online. Both purchasers and dealers have the possibility of requesting information on orders, for example on the status of an order. Stock monitoring and contract awarding and monitoring are done completely automatically.

The solution "takes note" of customer-specific conditions, for example, discounts and terms of payment. Osram Sylvania manages around 1.5 million condition records for their customers (customer-specific prices, discounts, bonus regulations, and so on). They form the basis of a complex set of rules for pricing. The very high level of personalization in pricing has another dynamic component: thousands of changes are made every day. All individual items of information on the payment system have to be continuously updated in accounts, in sales and on the web site. The SAP integrated e-business solution ensures that the prices and conditions on the web pages always coincide with the prices invoiced and of course only have to be maintained centrally.

Moreover, the integration of abundant technical information and documentation on Osram Sylvania products in the e-selling solution presents a great challenge. There are profuse amounts of data, product sheets, warning notices, technical drawings and descriptions of use available for each product. All of this information is of significance to customers and can therefore naturally be called up on the Internet.

Mass Customization: Online Configuration With Fiducia AG

Fiducia Informationszentrale AG is the biggest computer services center for credit unions in Germany. At the core of the company's service offer is the dialog oriented processing of accounting procedures for the affiliated credit unions. In addition, the range of services also includes the development of separate software solutions, implementation, training and consultation, as well as the centrally organized delivery of hardware and software to customers.

Customers can order hardware and software components, services and support services at the click of a mouse via the Fiducia service portal. They are always offered precisely the combination options of hardware and software that are permitted and/or are possible for the work center in question. By means of dialog, the purchaser is led to a product configuration, that both meets his requirements and is released by Fiducia. Detailed technical documentation is available for each product or component. For configurable products, the current price is determined and availability is checked. Later, during order processing, there is also the option of calling up the current status of the ordering transaction at any time.

With this online-solution not only have Fiducia optimized ordering, but have also ensured that up-to-date information is available at all times. Whereas in the past sales employees still had to be informed of all details of software and hardware configuration by conventional channels, thanks to the centralized maintenance of product changes, this information is now automatically available to employees and their customers online.

The full integration of frontend and backend applications produces a universal distribution channel and makes an important contribution to the cross-enterprise optimization of business processes.

Apart from improved service and the simplification and speeding up of the information and transaction processes, the work involved with order management is reduced. The potential savings brought about by optimizing processes and workflows could be as much as 95 % of order-related costs, that is, with the introduction of the comprehensive mySAP CRM E-Selling solution, costs can be reduced from $60 to $3 per order. With this considerable saving in order processing alone the investment will quickly pay for itself.

10   mySAP CRM for the Interaction Center

Overview

"The employee you need to talk to is currently at lunch, please call again later." A fateful, yet not infrequently-heard sentence that can damage a carefully nurtured customer relationship in seconds. The customer may well wonder who exactly is there for whom. Before long they may possibly move to another supplier who, in this age of electronic trading, is only a mouse click away.

Even if the customer chooses to be lenient, the enterprise has wasted an opportunity. Because now, as always, direct contact with the customer still offers an enterprise the best opportunity to answer questions, resolve issues, learn more about customers' needs and offer additional services.

Today customers expect outstanding, consistent service availability right around the clock and always of the same reliable quality. This can only be achieved with a customer relationship management system that opens all channels to customers and supports all forms and combined forms of sales, marketing and service processes. The adaptation of the entire enterprise to this new understanding of customer relationship management has become a goal of strategic enterprise management.

It is vital that the customer relationship management solution supports all forms of establishing contact, whether web-based, by telephone, fax or in person-to-person conversations. It is also important that all possible business partner roles can be portrayed. Today, customers can also be suppliers, competitors and employees. Representing the many different roles and, from this, formulating corresponding offers is the business challenge of the future. This is where the changeover from the traditional call center to the interaction center of the future occurs.

Call Center Becomes Interaction Center

The call center was traditionally a central place of contact between the customers and the enterprise. An enterprise has to provide its call-center agents with knowledge and accurate and up-to-date information on all customers. Agents need to be able to access this type of information at all times. Data on customer history, buying behavior and preferences allow the agent to interact efficiently and beneficially with customers. Traditional call centers that only work with telephones and provide agents with only rudimentary data on customers are a relic of the past. They have nothing to do with today's understanding of customer relationship management.

Customers demand very different forms of interaction. With declining customer loyalty – and the competition only a mouse-click away – today's challenge is to make it as easy as possible for the customer to interact with the enterprise. This includes all activities from supplying information on products and services to closing deals, tracking the delivery process and the request for services. This *Closed Loop Strategy* is the cornerstone of the mySAP.com architecture.

In this context the interaction center is the central medium for accessing all aspects of customer relationship management. It offers elements of operational, analytical and collaborative CRM. There is also close interconnection with the areas of Internet use and mobile technologies, which will be discussed in further detail throughout this chapter.

The switch from call center to interaction center is in line with the general trend towards optimizing value for customers with CRM solutions, as can be seen in figure 10.1.

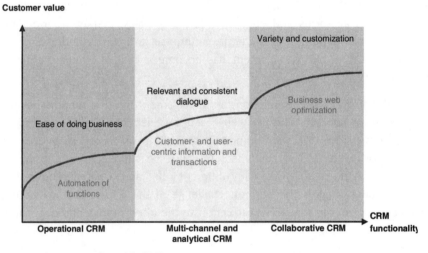

Figure 10.1 Customer value with CRM

Over the last ten years the subject of process automation has been prominent in many enterprises. Against this background call centers emerged, the purpose of which was to reduce transaction costs. Often these centers were picked from the enterprise itself. Determination of success was limited to factors such as transaction costs, length of conversation and turnover of personnel.

For a few years now enterprises have recognized that the quality of the call center has a significant influence on customer satisfaction. Customer behavior is changing. For years customers tolerated the fact that they had to call different numbers for questions of service, sales or sales processing. Today they insist that the agent contacted will control all of the processes and will have up-to-date information on the customer.

A customer who sends a fax on Monday, writes a letter on Tuesday, sends an e-mail on Wednesday, speaks with the board on Thursday and with a sales employee on Friday, expects that the interaction center agent contacted on Saturday is informed of all of these contacts and any agreements reached therein. In addition, he expects precise information on price, delivery dates, the availability of service employees and the order processing status.

This profile of the interaction center has nothing in common with the traditional call center. Agents have access to comprehensive knowledge on all business processes and are aware of their responsibility to the customer. If the call center of yesterday was only a sort of satellite organizational unit, today it stands at the center of customer relationship management. The traditional problem of high staff turnover in these organizational units must be resolved immediately, because these employees and their knowledge are among an enterprise's most valuable resources.

The change from call center to interaction center could not be more radical. The challenges to be faced include:

▶ The technological change from traditional analog telephone installations to web-based multi-channel systems

▶ The change from being a mere means of establishing contact to looking after the customer through all business processes

▶ The change from being a low-skill organization to become a highly qualified, team-oriented service organization

SAP's interaction center provides customers with the necessary technology and instruments for presenting business processes. As with all mySAP CRM components, the product is constantly being modified. New technologies, new business processes and new business ideas determine the structure of the solution.

The SAP Interaction Center Solution

The current version of *mySAP CRM Interaction Center* represents a milestone, in that for the first time all business processes are available to agents, constantly and via all channels (telephone, e-mail, web chat, and so on). To show technological leadership in the multi-channel capabilities often demanded by customers, SAP entered a development partnership with the market leader in multi-channel communication systems, Genesys. Within the framework of this cooperation it was possible to integrate Genesys's multi-channel solution both generally regarding the server and in the area of the program interface. Therefore, in addition to the traditional SAP interfaces, for the first time customers can access all communication channels. Figure 10.2 shows the linking of Genesys user interfaces in the mySAP CRM Interaction Center. Tab pages for contacting the agent via the channels *Phone*, *e-mail* and *Web Chat* can typically be seen.

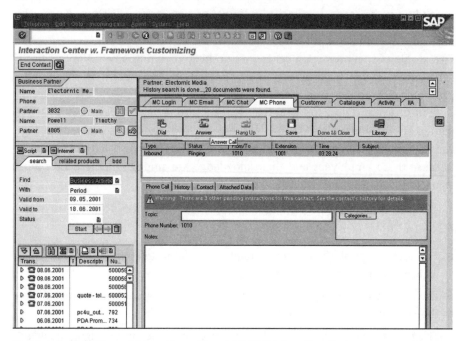

Figure 10.2 Multi Channel Interaction with mySAP CRM Interaction Center

Alternatively, the integration of other multi-channel systems can be done via an expansion of the existing SAP communication interfaces SAPcomm and SAPphone (see "Multi-Channel Interface Architecture" on page 176).

Another innovation is the *Alert Modeler* (see aslo chapter 7, "Customer Care" on page 114). It makes it possible to set business rules and, depending on checking of same, provide the agent with certain information or offer scripts to support the conversation. Therefore, for example, a delay in delivery can be pointed out right at the beginning of the conversation. The agent can approach this matter proactively and therefore structure the conversation situation better.

mySAP CRM Interaction Center is continuously being expanded. The business functions cover the requirements of today's specifications, but the next challenges can already be identified. In particular, investments in the system architecture offer the possibility of differentiating a company from its competitors. Among others, the following solution elements are currently being (further) developed:

► Process design and the shaping of the user interface
► Open interface architecture for linking multi-channel systems
► Volume and scalability
► Development platform
► Routing in interaction and workflow scenarios
► Management tools

The elements cited will be discussed in greater detail below.

Process Design and the Shaping of the User Interface

SAP is pursuing a consistent portal strategy for all products, with browser-based user interface in a thin client architecture. This design objective is also being pursued by Interaction Center. To achieve this requires replacing the *ActiveX Controls* in the user interfaces and a complete reshaping of the interaction model.

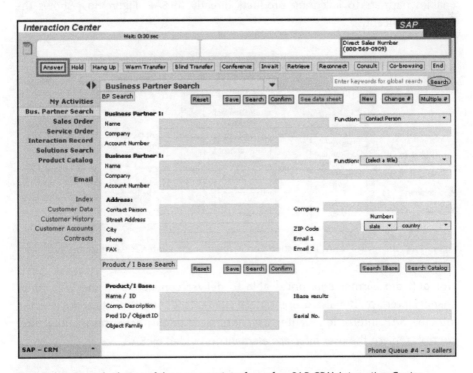

Figure 10.3 Example design of the new user interface of mySAP CRM Interaction Center

The objective is the design of user interfaces that make an intuitive use of the interaction center tools possible for experienced Internet or portal users. An example design of such a user interface can be seen in figure 10.3.

A user experienced in working with browsers immediately recognizes the navigation elements and the significance of the individual screen areas (*tiles*) and uses the different forms of field entry. Compared to traditional, program specific interfaces, training time is reduced considerably. First feedback studies with customers show a high level of acceptance among users.

The development of the Interaction Center user interface is being carried out in close coordination with the SAP subsidiary SAP Portals, since, ultimately, the Interaction Center is just one application of many in SAP Portals.

Multi-Channel Interface Architecture

In addition to the comprehensive integration of the Genesys family of products and the expansion of the existing communication interfaces, with *SAPmultiChannel* SAP is developing an open, certifiable interface architecture that enables partners to link their products directly to SAP. Figure 10.4 shows the solution concept.

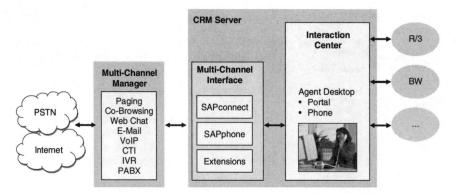

Figure 10.4 The mySAP CRM Interaction Center multi-channel interface architecture

Not only are partner enterprises able to deliver connectors to the SAP multi-channel interface, but also user interface elements (*Controls*), that can be inserted into the SAP Interaction Center user interface. In this case the manufacturer controls replace the user interface elements provided by SAP.

Volume and Scalability

Response times also play a decisive role in browser based architectures. Even the most attractive user interfaces miss the mark if they go over the magical limit of one second with the addition of server round-trip and rendering times. Moreover, there is also the response time of the entire system including access to data in the logistics and accounting systems.

For years, SAP has been setting the standard for the evaluation of volume and scalability in business applications. This includes the precise description and publication of business scenarios to be gauged, the documentation of the hardware, software and network infrastructure used as well as the complete presentation of all results and factors of influence.

In order to set standards in the Interaction Center sector too, SAP, together with the partner AMC technologies, published the first Interaction Center benchmark in June 2001. The infrastructure, the scenario and the response times are presented in figure 10.5.

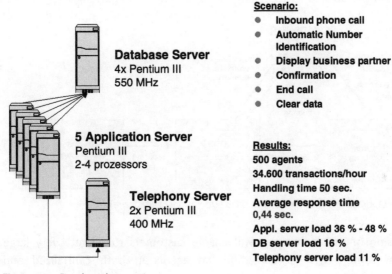

Database Server
4x Pentium III
550 MHz

5 Application Server
Pentium III
2-4 prozessors

Telephony Server
2x Pentium III
400 MHz

Scenario:
- Inbound phone call
- Automatic Number Identification
- Display business partner
- Confirmation
- End call
- Clear data

Results:
500 agents
34.600 transactions/hour
Handling time 50 sec.
Average response time 0,44 sec.
Appl. server load 36 % - 48 %
DB server load 16 %
Telephony server load 11 %

Figure 10.5 Benchmark scenario

In the benchmark analyses, 500 agents with an average call handling time of 50 seconds were simulated. In most customer situations an average handling time of a maximum of 3 minutes is currently assumed. This gives a figure of over 1,500 agents (with corresponding larger main memory on the application servers).

The outstanding result of the benchmark analyses is not surprising, because the underlying mySAP Technology architecture presents a further development of the successful R/3 base architecture.

At least one further problem remains to be solved though: Many customers use old systems that have to transfer data to the Interaction Center. This is particularly critical to performance if this data has to appear on the first screen in the Interaction Center during a customer interaction, that is, if the data cannot be dynamically reloaded.

To achieve a good response time in this case, the Interaction Center uses the *Operational Data Store* (*ODS*) from the SAP Business Information Warehouse (SAP BW). ODS is a flat data structure which permits very fast access both to individual records and to large record groups. ODS structures can be supplied with data from both SAP sources and from external sources. As soon as the data is in ODS its origin is of no significance as far as performance is concerned. To obtain the necessary data, the Interaction Center first of all accesses ODS and displays the resulting information. Only when a business object has been changed are the transactional SAP structures accessed. This is presented in figure 10.6.

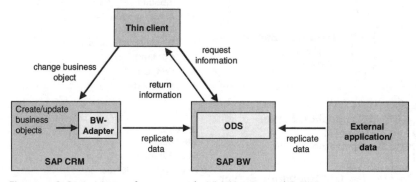

Figure 10.6 Optimizing performance with ODS (Operational Data Store)

The inclusion of this technology will enable customers to operate very large interaction centers with several thousand agents in both centralized and decentralized infrastructures.

Development Platform

Hardly any SAP customers use the mySAP CRM Interaction Center with the standard user interface supplied. In most implementation projects the user interface is adjusted to a greater or lesser extent. The motivation behind such investments can be explained by the very different business processes in enterprises and the different levels of training of the employees in interaction centers.

The user interface of some interaction centers is presented in the form of a cryptic control screen with text fields of a maximum of three characters in length. This displays comprehensive customer information in a very condensed display, something which requires long training times for employees. However, the call volume in these centers is very high. Other buyers of interaction center solutions make the user interface very simple to use, because they mainly rely on un-trained employees. In general it can be said that there is no ultimate user interface that will satisfy all requirements.

A frequently expressed wish from software customers is the use of Java as the development environment for the creation of the user interface. The reason for this is that trained Java developers are in abundant supply. However, at the same time customers expect that in a Java-based solution world the same development tools (incl. transport and maintenance control, transmission, and so on) that they know from the SAP development world will also be available.

SAP reacts to these requirements with the SAP Web Application Server and the Web Dynpro Technology. mySAP CRM Interaction Center is an internal SAP pilot customer of this technology.

Routing in Interaction and Workflow Scenarios

To offer customers the most suitable agent in each case, routing systems in communication installations are clearly going to have to know more in future about agents and customers. SAP delivers an open business routing interface that makes it possible to exchange both employee qualifications and data on customers. The advantage of this for enterprises is that there is no need for double maintenance of this data.

In a future level of configuration this interface will also be used for the synchronization of workflow and channel systems. In certain situations the router in the workflow system and the router in, for example, the telephone system, may come to different decisions. For example this could result in an agent forwarding a call to the second-level organization, the telephone system determines the most suitable agent, this agent's telephone rings too, but the related workflow object appears in the inbox of a different agent. In a synchronized global system, on the other hand, the SAP workflow system transfers the routing requirement to the telephone system.

Tools for the Interaction Center Leader

Currently, interaction center leaders mainly monitor the activities of their centers with the communication system statistics. These statistics show the state of the waiting queue, the agents' workload, length of call and other technical data about the channels. However, communication systems know nothing about customers and the business valuation of interactions.

On the CRM side, on the other hand, there is indeed a complete picture of the customer, but no information about how long an important customer spends waiting before an agent takes the call.

A combination of both reporting systems offers many advantages, such as a unified interface and a thorough view of all substeps in the customer interaction. This can be achieved, for example, with data extracts from the communication system being transferred directly to the SAP Business Information Warehouse. An appropriate statistic interface that would simplify the exchange of data is being planned.

Further Development

The following developments are set to influence the structure of interaction centers over the coming years:

▶ UMTS (Universal Mobile Telecommunications System) will be established as standard for mobile telephony, at least in Europe. Parallel to this there will be convergence between mobile communication end-appliances (for example, mobile telephones) and mobile computer systems. It can be presumed that transmission bandwidth will be around 2Mbit/s. The performance of these mobile appliances will be more or less similar to the performance of current desktop systems. Technically it will therefore be possible to have the functionality of the interaction center on a mobile terminal. This will eliminate the static interaction center limitations still common today. New models of employment and the construction of decentralized service centers in regions that are currently industrially disadvantaged could be the result.

▶ Within enterprises the use of technologies currently reserved for interaction centers will change. Although today it is already possible, only very few employees get relevant information on the caller when a call comes in. With enterprises increasingly orientating towards customer needs, all employees will get access to all communication channels, information on callers and solution databases. In this way interaction centers will lose their current boundaries. This trend also explains the close coupling between the Interaction Center and SAP portal technology pursued by SAP.

▶ In the area of speech-based applications (*Voice-Enabled Applications*) it would appear that a breakthrough has been made since 2000. The use of the latest technologies goes far beyond what is currently used in speech based ACD (Automatic Call Distribution) systems. In the context of the interaction center, we can envisage scenarios in which the voice recognition system analyzes the conversation between customer and agent and suggests any information that it deems relevant to the agent. This scenario seems particularly realistic because many conversations in interaction centers keep to certain patterns and catchwords. A further area of usage lies in the field of speech-based information systems.

11   mySAP CRM Solutions for Mobile Users

In the history of the development of the personal computer, a trend towards simplification and miniaturization could be observed right from the start. A prominent example of this development came at the beginning of the 1990's in the form of the laptop computer, which was to broaden the potential use of the PC and allow any person in any place to participate in e-commerce.

With the availability of handheld palmtop computers the term m-commerce emerged as an extension of e-commerce. At first, use of this new generation of appliances was limited to dealing with purchasing and payment transactions, a special form of m-commerce, so to speak. With the spread to all forms of interaction (for example, notifying mobile users with alerts, displaying reports, and so on) the term m-business or mobile business has become established.

mySAP Mobile Business is an extension of the mySAP.com solutions, offered by SAP to facilitate wireless integration. It permits mobile use of mySAP CRM applications. With a simple, step-by-step introduction of this technology, the normal IT environment and the application landscape in an enterprise is preserved and effective investment protection is given.

Wireless Data Processing as a Basis for Mobile Business

There is a lot to indicate that after the introduction of Internet into the home, the next big technological thrust will be wireless data processing. With wireless data processing, existing information technologies and processes are combined and are generally made available for everyone. In the future almost all mobile telephones will have an Internet browser. Both cell phone manufacturers and analysts offer parallel projections on the spread of wireless devices for Internet use and estimate that they will overtake fixed PC's by the year 2004. According to their projections, the total number of Internet-enabled cell phone users will already be in excess of 200 million by the year 2005.

There are different ways to achieve mobile data processing. In general, the term *wireless* is used to refer to the use of a radio contact for transferring data. However, radio contacts are still associated with high technical requirements together with limited availability and reliability. As a result, in m-business all possibilities for dispensing with cable connection in order to execute a transaction, call up information or a local PIM (Personal Information Manager) function, for example, calendar or e-mail, on a mobile device are considered.

Radio connections can be characterized by their range of coverage and for the techncial capacity required for them to operate. In the CRM environment the following technologies are of particular interest:

▶ **Bluetooth (Personal Area Network)**
Wireless networking in a local area for cell phones, PDAs and computers

▶ **WLAN (Wireless Local Area Network)**
The possibility of linking mobile users in a Local Area Network (LAN) using wireless connections

▶ **WAP (Wireless Application Protocol)**
WAP was devised to link the Internet with mobile devices and was drawn up in detail by the WAP Forum, under the leadership of a consortium made up of representatives of Ericsson, Nokia, Motorola and phone.com. The WAP Forum works in close collaboration with the Internet standardization committee W3C.

After Internet cell phones, PDAs (Personal Digital Assistants) are the second largest group of devices, with a growing market and a certain lifestyle flair, both for discriminating consumers and professional users. The synchronization of such devices with central data processing by means of a cradle (insertion module) and gateway PC or an infrared interface in association with an appropriately equipped cell phone is already common since the introduction of the first PalmPilots in 1997.

This variety of appliance and connection options requires a standard architecture for mobile applications. Apart from the lack of stable medium-term standards, different regional strategies also give rise to a confused landscape of vendors. As long as there are new types of device appearing almost every month, it will be difficult to find a suitable development environment. In addition there are different ways to deal with the demands on mobile applications. Below we will explain how SAP is setting out the route to standardization with mySAP Mobile Business.

Examples of the Uses of Mobile Applications

With the implementation of mobile business solutions, enterprises can raise their overall efficiency appreciably:

▶ The possibility of using modern software application systems is extended to more people and locations (non-technically-minded employees can also get to grips with new mobile devices).

- The selection of device for each individual employee is done in consideration of cost and use (cell phones, palmtop or pocket PCs, handheld PCs, shockproof devices).
- Routine field tasks – such as determining times and costs or reading order or device numbers can be automated. Productivity increases and at the same time, the occurrence of errors falls.
- Employees can access enterprise data and processes relevant to their work, from any place and at any time.
- Data entry occurs immediately at the place of origin and allows the company to react to customer wishes immediately.

The implementation of mySAP Mobile Business allows all mobile employees to optimize their work and to use rationalization possibilities by means of wireless interaction on the basis of a standardized architecture. Two examples of this follow.

The Traveling Salesman (Van Sales)

A sales representative visits customers in his sales area every day with a particular product offer in his vehicle (*Van Sales*). For each visit he registers the number and type of products sold and all special agreements and price discounts. With manual processing, mistakes are always possible. Such errors can lead to customer inquiries, lost orders and additional administrative costs. Depending on training, sector and individual entitlements, personal computers – from laptops to high-end mobile phones – can be the solution. Mobile business solutions and technologies offer concrete options for this. Now the field sales employees can be supplied with inexpensive palmtop devices or – if necessary – with lightweight high-tech laptops. The salesperson can be informed of canceled appointments, new products or advertising campaigns while away from the office. If the mobile device can also give the current location of the employee, a new visit can even be scheduled with a potential customer in the same area to make the best possible use of time. The field sales team can create orders on the spot and check on possible delivery schedules immediately. Up to now this was only possible in a systematic manner at the end of the day. Backend systems can carry out plausibility checks, verify discounts given against guidelines or bonus agreements, and immediately indicate further sales opportunities in conversations with customers.

The Service Technician

Service technicians are responsible for maintaining and, if necessary, restoring the functioning of devices, machines and manufacturing installations. To be able to perform these tasks efficiently, they must possess knowledge on the components and know how quickly and at what times service work has to be carried out, in accordance with service contracts. Mobile service solutions make this information available at the usage site at any time. All details on usage site, customer, equipment and problem description are available. Once the work has been completed it is only necessary to enter work time and material for invoicing and the history. The times and materials entered can immediately be passed on to human resources and materials management. The company can observe work progress, determine completion and monitor each escalation. Both the technician and the customer service leader are better informed and can therefore provide a more reliable service.

Mobile Business With SAP

SAP has both transferred existing functions of mySAP.com to the new generation of mobile devices and also developed completely new services, specially designed for mobile users. With this SAP can build on two important advantages over other mobile solution providers:

▶ A large customer base which makes the development of widely applicable, powerful and robust solutions economically viable.

▶ A comprehensive collection of integrated business processes which do not have to be designed from scratch; simply adapted to mobile use.

Standard Architecture

mySAP Mobile Business is integrated into mySAP.com regarding both content and architecture. The objective of mySAP Mobile Business is to build on the existing (solution) knowledge in the user enterprise, without restricting the possibilities of new technological developments.

Whereas in recent years the processing of information throughout the enterprise took place in a tested environment and SAP had become the de facto standard for client-server business applications, the wireless age calls for a new, integrated architecture, suited to the distinctive features of all mobile systems involved and simple to implement. The standard architecture for mobile enterprises, the *Mobile Engine,* is aimed at achieving this objective.

Mobile Engine standard architecture creates a platform-independent framework that enables mobile devices such as Palmtop computers, Personal Digital Assistants (PDA) and laptops to execute business applications offline and to synchronize data with an SAP system via a normal Internet connection.

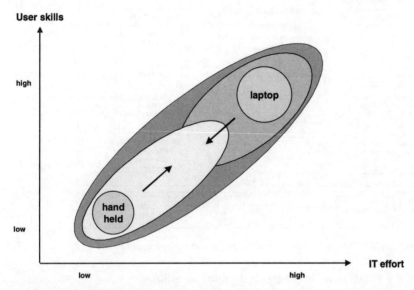

Figure 11.1 The solution area of mySAP Mobile Business

Technological Options for mySAP Mobile Business

In the development of mobile solutions the following two questions have to be answered:

Should the mobile solution be integrated into a portal?

If an enterprise decides only to enable some processes for mobile use, implementation will be simple because the process does not have to be integrated into a mobile portal. However, this normally restricts the solution to one specific device. A solution based on a portal is more versatile, even if initially there is more work involved in implementation. The portal gives the user access to a wide spectrum of functions. The user only has to log on once, not repeatedly, for various different applications. The portal identifies the user and offers him functions and information suited to his needs. It contains certain standard functions, for example, a calendar.

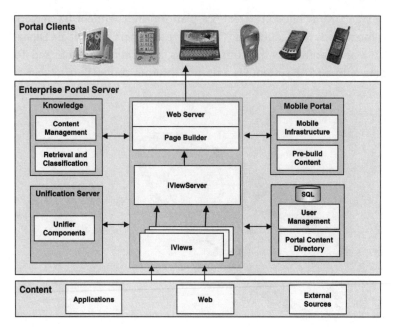

Figure 11.2 mySAP Mobile Business – mobile portal and mobile applications

Should the solution be implemented online or offline?

With mySAP Mobile Business, companies can use both online and offline applications.

Offline applications can be installed practically everywhere and a dial-up to the central computer is required only occasionally to synchronize data (see also chapter 17, "CRM Middleware" on page 278). Offline scenarios, however, still require locally installed software (Mobile Engine and the necessary application functions) and local data storage. While this poses no problem for notebooks, more compact devices may perhaps not provide the necessary speed or capacity.

The key advantage of online applications is the real-time nature of processing. The user has the most up to date information available and data entered by him are immediately accessible by all those involved and can immediately be processed further. Furthermore, online applications can use the entire functionality and performance power of the enterprise's internal information processing.

However, the processor performance of mobile applications and the bandwidth of mobile telephone networks limit the range of functions that can be supported effectively. New technologies such as UMTS should soon help to overcome these obstacles.

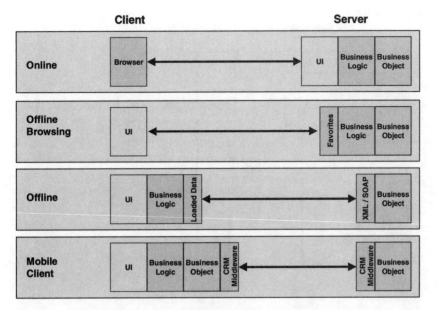

Figure 11.3 mySAP Mobile Business – online and offline

Although the processor speed and data capacity of mobile devices is continuously being improved, the difference in performance between these devices and PCs should not be disregarded. As a result, online applications should be kept relatively simple.

In some cases, online applications simply cannot be implemented from a technical point of view. A gas controller working in a cellar, for instance, would frequently be unable to connect to a cellular telephone network. A further disadvantage is the expense of prolonged telephone connections, although this problem should be solved by the extension of GPRS (General Packet Radio Service) networks.

In some, but not all cases, the offline/online dilemma can be resolved. Packet-based data transfer services, which restore lost connections, can dissolve the clear separation between offline and online applications. Some online applications allow the user to go offline for a short time during which web pages and input forms are buffered. This does not include complicated synchronization mechanisms, but works well in many business situations.

In general, offline use is recommended in cases where the connection to the backend system cannot always be guaranteed or is too slow or expensive. If, however, priority is given to real-time access, the online solution should be given preference.

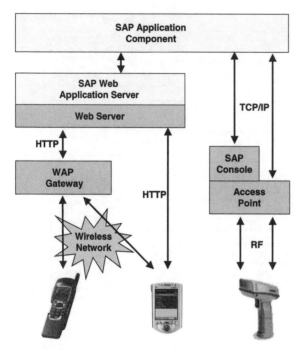

Figure 11.4 SAP Mobile Business online architecture

Data Security in m-Business

It should come as no surprise that, with technologies that allow universal and 24 hour access to business data, questions of data security arise.

Standardization consortiums (for example, WAP Forum), SmartCard makers (SWIM Cards), infrastructure providers and device manufacturers work together to analyze, identify and find suitable measures to rule out any possibile misuse. SAP is working in close collaboration with all competent parties to guarantee the security of mobile solutions. In addition, SAP is helping customers to identify and eliminate possible weak points and can act as advisor or mediator in negotiations with cell phone companies, for example.

Mobile Sales and Mobile Service

The laptop solutions *Mobile Sales* and *Mobile Service* are closely linked to each other. Both components share the same technical platform and have access to the same components (for example, customer and potential customer administration, contact person, material master data, calendar). Thanks to this close linking, enterprises can utilize and foster the synergy effect between the areas of sales and customer service.

Guaranteed Consistency of Data With Seamless Integration

Communication and data exchange between Mobile Sales, Mobile Service, the CRM server and the other mySAP solutions are controled by CRM Middleware and use the principle of data replication (see also chapter 17, "CRM Middleware" on page 278). All data relevant to mobile applications are held on a separate logical database on the CRM server.

This database also serves as backup for local datasets on laptops. From Middleware, the data is distributed to local clients or to the mySAP family of products on the basis of centrally defined distribution keys. Whereas connection to the mySAP system permits permanent data exchange, data reconciliation with mobile clients is carried out every time the field service employee dials up via a temporary online connection (for example, telephone or data network). To minimize data transfer times, in principle, only those data fields that have changed since the last reconciliation are transferred.

The seamless integration of mySAP CRM with the other mySAP solutions guarantees the consistency of all data within the entire sales process. For example, an order created at the customer's premises on a laptop is transferred with all data (price, configuration, texts, graphics, and so on) to mySAP CRM where it is then available for further processing. Hence the need for time-consuming repeated data entry is averted.

SAP's Mobile Sales Solution

With the frontoffice-oriented application *Mobile Sales*, field sales employees receive the infrastructure necessary for efficient customer relationship management. They are therefore in a position to react more efficiently and more flexibly to the continuously growing demands of their customers. They are able to access all information relevant to sales, whether they find themselves at their work center in the enterprise or on-site on the customer's premises.

In Mobile Sales, transparency goes far beyond current, market-related events. Comprehensive and detailed information allows for fast reactions to short-term changes in the market. Integrated processes speed up all processes from initial customer contact through drawing up a quotation and order entry, right up to delivery and service. Sales processes and sales projects can be controlled and coordinated more efficiently.

The possiblities of Mobile Sales motivate the employees in field service and increase their productivity, because they have all relevant information available at the crucial moment. With the click of a button field sales employees can call up an integrated view of customers, potential customers, services, competitors, activities, contacts, quotations and much more. In addition, sales material can be provided in electronic form (for example, presentations and the latest product brochures).

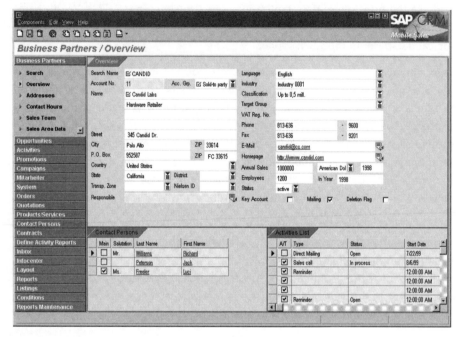

Figure 11.5 The mySAP CRM Mobile Sales user interface

Integrated Components

With comprehensive functions and integration with all solutions in the mySAP.com e-business platform, the business scenarios in mySAP CRM fulfill all the requirements of sales departments. SAP's Mobile Sales solution supports the field sales team with the following key functions:

▶ Business partner management

▶ Contact information

▶ Activities management and calendar

▶ Products and services

▶ Opportunity management

▶ Quotations

▶ Orders

- ▶ Pricing and product configuration
  SAP Internet Pricing and Configurator (IPC), linked into Mobile Sales, offers comprehensive configuration functions for single and multi-step product configuration. It brings the power of a variant configurator offline to the field service employees' laptops.

- ▶ Infocenter
  The Infocenter is a collection point for internal and external information (*Web Content*), which can be accessed via push-services and subscription mechanisms. In this way, relevant information is actively made available to mobile employees.

- ▶ Campaigns

- ▶ Customer agreements

- ▶ Reports and analyses

- ▶ Territory management
  mySAP CRM supports automatic data replication, geared towards sales territories, on the mobile laptops of field sales employees using CRM Middleware.

Adjusted to Meet Individual Needs

To minimize the implementation work involved with Mobile Sales, pre-configured solutions are supplied (see also chapter 15, "Best Practices for mySAP CRM" on page 247), which take specific sector requirements into account, such as the consumer goods industry, the investment goods industry and the pharmaceutical industry.

SAP's Mobile Service Solution

Mobile Service is specially designed to meet the requirements of technical customer service on site. Service technicians get a complete overview of installed bases, current and closed service orders, contracts and other information relevant to customer service.

The following functions are supported by Mobile Service:

- ▶ **Creation and awarding of service orders**
  The field service technicians download their service orders onto their laptops from the CRM server. The service orders and messages assigned to an employee are then listed in his calendar. He can search the service orders for different criteria and sort them according to personally-defined criteria for a better scheduling of his work.

▶ **Processing service orders**

After performing a service job the service technician can complete the necessary service order confirmation. Mobile Service supports the following confirmations:

  ▶ **Time confirmation** – time spent traveling to and from site and repairing equipment

  ▶ **Material confirmation** – planned and non-planned materials used for the service order

  ▶ **Technical confirmation** – detailed report of activity on each service item, cause of problem and measures taken to solve problem

The service technician can also print out activity reports for the customer.

SAP's Mobile Business Applications for Handheld Devices

Apart from powerful mobile laptops, small handheld devices play an ever-increasing role in the shaping of mobile application solutions. The following examples present *handheld scenarios* that optimize the limitations of these devices and which are already being realized in diverse CRM customer projects.

Handheld service

The scenario includes the following functions:

▶ Allocation, acceptance and execution of service orders

▶ Search and display of business partners

▶ Absence time and productive time

▶ Personalization

▶ Field sales

▶ Sending e-mails

▶ Offline processing

Handheld sales

The scenario includes the following functions:

▶ Entry, modification and release of orders

▶ Search and display of business partners

▶ Personalization

▶ Opportunities and quotations

▶ Activities

▶ Sending e-mails

▶ Offline processing

Travel management with handheld devices
The scenario includes the following functions:

▶ Booking flights, hotel, rental car

▶ Cancelation of travel plans (in part or in whole)

▶ Display overview of travel plans

▶ Display details of itinerary

▶ Entry of expenses

Time management with handheld devices
The scenario includes the following functions:

▶ Entry of activities and allocation to projects (Cross Application Time Sheet, CATS)

▶ Entry of absence with confirmation workflow

▶ Entry of time stamps and breaks

▶ Access to information on leave, such as time offset, special leave, premium wage account

Purchasing with handheld devices (for example, for mobile users on customer service)
The scenario includes the following functions:

▶ Procurement for maintenance tasks

▶ Manager's inbox (workflow)

▶ Access to purchasing catalogs with integrated shopping basket

▶ Mobile business intelligence

▶ Offline use of SAP BW reports

The Future of M-Business Applications

The sector of mobile applications is still very much in the infant stage, with new ideas and technology emerging practically every day. The trends for the future outlined below seem to be the most noteworthy at present.

Smart Labels (RFID)

Smart labels (*Radio Frequency Identification, RFID*) are extremely compact devices with processors and sensors which can register, enter, aggregate, save and transfer information on external conditions such as level of light, speed, temperature, humidity, geographical location and much more. They are particularly suitable for tasks in transport and warehouse logistics. They can, for instance, monitor quality standards. They can be attached to freezer packaging and send signals on the observation of the cold chain to a central office so that in the event of a raise in temperature, correction measures can be set in motion immediately. The attributes of smart labels can also, for example, be read to create a pick-list in a picking process.

Intelligent Device Management (Embedded Systems)

The term *intelligent device management (embedded systems, smart appliances)* refers to microchips that are built into normal trade items of practical use to make the characteristics or functions of these devices accessible to third parties via the Internet. So, for example, machine control in a vending machine can monitor or trigger non-cash payment procedures, refilling or any necessary maintenance work via a normal web-server.

Personal Microsystems (Personal Devices)

Personal microsystems are powerful devices that use conventional computer technology but are integrated into personal circumstances of daily use. These computers may, for example, come in the form of a wrist watch, a glove, a hat band among other things. They allow for hands-free work while also offering support in the form of services or information processing, which the user can call up with a simple movement of the hand or eye contact. Therefore, for example, a warehouse worker can check the identity of a package by touching it, to ensure that the correct pieces are being selected for delivery.

12   Collaborative CRM for Cross-Enterprise Cooperation

Introduction

Enterprises can only accomplish lasting competitive advantages if their product and service offers convince the customers and are completed by suitable business partners. In the long term, high offer quality and cost leadership can only be achieved with the help of successful collaboration with partners (component suppliers, distributors and other partner enterprises). To preserve their competitiveness, enterprises must integrate their business processes even closer with those of their customers, suppliers and business partners. The need for efficient cooperation has changed from implying integration within an enterprise, to meaning integration beyond enterprise boundaries. With interlinked cooperation between several partners in a CRM solution, collaborative business processes for the marketing, sales and service of a product can be arranged within an enterprise or between enterprises. This is feasible if the most homogeneous and integrated systems, data and interfaces are used [Bond 1999].

The special advantages of CRM arise if such collaborative business processes are achieved with the implementation of a CRM solution. This adjustment can happen within an organization (*intra*) or, on the other hand, between organizations (*inter*). With such collaboration, CRM processes can be linked to each other in a meaningful way and their efficiency and effectiveness can be strengthened (see also [Porter 1986]).

mySAP CRM offers many possibilities for the inclusion of business partners in cooperative business processes. Examples include collaboration with sales partners (*Partner Relationship Management, PRM*) and various other scenarios in *E-Marketing, E-Selling* and *E-Service* (see chapter 4, "Collaborative CRM" on page 34). Specific portal environments can be arranged for business partners with the help of the standard tools available.

Collaborative Business Maps

SAP has developed a methodology with which the new opportunities for electronic and cross-enterprise collaboration can be appropriately described and documented using specific solution models – known as *collaborative business maps* (*c-business maps*). Collaborative business maps show at which point the business process and information system of one enterprise interlinks with the process and system of another that is also taking part in the same process [SAP 2000].

The c-business maps document the possibilities for developing shared business processes together in detail and in so doing define model solutions for different industries and areas of business application (for example, customer relationship management, supply chain management, finances, human resources, and so on). Collaborative business maps include both the business management standpoint and economical value as well as various different aspects of the process structure (such as process and organizational structure, business information to be exchanged, and so on) and relevant information for the concrete implementation of such a joint process flow and the linking of same into an existing application environment. The instruments for realizing and implementing a collaborative business map are provided by *E-Business Solutions* in the mySAP.com platform [Hack 2000].

To date SAP has developed more than 170 c-business maps. The aim of a collaborative business map is to use an easy to understand graphic – what is known as the *zipper presentation* – to portray how the different enterprises and participants work together and to document the resulting value added potential. With the help of the SAP method, enterprises are in a position to identify qualitative and quantitative value added potential within their value added chain and thus achieve the best possible value for all those forming part of a c-business map.

The business value arguments for the corresponding collaborative business processes are put together on the basis of extensive implementation experience, conversations with customers and independent expert analysis. They are quantified and documented as a central component within c-business maps. The business value for all parties taking part in a collaborative business process is considerable and diverse. Apart from specific value arguments for the business process in question, cross-enterprise collaboration and integration generate the following for all participating business partners:

▶ Competitive advantages thanks to shorter time-to-market cycles

▶ New, innovative business models and processes

▶ Potential for growth, for example, with customer-specific service offers

▶ Faster exchange of information

▶ Higher quality information

▶ Cost advantages (see also [Brandenburger 1996])

The c-business method follows a logical top-down strategy which makes a comprehensive analysis of the electronic business process possible – beginning with the business contexts, through the process structure right through to component realization in the implementation project. The collaborative business maps not only define cross-enterprise processes but also generate the prerequisites for the problem-free implementation of these processes and evaluate the potential business value and *Return on Investment* that occurs with this solution. In particular they provide detailed information on the respective tasks, roles, system interfaces and even on the business documents needed for the e-business process. The XML code or attributes needed for the implementation of this process are also defined.

Collaborative business maps are described in full with the help of four different viewpoints – *Business View*, *Interaction View*, *Solution View* and *Component View*:

▶ **Business View**

The *Business View* gives information about the participating business partners and offers an overview of the extent and general flow of collaboration between the parties involved. In particular, the business view also documents the business arguments in the sense of arguments of value and value added potential that can be achieved for the participants. These form the basis for an investment and yield calculation.

With the help of the *zipper presentation*, figure 12.1 describes the business connection between the participants within the collaborative business process *Configure to Order*: An order with a corresponding configuration is created in conjunction with the customer's specification. The requirements associated with this form a part of material requirements planning. As a result of the ensuing material requirements planning, external procurement processes are triggered if necessary. After the goods have been produced in accordance with the configuration specified, they are shipped and finally invoiced. The business scenario comes to a close when the customer pays for the goods.

▶ **Interaction View**

The *Interaction View* illustrates the interdependence between the individual activities within the entire process and also the exchange of information between the business partners. The business documents exchanged between the business partners involved are defined and specified.

The interaction view offers a lot of additional information, such as user roles (for example, marketing manager, field sales employee) that are responsible for certain tasks within the context of the joint business process.

▶ **Solution View**

The *Solution View* describes the process design on a very detailed level so that the individual process steps involved in the business scenario are visible. In solution views the outstanding characteristics of the mySAP integrated e-business platform become particularly clear. Several solutions such as mySAP CRM, mySAP SCM and mySAP FI work together optimally in the context of the

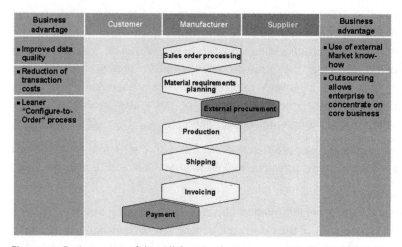

Figure 12.1 Business view of the collaborative business map "Configure to Order"

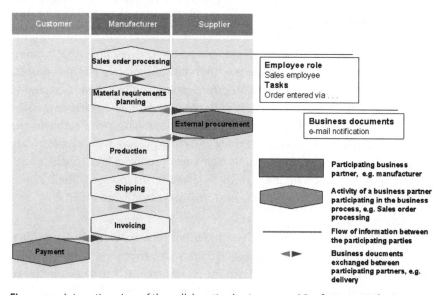

Figure 12.2 Interaction view of the collaborative business map "Configure to Order"

e-business platform mySAP.com and in this way allow for the perfectly smooth integration of a global solution. The advantage for SAP customers lies in the possibility of integrating new processes into an existing application landscape. Unlike other e-business solutions, with mySAP.com SAP offers an integrated e-business platform to achieve this.

▶ **Component View**

The *Component View* unites the IT application landscapes of the participants in a cross-enterprise business process in a consistent representation. It describes the application components necessary for the system support of the business

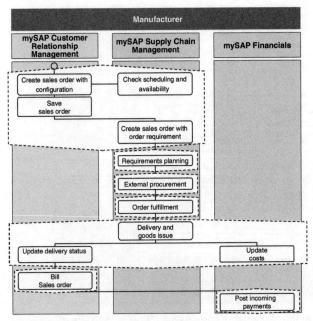

Figure 12.3 Solution view of the collaborative business map "Configure to Order"

process. Among other things, activities are sub-divided into relevant individual steps, carried out within the relevant applications. In addition, the component view contains information on release requirements and is the basis for the subsequent technical conversion.

Adapted to meet the information requirements of different addressee groups (management, department, IT specialists), these different views guarantee a consistent transition from the business contexts through to the system conversion into an IT application landscape.

Further information on model solutions for cross-enterprise cooperation networks can be found on the Internet under *http://www.sap.com/c-business* or on the SAP Service Marketplace under *http://service.sap.com/c-business*.

Examples of Collaborative Business Processes in mySAP CRM

Two examples of collaborative CRM business processes are presented below as a business view of a c-business map:

▶ Marketing management: campaign management
▶ Mobile sales: customer visit and order entry

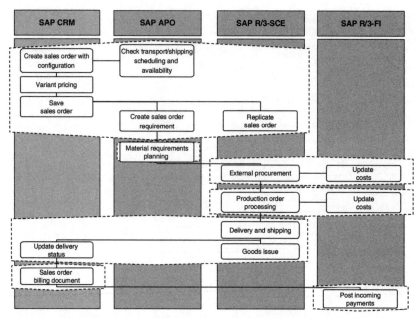

Figure 12.4 Component view of the collaborative business map "Configure to Order"

Collaborative Marketing Campaigns – Planning and Management

This c-business map shows how three possible participants in a marketing campaign – an external data provider, a manufacturer and a mailing provider – can work together for the successful execution of a marketing campaign. Figure 12.5 illustrates the advantages of the collaboration. The result is a complete marketing campaign that is carried out efficiently and effectively.

The goal of this c-business map is to represent the complete process of executing a marketing campaign,which begins with a campaign analysis and subsequently runs through campaign management to the conclusion. This scenario can, for example, be used by a product manufacturer or a dealer.

The marketing manager who initiates the marketing campaign first of all gets an overview of current sales figures, supported by the SAP Business Information Warehouse. External analysis data, supplied by a market research company, is included in the analysis. Taking market development, marketing requirements and the potential behavior of competitors into account, the marketing manager identifies those products that should be promoted with the marketing campaign. He defines the campaign name, when it will start, how long it will last and the finishing point.

After agreement with the marketing manager, the sales manager defines the campaign target group, with the help of an expert selection of customers and /or potential customers. Then, the campaign and the target group are once again checked, discussed and confirmed. Afterwards, the mailing activities are generated and are forwarded with the support of an external *Mail Shot Provider* (a service provider that sends the e-mails). After the campaign has been executed the marketing manager then oversees the campaign and the status and execution of the individual mail shots. At the end of the campaign cycle the marketing manager and the sales manager can evaluate the effectiveness and efficiency of the campaign and allow this experience to flow over into subsequent campaigns.

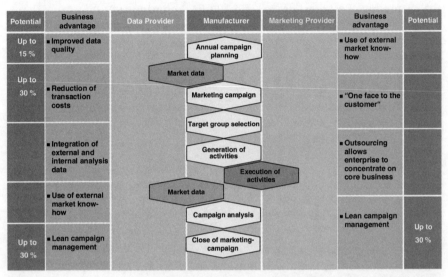

Figure 12.5 Business view of the "Collaborative Marketing Campaigns" c-business map

As can be seen in figure 12.5, different qualitative and quantitative improvements occur in the business process. These include:

▶ Improved quality of data because of data consistency

▶ Reduced transaction costs because of improved collaboration

▶ Integration of external and internal analysis data

▶ Provision of external market know-how

▶ Lean marketing campaign planning and execution

▶ Concentration on campaigns through outsourcing

▶ One face to the customer

Mobile Sales – Customer Visit and Order Entry

This c-business map shows how a field sales employee of a manufacturing concern plans and executes a customer visit, and how the quotation entered is processed as a sales order. Figure 12.6 illustrates the advantages of the collaboration. The result gives an overview of the most important activities of the daily work of field sales employees, put together by Mobile Sales as a process.

In addition, the *Mobile Sales* c-business map is available as a pre-configured best-practices solution (*Best Practices for mySAP CRM*). Best Practices for mySAP.com are pre-configured contents (Business Content) that support and speed up the conversion and implementation of the processes described in c-business maps (see chapter 15, "Best Practices for mySAP CRM" on page 247).

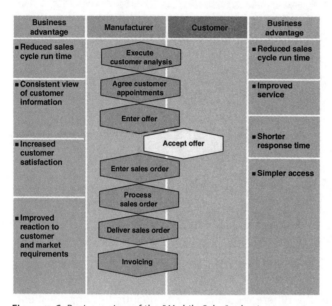

Figure 12.6 Business view of the "Mobile Sales" c-business map

The objective of this c-business map is to present all of the processes – from the visit to the customer through the entry of the sales order – that are typical activities for a field sales employee in a manufacturing concern.

Starting with an analysis of the most recent sales figures for customers in his area, the field sales employee plans customer visits. For some customers, for example, those whose sales figures have dropped considerably, the field sales employee checks the customer history for earlier activities, contact people, opportunities, quotations and orders, and also takes current promotions and campaigns into account.

He arranges an appointment with the desired contact person. During the visit to the customer's premises the field sales employee can maintain customer data, present product offers and, if appropriate, define follow-up activities. A central process is the creation of an order after the acceptance of the corresponding offer. The offer is transformed into an order. Subsequently the order is forwarded to the office-based personnel. Sales and distribution can confirm the picking, packing, shipping and the invoicing process. The field sales employee can track the order status at any time.

As can be seen in the presentation of the processes as a c-business map in figure 12.6, various different qualitative and quantitative improvements occur in the business process. These include:

▶ Shortening of the sales cycle
▶ Consistent customer data
▶ Increased customer satisfaction
▶ Quick reaction to changes in the market and customer wishes
▶ Improved customer service thanks to improved reaction possibilities

Collaborative Business Maps as a Basis for Calculation of Business Profitability

As the examples above demonstrate, the advantages of integrated, shared business processes are documented as business value and in the form of value-added potential on both sides of the business view of a c-business map. For example, for the business scenario *collaborative marketing campaigns* a reduction of up to 30 % in transaction costs is calculated. This is percentage information which makes it possible to adapt the relevant improvement potential (for example, up to 20 % increase in turnover with cross-selling) to each enterprise's own circumstances. The expected improvement potential and percentages are determined and validated in the context of expert meetings, customer projects or independent research.

In this way, before implementing of a c-business process, business partners can check how high the possible return on investment in the realization of such a business process can be, using suitable business application software. The improvement potential for each business partner in a certain area (for example savings in operative costs) can be calculated by simply multiplying the actual basis by the expected improvement potential percentage. The total value for the individual business partners is calculated by adding the quantified business potential to a total value potential. This value provides the basis for management's investment decision on whether or not to actually go ahead with the corresponding implementation project.

The E-Business Case Builder

In order to permit and facilitate a quantitative calculation of the customer-specific value to be expected with the implementaion of mySAP.com solutions, SAP has developed the *E-Business Case Builder*. The E-Business Case Builder offers a transparent and structured method of procedure for calculating the return on investment (ROI). Taking the specific customer situation into account, the tool enables a plausible and structured method of procedure for generating a profitability analysis (known as a *Business Case*) for an envisaged software solution. The tool offers an integrated and transparent method of procedure and also guarantees that it will be possible to compare results.

The E-Business Case Builder is organized in three sections:

▶ Industry analysis (from an independent source)

▶ Identification of a solution

▶ Generation of a return on investment within the context of a business case.

With the help of E-Business Case Builders, the customers can analyze and document their own specific situation. Subsequently, these requirements can be compared with the portfolio of solutions in mySAP.com. Within the portfolio of over 170 c-business maps there are approximately 40 c-business maps with CRM processes, as described above. In addition, many of these processes are adapted to suit specific industries, so they respond to the special needs and requirements of the industry in question.

Finally, with the help of the E-Business Case Builder, a corresponding investment calculation can be set out for the solution selected. Values based on experience from previous, successful implementation projects can be used as default values. Within the framework of the structured method of procedure, customers can add calculations related to their own special situation, and as such the expected improvement value is adapted to suit that customer. With the help of the entry of key values (known as *Key Performance Indicators*, *KPIs*) and balance sheet values, a business case or profitability analysis can be determined quite accurately and in a very short time. The result is presented in what is known as a *Collaboration Scorecard* (see figure 12.7).

The Next Step: Distributed Order Management

A further collaborative business scenario, available after Release 3.0, deals with order processing in divided environments. Self-contained enterprises that carry out all functions of order fulfillment in-house are increasingly being replaced by dependency networks between different business partners participating in the

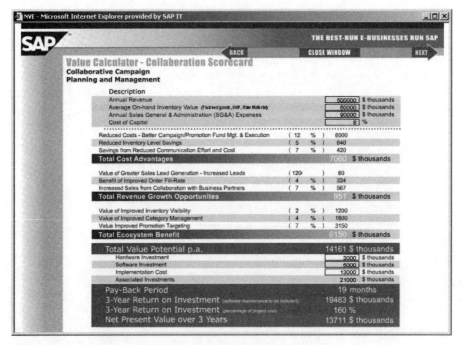

Figure 12.7 E-Business Case Builder: Collaboration Scorecard

order fulfillment process. The aim of the new mySAP CRM service *Distributed Order Management* is to coordinate the order fulfillment process taking different internal and external partners into account and to work in collaboration with any SAP and non-SAP systems. Important business aspects involved are:

▶ Support of third-party business transactions in which a customer is not supplied directly, rather by a business partner or from a different plant.

▶ *Order Split*, that is, different component suppliers for a single order item

▶ Creation of one overall invoice for each order

Distributed Order Management is based on SAP's new *Master Data Management* for heterogeneous system landscapes (see chapter 17, "Master Data Management" on page 283).

13   Analytical CRM – Decision Making Support for Departments and Business Management

Introduction

The basic objectives of customer relationship management are

▶ *Extending* customer relationships by winning new and profitable customers

▶ *Lengthening* the relationships with existing customers by concentrating the resources available on real value added customer relationships

▶ *Deepening* customer relationships by transforming unimportant customers into highly profitable business partners

To achieve this and to make the interaction process with customers as efficient as possible, enterprises need measurement and analysis procedures to evaluate their customer relationships. These are provided by analytical CRM applications which give enterprises answers to questions such as:

▶ *Expanding* customer relationships

  ▶ What type of customers should be won?

  ▶ What type of customers will contribute to the future growth of the enterprise?

  ▶ What new customers might be interested in what the enterprise has to offer?

▶ *Lengthening* customer relationships

  ▶ Which customers should be maintained if possible?

  ▶ Which customers make the most significant contribution to profits?

  ▶ Which customers threaten to move over to the competition and why?

  ▶ Which customers are not satisfied with the enterprise's products and services?

▶ *Deepen* customer relationships

  ▶ For which customers could the share of the wallet be increased?

  ▶ Which products and services are of interest to a particular customer?

  ▶ Which products are normally bought together? What cross-selling possibilities should be taken into account?

Analytical CRM applications provide all the necessary functions for gauging, forecasting and optimizing customer relationships. The following steps are important for the successful use of analytical CRM applications:

- Firstly, all of the relevant customer information, from the various different sources, channels and communication paths must be brought together in an integrated customer knowledge base.
- A comprehensive system of analytical methods for gauging and evaluating customer relationships and for answering business questions related to customers helps to gain insights from the extensive data.
- The use of analysis results for optimizing CRM processes, customer interactions and customer-oriented planning means that these insights can be used by all employees in marketing, sales and service.

And not least of all, it is wise to take customer-related key figures into account in business management and to link customer value with enterprise value. With the help of analytical CRM applications, in association with a constant updating of experiences gained in dealings with customers, enterprises gain a solid understanding of their customers and can optimize their customer relationships via all channels and paths of communication.

The Structure of Analytical CRM Applications

Analytical CRM solutions can be used in different business sub-areas:

- Marketing (*Marketing Analytics*)
- Sales (*Sales Analytics*)
- Service (*Service Analytics*)
- Customers (*Customer Analytics*)
- Products (*Product Analytics*)
- Interaction channels (*Channel Analytics*)
- Marketplaces and Internet (*Marketplace and Web Analytics*)

These analytical sub-applications serve different objectives in part. For example, customer analytics concentrates on customers and leads to a better understanding of customer requirements, customer behavior and customer value. Analysis applications for marketing, sales and customer service give information that help to better understand, plan and evaluate the individual phases of the customer lifecycle (customer acquisition, sales, shipping, service). Channel analytics, finally, give answers to channel specific business questions, such as the acceptance of web access or the efficiency of the interaction center.

Figure 13.1 shows the individual functional areas of an analytical CRM solution and how they are interrelated. Each functional area contributes to the attainment of a good understanding of customers and a deep insight into customer relationships. This information can be used in all customer interactions at all times.

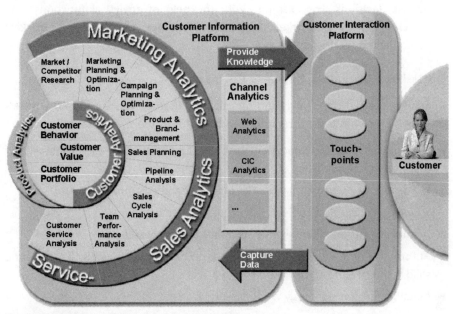

Figure 13.1 Business architecture of analytical CRM

Value Added Potential of Analytical CRM Solutions

The introduction of analytical CRM opens a huge value added potential to enterprises with the possibility of immediately improving enterprise results. The objectives pursued by analytical CRM are presented below.

Understanding Customer Requirements and Behavior Patterns

Analytical CRM helps enterprises to better understand customer requirements and preferences and to identify recurring behavior patterns. This forms the basis for the following points:

▶ Gaining new, profitable customers by "cloning" the best customers

▶ Deepening the relationship with existing customers with personal and individual dialog

▶ Optimizing cross-selling and up-selling possibilities

▶ Maximizing customer loyalty so that customers showing a tendency to move can be recognized and countermeasures can be implemented in time

Optimizing Enterprise Decisions

Analytical CRM can make a significant contribution to the optimizing of strategic enterprise decisions. For example, with the help of analytical functions new tendencies in important markets can be identified. Investments for these markets can be organized correspondingly.

Optimizing Operative Business Processes

In addition, analytical CRM is an important catalyst for gearing the enterprise's operative processes toward customer wishes. This includes, for example:

- ▶ Focusing resources on important customers and maximizing the profitability of customer relationships by
    - ▶ Purposeful investments in marketing, sales and customer service
    - ▶ Focusing attention and services on profitable customers
    - ▶ Improving internal enterprise efficiency and processes
- ▶ Automating and individually planning customer interactions on the basis of a solid customer knowledge
- ▶ Matching business strategy with marketing, sales and service strategies.

Investigation has shown that the profits of companies could sometimes be as much as doubled if they held on to even a small percentage of their customers for longer. The Gartner Group estimates that it costs up to 10 times more to replace a customer with a new one than to keep an existing customer [Lassmann 2000].

Functions of Analytical CRM Solutions

Analytical CRM solutions offer an extensive and functional range of analytical and supporting functions. These include:

- ▶ Recording and consolidation of all relevant customer information
- ▶ Gauging and analyzing customer relationships
- ▶ Optimizing interaction with customers
- ▶ Customer-centered planning and business management
- ▶ Support of operational procedure

The following sections present these functional areas in detail.

Recording and Consolidation of all Relevant Customer Information

The basis for such an analytical CRM solution is an integrated knowledge base on all an enterprise's customers. In the past this information was only available in fragments and dotted like islands throughout the entire enterprise and its different departments. An important requirement for analytical CRM involves combining this information both from a business and from a technical point of view.

Today, there are many new ways that a customer can come into contact with an enterprise. As a result there is a previously unknown wealth of sources of information. For analytical solutions this means that they must go further than the provision of a reliable platform for the creation of a customer knowledge base. It is also important to integrate and bring together customer data from all customer interactions via all channels of communication. It would be a bad approach to limit customer assessment to individual channels of communication. This view of customers, consolidated via all channels, can then give information on, for example:

▶ Customer reactions to certain marketing campaigns

▶ Customer priorities on the web store

▶ Customer questions received in the interaction center

Apart from just the information on customers, analytical applications should also take external sources of information into account in the integrated knowledge base, for example:

▶ Market data on the customer base

▶ Company data on competitors who maintain relationships with the same customers

▶ Internet surveys with which internal customer data can be amplified to include details on customer satisfaction and customer preferences

▶ Data from clubs or organizations with similar interests

Finally, the linking of analytical applications to the backend system should not be overlooked, where supplier and shipping data, together with all activities related to customers, are evaluated monetarily and merged to produce a consistent image of the success of the enterprise and customer profitability.

All in all, the customer knowledge base takes in a wealth of data, as can be seen in figure 13.2.

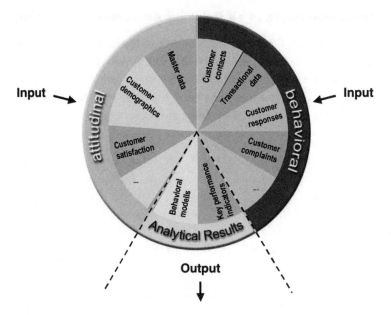

Figure 13.2 The customer knowledge base

Gauging and Analyzing Customer Relationships

A solid analysis of existing customers is often the best basis for the development of customer-oriented marketing, sales and service strategies. This insight is reflected in a fundamental marketing maxim:

The more one knows about one's customers, the easier it is to offer them the goods and services they are looking for.

Successful enterprises can anticipate and even shape and influence customer needs. However, the investment in the customer group necessary for this is not possible without knowledge of:

▶ Customer behavior (preferences, priorities, activities, and so on)

▶ The value of certain customers with regard to customer profitability, customer lifetime value and potential sales that can be expected for the future

▶ The make up of the customer group

Modeling Customer Behavior

Modeling customer behavior provides an enterprise with further information about who their customers are. From observing customer behavior, customer profiles can be created and recurring behavior patterns can be identified. The information gained in this way can be used for the generation of forecasting models to identify attractive and profitable customers and to link them with the enterprise long-term.

Modeling customer behavior supports the following activities:

▶ *Definition of homogeneous customer segments* and decision making in marketing, sales and customer service. Analysis methods such as forming clusters and customer scoring (evaluation) with proven methods such as RFM (see "Application Scenarios" on page 225) are useful tools for this.

▶ *Winning the best new customers* by evaluating the profile of the top existing customers. In this case, methods such as scoring and decision trees that structure the dataset hierarchically, are also helpful for identifying the customers who generate the most revenue and who should, for example, be approached in the next marketing campaign.

▶ *Increasing sales with existing customers*, who are presented with offers that meet their requirements exactly. Analysis methods such as association analysis (for example, product association: examining which products are usually purchased together) help in making full use of cross-selling and up-selling potential.

▶ *Holding on to profitable customers* by recognizing the behavior pattern behind their purchasing behavior. Analysis methods help in identifying tendencies and patterns of customer behavior. Based on this, for example, warning signs that individual customers may stray can be recognized. Data mining methods such as, for example, decision trees are particularly suited to this type of entrepreneurial analysis and provide an ideal method for gaining knowledge in this area.

The business value of analytical CRM depends greatly on ready-made, ready to use models and methods which help to answer customer oriented questions. Key figures such as

▶ Customer satisfaction index (gauging customer satisfaction)
▶ Customer retention index (gauging the strength of customer ties)
▶ Retention Rate
▶ Share of Wallet
▶ Response Rate

help in measuring and influencing the quality of customer relationships (see also chapter 4, "Analytical CRM" on page 35).

Assessment of Customer Value

Customer valuation is a central component of analytical CRM. It helps enterprises to concentrate their limited resources on the best and most valuable customer relationships. In general, customer valuation includes the consideration of customer profitability, customer lifetime value and the *customer rating*.

Customer profitability

One of the most common and most important key figures in customer valuation is customer profitability. The simplest way to generate this figure is to calculate the difference between sales and revenue for each customer. Many CRM solutions offer this type of *margin reporting* and recognize that this alone is not enough for a solid evaluation of customer profitability. Rather, a *contribution margin analysis* is necessary. It provides a consistent image of customer profitability from product and sales costs, taking into account different forms of revenue (see figure 13.3). Modern software solutions also link process cost calculation with customer profitability – with only minimal manual work involved. As a result there is an extremely simple allocation of customer related costs (for example, costs for customer visits, customer support or campaigns) to the customer in question. Of course customer profitability does not replace product profitability, which is also essential for the success of an enterprise.

Volume	30 ST
Gross sales	**500**
- Sales deductions	20
Net sales	**480**
- Product costs	250
Contribution Margin I	**230**
- Direct sales costs	20
- Campaign and promotional costs	10
- Customer related order costs	10
- Customer related shipment costs	40
Contribution Margin II	**150**
- Customer visits	30
- Customer support	10
- Customer care	50
Contribution Margin III	**60**

Figure 13.3 Customer profitability

Customer lifetime value

The customer listing – the most important business capital of many enterprises – does not appear on financial statements. Nor do the financial statements reflect the most difficult and most expensive sales procedure: namely, the customer listing.

If the enterprise has won the trust of a customer just once, then the door has been opened for many subsequent sales. In addition, further new customers can be won through customer recommendations. Customers should therefore also be considered as an investment, on the basis of which decisions are taken that can be evaluated and, finally, must also be protected.

Customer Lifetime Value refers to the real net profits that an enterprise can attain with an average new customer in a certain customer segment over a certain number of years. This is the true value of a customer, which should be taken into account when deciding on investment in new customers. Unlike customer profitability, based on a calendar period viewpoint, the customer lifetime value, based on a lifetime period, gives a measure of how much an enterprise should be prepared to invest in efforts to win new customers.

Customer profile and customer scoring

The generation of customer profiles with suitable classification, for example, ABC analysis (descending ordering of customers according to sales, contribution margin or profit), allows for an in-depth look at the structure of an enterprise's customer base.

In customer evaluation – customer scoring – various different customer-related aspects with different weighting go into a comprehensive appraisal of the individual customer. The sales potential and satisfaction of all customers can, for example, be evaluated and merged together in a single evaluation key figure for each customer. The results of this analysis give a valuable basis for the allocation of marketing, sales and customer service resources to individual customers.

Subjective assessments are not completely excluded in this type of overall evaluation of customers. On the other hand, customer scoring offers the great advantage of allowing fast and efficient evaluation of customers which can, for instance, be used in the interaction center or in the service area immediately. Moreover, this type of key figure can also be used as a basis for considering the composition of the customer portfolio.

Optimizing the Customer Portfolio

For strategic decisions in the area of marketing, sales or customer service, each individual customer is not normally examined for particular characteristics, but the composition of the customer base as a whole is used as a basis for decision making. The analysis of the customer base with a suitable classification of the customer profile, the *customer portfolio*, is an important tool for optimizing the make-up of the customer base. For example, customers could be sorted into different categories based on the key figures *attraction of customer* and *intensity of the customer relationship* (see figure 13.4). Additional key figures such as customer lifetime value, customer scoring or strength of the customer relationship are available for evaluating customers or customer groups, and can help to decide on the most suitable measures to be taken to optimize the customer portfolio. This can be used for the focused acquisition of new customers or for securing existing customers.

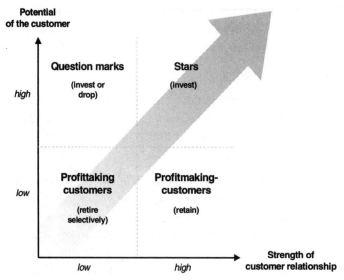

Figure 13.4 Customer portfolio

Optimizing Interaction With Customers

In the cases mentioned below, knowledge of customer preferences and priorities, as well as knowledge of customer value, contribute to the fact that different customers are approached in a manner appropriate to them and limited enterprise resources are concentrated on the most attractive customers:

▶ **Selling in the interaction center**
Providing employees with knowledge on customers' credit worthiness rating, attraction and satisfaction

▶ **Forwarding in the interaction center**
Passing customer service calls on to the most suitable person in the service center, depending on the customer rating and customer value

▶ **Marketing campaigns**
Optimizing target groups by using customer samples which give information on the expected reaction rates

▶ **Web store**
Presenting personal product recommendations or special offers to certain customers

It is of particular importance that the information gained on customers is made available to the corresponding employees in marketing, sales and customer service at the right time to be of assistance in decision making. For this, electronic forms or – in innovative enterprises – information portals are necessary, which consistently report customer analysis results to all enterprise areas and via all communication channels. Furthermore, business processes must be arranged in such a way that the necessary information is also made available quickly and easily for processes in, for example, operational CRM or the interaction center. For a quick and clear interpretation of analysis data, traffic light or symbol presentations can also be used.

Analysis data form a good basis for the increased automation of customer interactions. Especially in the web store, comprehensive knowledge about customers and their behavior can be used to help draw up business rules for optimizing and for individually shaping customer dialogs. In this way product proposals can be individually geared to meet the requirements of individual customers.

However, enterprises should not try to optimize the contact channels with their customers individually or one after the other (for example, first the web page and then the interaction center). Rather, the goal of interaction management is to integrate all interaction channels and optimize them collectively, in what is known as the *channel mix*. Enterprises, for example, often conduct the customer acquisition phase via the Internet and then in the sales and order fulfillment phases incorporate other channels as well.

Customer Centered Planning and Business Management

"In competitive markets, it is not enough to concentrate on market share and revenue growth. A superior business model unites outstanding knowledge about customers and profits with a large quantity of imagination." [Slywotzky 1998]

The close connection between customer value and shareholder value is based on the fact that the market value of an enterprise depends to a great extent on the value of its customer base. Enterprises must reconsider how they can win and retain customers in strongly contested markets. Every enterprise must learn how it introduces and implements customer-centered strategies successfully.

The *Balanced Scorecard* developed by Robert Kaplan and David Norton [Kaplan 1996] is a method for implementing this type of business strategy in terms that are easy to understand, communicate, monitor and implement. It presents management with a comprehensive key indicator system for running the enterprise. The key figures generated are not only related to finance; non-monetary values such as customer satisfaction and the enterprise's ability to innovate are also taken into consideration. These values can be calculated for complaints, returns or the number of new product developments over a certain period of time. All values are set in relation with each other so that both short-term needs for action and long-term business strategies can be derived from them.

To transfer enterprise objectives into concrete marketing, sales and customer service strategies and into operative goals, modern management systems support the following steps:

▶ Analysis of weak points and scenario planning

▶ Formulation of transparent strategies

▶ Communicating the strategy to the whole enterprise

▶ Coordination of enterprise strategy with employees

▶ Linking objectives with the annual budget

▶ Definition and coordination of strategic initiatives

▶ Carrying out regular performance checks with feedback and, where necessary, adjusting strategies

The implementation of a strategic management system (*Strategic Enterprise Management*), in combination with analysis functions and key figures from analytical CRM is an adequate base for synchronizing enterprise management and enterprise strategy.

Support of Operational Procedure

In many companies the implementation of CRM solutions is limited to the automation of marketing, sales and customer service with the help of operative front-office CRM applications. For example, operational CRM puts sales employees in a position to serve customers efficiently and provides the prerequisites for ensuring that customer interactions are synchronized through all channels. However, if enterprises want to ensure that these efforts provide the best possible results, they should combine operational CRM with analytical CRM, because the latter aims at much more than simply generating analysis results and key figures. Knowledge about customers and customer behavior gained through analysis must increasingly be made available to the relevant employees, systems and processes in the enterprise for their daily work. Detailed information about customers is only of value to an enterprise if these insights can really be used and elaborated on in the day-to-day activities of the enterprise.

To allow for a continuous improvement and optimizing of the processes in marketing, sales and customer service, a *Feedback Loop* must be put in place, as demonstrated in figure 13.5. For CRM solutions, the seamless integration of analytical aspects into operational processes means:

▶ Taking analytical results into account in customer oriented planning

▶ Increasing employee productivity with precise and correct information

▶ Using analytical results for optimizing marketing, sales and customer service processes and intelligent customer interaction

Analytical CRM as a Component of mySAP CRM

Overview

SAP's solution for analytical CRM is an open analysis platform, based on the SAP Business Information Warehouse (SAP BW). SAP BW bundles and integrates all relevant customer information from a number of different sources with the help of suitable data extractors. A wide range of analytical applications with business methods, data mining techniques and interfaces to other non-SAP products use

Figure 13.5 Feedback loop for operative and analytical CRM

the customer knowledge base for all types of analytical procedures. Characteristics of SAP's solution for analytical CRM are:

▶ The user works with a browser-based portal, prepared by mySAP enterprise portals. This user interface permits easy access to all analytical results, exceptional situations and additional functions.

▶ A vast selection of key figures (Key Performance Indicators, KPIs) is available to the user for analyzing customer relationships.

▶ SAP functions for analytical CRM are fully integrated with SAP's extensive solution for enterprise analysis along the value added chain. This is true for both SAP Business Analytics and SAP's Strategic Enterprise Management solution (SAP SEM).

Analytical Functions in mySAP CRM

Analytical CRM as a component of mySAP CRM is an integrated package of analysis applications with which customer data can be transformed into strategic information, and as a result customer relationships can be gauged and optimized. These analysis applications are made up of more than just ready-made, instantly usable reporting applications and flexible, adjustable OLAP analyses. Whereas this type of analysis is frequently concerned with the past, analytical methods must also deal with the future and forecast customer behavior or customer lifetime value. In this way they can contribute greatly to current decision making processes.

The analytical functions of mySAP CRM include:

▶ Customer knowledge base

▶ Customer analytics

▶ Marketing analytics

▶ Sales analytics

▶ Service analytics

▶ Channel analytics

These functional areas are presented briefly below.

Customer Knowledge Base

The customer knowledge base unites all relevant customer information and is embedded into SAP BW. The data model used in conjunction with SAP BW guarantees the availability of this information in all analytical applications. Data from the following sources are brought together in the customer knowledge base:

▶ Customer interactions via all channels and media of communication

▶ Internal systems (CRM, SCM, Backend, and so on)

▶ External sources (market data, competitor data, Internet surveys, and so on)

▶ Analytical results

Customer Analytics

Customer analyses offer a range of methods for analyzing and evaluating the customer knowledge base and for using this data to gain insights. In order to develop a good understanding of the customer, various solutions are available for modeling customer behavior (*Customer Behavior Modeling*), for calculating customer value and for analyzing the customer portfolio.

Marketing Analytics

Marketing analytics offer numerous evaluation possibilities:

▶ Market studies and research on competition help to discover new market opportunities and to estimate the potential they hold.

▶ Tools for marketing planning and optimization, support management and marketing management in measuring and planning marketing performance according to time, area, distribution channel, and so on.

▶ Tools for campaign planning and optimizing go beyond the mere planning of campaigns in the narrowest sense, in that they simulate results and monitor success during the execution. Gauging can be carried out with the help of reaction quotas, contribution margins per campaign, conversion quotas, the campaigns' ROI, and so on.

▶ Product and brand analytical functions offer the full range of product-related planning and analysis possibilities, with which the performance of individual products or product groups is controlled and optimized.

Sales Analytics

Sales analyses supply the answers to numerous entrepreneurial questions:

▶ Sales planning tools offer an extensive platform for planning, forecasting and simulating sales figures and profits.

▶ Pipeline analyses help in the evaluation and forecasting of pipelines and opportunities, offers and contracts, to allow for a better exploitation of possible sales opportunities.

▶ Sales cycle analyses support the acquisition of insights throughout the entire sales process – starting with leads through opportunities, to order fulfillment.

▶ Team performance analyses establish the performance of sales organizations, distribution channels and sales areas and how successful sales activities have been.

Service Analytics

Service analyses supply a whole range of answers to all questions related to service – from customer satisfaction to product quality and trends in complaints, to statistics such as completion rates and work load in the service department. Detailed analyses of service revenues and costs help to optimize the performance of the service department.

Channel Analytics

Channel analytics offer analysis functions adapted to suit individual channels, for example, for the web or interaction center. The information gained in this way about customer interactions is also stored in customer knowledge.

Web analyses include, on the one hand, technical analysis of access figures and performance. In this way enterprises can find out what happens on their web site and what areas are of particular interest to customers. More important however, are the *business analyses*, with which enterprises can see the purchasing behavior of their Internet customers and can determine different measurement values such as conversion quota, number of one-off visitors and frequency of visits.

Analyses for the customer interaction center help to estimate the performance and workload of the center.

Application Scenarios

The following scenarios document how analytical applications can contribute to successful customer relationship management along the customer life cycle.

Acquiring new Customers and Customer Lifetime Value

The issue of acquiring new customers involves different questions that should be answered:

▶ Which new customers have the potential to become top customers in the future?

▶ What distinguishes them? With what offers can these customers be best approached?

▶ How advisable is it to invest in a corresponding campaign or advertising measures?

These questions cannot of course be answered with analytical applications alone, well known marketing methods are required here first of all. Yet analytical CRM can also make a contribution:

▶ First of all it is necessary to analyze the market and, for instance, with the help of external data providers such as Dun&Bradstreet (compare, for example, [Bader 2001]), determine market penetration and ultimately the potential of possible prospective customers. The analytical application *Market analysis* helps not only to find the best potential customers but also gives additional information on how these should best be approached.

▶ In addition, the customer profile also plays an important role. Answers are needed to the question on what makes an enterprise's best customer segments stand out. So, for example, it is wise to describe the best customers on the basis of age, sex, location, income or even type of contract and ultimately identify the potential customers that promise the highest revenue.

▶ Customer segments generated in this way can be evaluated with respect to their customer lifetime value. The customer lifetime value can give exact cutoff points as to how much an enterprise should invest in a customer belonging to a particular customer segment.

Retaining the Best Customers in the Enterprise

The comprehensive key figures in analytical CRM such as, for example, customer profitability, customer lifetime value or customer score values, are particularly useful for determining the value of existing customers or customer segments. Analytical CRM helps to understand the profile of the best customers and to use this information gainfully in sales and marketing. For example, in the context of customer behavior modeling it may be seen in a decision tree analysis that customers in the 30–40 age group, who are *single* and with contract type *XY* are very often *top customers*. Also, on further analysis, it emerges that these groups place particular importance on good service and on the reliability of products. *Analytical CRM* supports the answering of these questions with data mining procedures on the one hand, or on the other hand, with classical web surveys which can lead to the results mentioned above.

The next step in customer retention management involves developing effective measures that can better link precisely these customers with the enterprise. Such measures can extend from targeted marketing campaigns that can influence these customers' perception, to deliberate offers of specific products and services, right through to a better integration of the customer in cross-enterprise processes.

Taking Full Advantage of Customer Potential With Up-Selling and Cross-Selling

Another way to increase customer satisfaction and to ultimately ensure that the customer does not stray is to identify cross-selling potential and to exploit it to the full. Analytical CRM offers comprehensive analytical methods for examining cross-selling behavior and using it to forecast customer buying behavior.

The association analysis is the most important data mining procedure for analyzing shopping baskets and identifying cross-selling patterns. The resulting combinations of products or product groups serve as a starting point for campaigns or for putting together new offers (*bundling* or *category management*).

Cross selling analysis can be carried out for different customer segments (target groups) or for individual customers to consider the different buying behavior of these target groups (or individual customers). Geographical differences can also be taken into account in the examinations, at the end of which precise recommendations for marketing action can be developed, as by then it is clear which customer segment buys which products.

Optimizing Direct Mailing Campaigns With the RFM Method

In the past, mailings with high circulation and a minimal response rate of less than 2 % were not unknown. Often offers were sprinkled around as if from a watering can and the sales achieved could not cover the high overall cost of the actions. This type of indiscriminate marketing not only incurs high costs, but often it even goes as far as annoying customers.

With the integration of customer, product and market related data, analytical CRM can now contribute significantly to the successful and well directed execution of a campaign. The following example of the *RFM method* should help to demonstrate this.

▶ R(ecency)

▶ F(requency)

▶ M(onetary Value)

This method is based on the assumption that the response quota depends greatly on when specific customers last made a purchase, how often they buy and how high their purchasing value is. With analytical CRM, customer transaction data can be used to determine what are referred to as *RFM segments*. These are customer segments that display homogenous behavior patterns in relation to the criteria mentioned above.

In the context of a segment evaluation an expected response rate can be forecast for each RFM segment. These insights can either be derived from previous campaigns or can be based on a test campaign.

RFM segments are much more effective at forecasting than models constructed from demographic characteristics such as age, income or real estate ownership. This is based on the fact that demographic models respond to the quesion of who the customer is and not what he does. Forecasting purchasing behavior on the basis of previous purchasing behavior, on the other hand, proves to be a superior marketing tactic.

RFM segments are sorted according to their expected response rate. The important business question of optimizing the campaign is:

How many customer segments should marketing employees include in the campaign to achieve optimal campaign results?

The optimal size of the campaign can be determined by taking the expected response rate, the expected revenue and the costs of the campaign into consideration.

The particular advantage of analytical CRM lies in the fact that this optimizing process is fully and seamlessly integrated into campaign management in operational CRM. There, the segment builder makes it possible either to carry out a manual preselection of target groups or, if desired, to base target group selection on existing RFM segments. This target group forms the population to which the RFM method described above will be applied.

Reducing the Risk of Straying

To help identify customers as early as possible who may be lost and to address the situation appropriately, analytical CRM offers the following solution, comprising two parts:

▶ On the one hand, it is very important to carry out evaluations that take into account straying behavior in individual customer segments, within the context of monitoring customer status. For this, analytical CRM generates a rules-based customer status, which indicates which customers are inactive and therefore in danger of drifting. Retention rates generated in this way show which customer segments are particularly affected by problems of straying.

▶ To be able to combat proactive risks of straying it is also very important to understand better the reasons for and also the patterns in straying behavior. Again, data mining can be of great assistance here.

Example Three months before the expiry of a cell phone contract, a cell phone company would like to know which contract parties are likely to cancel their contracts. Not all customers should be contacted – as this would carry the risk that some customers would only at that point realize that they can choose to terminate the contract and then do so – only those customers who it is feared will be lost and with whom it is hoped to extend the contract should be contacted.

With this sort of well-directed customer selection, the costs of a campaign can be minimized. To identify customers that may be lost, the behavior of customers in danger of straying should first be identified. Characteristics describing this behavior are ascertained. These are socio-demographic data, on the one hand (for example, address, region, details on neighborhood or profession), notes on the cell phone contract, on the other hand (for example, calls peak time, calls off-peak time, cell phone model, price of phone or type of contract).

These characteristics are analyzed with the data mining decision tree, to determine whether the customer will stray, and what the probability of this is. The segments calculated then give a description of the potential straying candidates and the probability that they will cancel their contract. Such a result could read, for example: *Private customers, under 40 years of age who own a telephone costing over $180 have a 75 % probability of canceling their contract.* All further segments can be described in this way.

With subsequent segmenting (in which customer lifetime value plays a decisive role) the customers in danger of straying and profitable customers (the top customers in this segment) can be identified. So, corresponding measures to avoid this changeover can be planned, introduced, executed and reviewed. This is done by transferring the identified and evaluated segments to campaign management. This will also further optimize the customer portfolio.

Market Tendencies

The Internet offers many possibilities, as yet not fully exploited, for interaction with customers and for the coordination of cross-enterprise business relationships. The spread of the use of mobile applications and devices will strengthen this tendency even further. Future solutions for analytical CRM will be strongly influenced by the following trends:

▶ Move from customer analysis to relationship analysis

▶ The evolution from conventional marketing to real-time marketing

▶ The growing importance of analytical CRM for performance management in enterprises

▶ Marketplace analytics (determination of future key trends using analysis on electronic exchanges)

From Customer Analysis to Relationship Analysis

The clear tendency towards enterprise networks, with the externalizing of business processes and cross-enterprise collaboration creates a growing need for analysis functions that extend beyond the traditional boundaries of enterprises. Enterprises that fulfill their customers' requirements and at the same time want to increase their profitability need to get an overview of the entire value-added chain – from the product through to customer service. In addition collaboration beyond enterprise limits requires that the partners and suppliers have all necessary information. With this type of cooperation all stand to gain in the value-added chain, because the competitive advantages achieved in this way are much greater than could be achieved by each individual enterprise alone.

From this perspective, enterprises must include their suppliers, partners and employees in all analyses; concentrating on customers alone would not be sufficient. This is particularly true for integrated enterprise networks. For example, making shared master data available to business partners is one of the most important prerequisites for converting pure customer analyses into analyses of enterprise relationships.

From Conventional Marketing to Real-Time Marketing

Marketing systems are evolving from database marketing, based on conventional campaign management, to a new, interactive marketing approach, geared toward individual customer requirements. Accordingly, marketing is today moving away from being a data-oriented, outward-directed, mass processing procedure, to event-driven interactions in real time [Martin 2000]. Great technological leaps mean that enterprises are in a position to carry out current, interactive marketing and to woo customers specifically with offers and products that are tailored to meet their individual requirements. In this way every interaction between the enterprise and customers can be used as a marketing opportunity.

A repository of analysis results and behavior patterns, independent of channel, forms an excellent basis for personalized customer interactions. According to how much information customers give away about themselves, web pages or, for example, dialogs with customers in the interaction center can be dynamically adapted and arranged to suit the individual preferences and interests of the customer. The automating of this type of marketing requires intelligent interaction management that uses existing analysis models dynamically, to identify optimal marketing interactions in each case.

The Increasing Importance of Analytical CRM for Enterprise Management

With CRM's development from being the project of one department to becoming a business strategy, analytical CRM now receives more attention from management, who consider CRM statistics – together with financial statistics – as important indicators of the financial performance of enterprises [Morris 2000]. With the integrated Balanced Scorecard solution enterprises are well prepared to face these challenges.

Markets, which are changing faster and faster, also influence planning methods in marketing, sales and customer service. Planning is gradually evolving away from retrospective budgeting, based on a certain point in time, toward rolling, continuous forecasting models. For example, behavior patterns gained from past data is used to forecast future behavior. SAP's linking of the analytical CRM solution to planning and forecasting models will gain increasing importance as enterprises become more aware of this change.

The Increasing Importance of Marketplace Analytics

Cross-enterprise collaboration in e-business places high demands on the merging of information about customers, partners and suppliers. Commercial web sites, electronic marketplaces and online exchanges will develop further and the externalizing of business processes will push ahead. As a result of this the increasing need to optimize business processes over the entire logistics chain, the shared use of information between partners and the development of corresponding analytical solutions will all continue. New solutions for marketplace analysis will play a more important role in analytical CRM in future solutions. The exchanges that SAP is currently implementing with partners already cover new challenges in analysis. With these pilot projects, new outline examples of cross-enterprise collaboration are already beginning to emerge.

14   Workforce Management with mySAP CRM

What is Workforce Management?

Employees in the interaction center, service technicians, sales employees, support personnel, and so on, all participate in some way in an enterprise's production process. The term *Workforce Management* refers to all business processes that affect the management and planning of these people in the production process. These include:

▶ Planning human resources with particular ability profiles for certain tasks at particular times, including exact forecasts and time schedules

▶ The inclusion of time and attendance data, together with individual requirements, in the planning and scheduling processes

▶ Evaluating the productivity and performance of employees and managers

▶ Identifying training needs and opportunities for employee development

▶ Management of motivation and performance incentives for employees (*Incentives & Commissions*)

To understand the role of Workforce Management in CRM, first of all it is necessary to answer the question as to why the related tasks are not resolved in the human resources system or in resource planning in the production system.

Why is Workforce Management Part of CRM?

Basically, Workforce Management is different from human resources (HR) systems in that it deals with the requirements of production or service processes, something that is not necessarily the case for HR systems. Human resources is concerned with the employee as a whole, with all his experience and history in the enterprise. In Workforce Management the employee is only considered as a resource in the business process.

So why does Workforce Management not form a part of traditional production systems like, for example, Supply Chain Management (SCM)? The reason is simple: People require different solutions than materials. Each person is unique. SCM traditionally concentrates on materials, consumables, or machines. These inanimate objects are always homogeneous, while people are generally heterogeneous and as a result each one needs an individual process.

Every customer relationship is primarily about people. This is why Workforce Management is of such importance in CRM processes. People accept sales orders over the telephone, complete project tasks or carry out field service activities. People prefer to do business with people that they know and trust. People make deals with each other if customer service is good. The cultivation and maintenance of relationships through good customer service is a widely recognized business objective. Workforce Management is the CRM tool with which the human resources of an enterprise are directed toward this objective.

The mySAP CRM Workforce Management Solution

Workforce Management will be available with the follow-up release of mySAP CRM 3.0 and supports all activities related to workforce planning, regardless of whether the human resource is a consultant, a field service technician, a service employee or all three at the same time. The basis of Workforce Management is the close cooperation with the mySAP.com solutions mySAP BI and mySAP HR.

The activities supported by Workforce Management in mySAP CRM include:

▶ **Planning workforce requirement**
Planning how many full time employees with what knowledge will be required at what point in time

▶ **Recruiting personnel**
Establish how the work to be done can be assigned and what recruitment measures are necessary

▶ **Organizing personnel**
Assign employee resources to requirements. How high are the estimated employee costs? Can the activities of employees and their performance be tracked?

▶ **Motivating personnel**
Acquire personnel, motivate them and bind them long-term to the company. Use of performance incentives and bonus systems

▶ **Developing personnel**
How can employees develop their own careers? What concrete possibilities for career development are available?

▶ **Equipping personnel**
Equipping employees with a suitable working environment so that they can carry out their duties as well as possible.

▶ **Analyzing workforce planning**
Use of analysis, reporting and simulation applications to optimize workforce planning

Interaction Center

Interaction centers support customer interactions via different contact channels and, if necessary, 24 hours a day. mySAP CRM's Workforce Management ensures that the necessary personnel are available at the appointed time and in the required number. For this, management can use the following services:

▶ Long-term business and capacity planning

▶ Long-term personnel, budget and service level planning

▶ Maintenance of employee data, integrated with mySAP HR

▶ Short-term planning and assignment of employees to specific tasks and dealing with exceptional situations (for example, an employee to which work has been assigned falls ill)

▶ Real-time monitoring (absence times, waiting times, and so on) and intra-day forecasts

▶ Transaction analysis after period-end close, taking budget, transaction objectives and employee performance into account

▶ Administration of several business locations

▶ Comprehensive reports and analyses

In mySAP CRM, Interaction Center forwards all relevant and up-to-date information necessary for generating precise and complete work plans to the Workforce Management application.

Forecasting personnel requirements can be done with the help of business activities via all channels, taking into account historical workload volumes, strategic enterprise goals and local objectives and experience. Short-term and long-term forecasts can be viewed, created or adjusted once a particular planning stage has been reached. As Workforce Management is an integral component of mySAP CRM, these forecasts or personnel plans can be forwarded to other business areas, for example, to support recruitment and budgeting.

As soon as a requirement is forecast, management can generate an optimal work plan based on different, configurable objectives. A work plan can, for instance, take into account particular knowledge requirements, personnel regulations, employee wishes or tried and tested practical rules. Depending on the level of complexity desired, these aspects can be weighted differently in the planning process.

Field Service

With the *Resource Planning Tool* (see chapter 7, "Field Service and Resource Planning" on page 123) the resource planner has the possibility of allocating service orders to field service employees on the basis of certain guidelines (for example, Service Level Agreements), geographical considerations, availability and personal knowledge and equipment requirements. Alternatively, automatic allocation can be carried out.

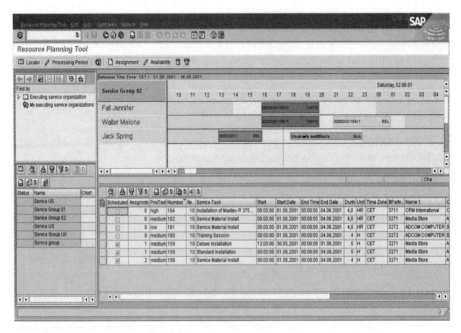

Figure 14.1 Resource planning for field service

Based on integration with mySAP HR, the resource planner can provide information on the availability of individual employees. Mobile communication services such as pagers and SMS allow the planner to forward up-to-date information on service employees' current schedules and any possible emergencies that may arise. Schedules are presented to the field service employees in SAP calendar format or in Microsoft Outlook or Lotus Notes. Field service employees can send status details on tasks back to the resource planner, for example, *accepted*, *rejected*, *completed*, *on site*, and so on. In addition the field service employee can report work times, material used, any damage codes, travel times and expenses.

Jobs can be allocated automatically, for example, by an agent in the interaction center or manually by the resource planner. In allocating jobs both the customer's interests (preferred visit time, service level agreements, and so on) and the optimization of the service processes should be taken into account. The resource planner can gain further flexibility by allocating several different employees from the same team to the individual items of a service operation. Furthermore, different resource planners can access planning data for employees that can be included in plans together. With future ATP (Available to Promise) functions, resource planners will also be able to ensure that the field service employees have access to the material needed to execute the task.

Consultant Scheduling

Today, many jobs are planned and executed in the form of projects. Many different types of collaborators take part in these projects; internal employees and also external consultants. The allocation of consultants to project tasks, taking into account their availability and individual skills, is a task of Consultant Management in mySAP CRM.

A resource planner in a consultancy has the possibility of definite planning of customer jobs for certain employees (*Hard Booking*) and in so doing, making use of the possibilities of integrating with different project management and schedule applications such as Microsoft Outlook and Lotus Notes. For long-term planning the functions for conditional planning (*Soft Booking*) can also be used, with which personal resources can be reserved on the basis of abilities, availability or preferences, without actually assigning the task to a particular employee.

15   Implementing mySAP CRM in Enterprises

Introduction

The Gartner Group's study on the reasons why CRM projects fail demonstrates the need for a strategy for the successful implementation of CRM [Nelson 2001]. According to the experts, the most noteworthy causes of failure are inadequate planning, the lack of an implementation strategy and the resulting problems of acceptance. Often CRM initiatives are started without a clear understanding of the extent of the necessary changes involved beforehand. Inadequate integration and a lack of interest on the part of top management, together with imprecise and impractical objectives are other mistakes that can lead to the failure of the CRM implementation.

For a successful CRM implementation project the following measures should be taken from early on:

▶ Anticipate changes in business processes

▶ Include end-users of the CRM software

▶ Piece together a clear project organization

▶ Use an implementation methodology specifically geared to CRM, which will serve as a basic introduction for the whole of the CRM implementation project and will be based on experiences, from successfully-completed CRM implementation projects.

Factors of Success in the Implementation of CRM

The most important factors contributing to the success of CRM implementation projects are:

▶ **The acceptance of the CRM software in the enterprise**
Often, end-user functions are implemented in a CRM project first (*end-user efficiency*), before the system is developed further. Gradually, more and more employees become users of the CRM solution (end-user and *team efficiency*), which finally supports entire processes within the enterprise and between enterprises (internal enterprise efficiency and cross-enterprise effectiveness). Given that these employees will not only have to work with new software, but will often also have to deal with a new organization structure, it is important that end-users are included in the project and in the implementation method as early as possible. Otherwise it is very probable that there will be resistance from end-users later.

- ▶ **Strategy and project planning**
  Some enterprises have such time pressures when implementing a CRM system that they lose sight of the overall strategy. It is therefore very important that enterprise and IT strategies are concurrent. Combining the requirements from the enterprise point of view with those from the IT point of view is the starting point for project planning.

- ▶ **The support of top level management**
  In view of the far reaching effects of the implementation of the CRM solution, the support of top level management is absolutely necessary. The managers involved must have access to CRM know-how (*Content Promoter*) and also have a position in the enterprise from which they can implement decisions (*Power Promoter*). The management has to make clear statements on the execution of the project.

- ▶ **Establishing factors of success**
  Factors of success and goals must be established at the beginning of the project. The project should be called to a halt as soon as possible if these factors cannot be achieved.

- ▶ **Cooperation with end-users**
  The systems used can in certain circumstances be very complex and as a result it is necessary to work in collaboration with technicians and end-users regarding specifications and requirements. This cooperation should be in the form of continuous team work.

- ▶ **Detailed description of the project plan**
  The project plan for the implementation of a CRM solution must give details of the objectives, methods, visions, people responsible as well as scheduling and resources (employees, budget, and so on).

- ▶ **Expert knowledge**
  In a good project plan it will also be established when which person will be needed and whether or not external know-how is necessary. In view of the fact that analysis is done with regard to business processes, one person should be selected as being responsible for each central process (for example, campaign management).

- ▶ **Development of a documentation and communication plan**
  It is necessary to have a communication plan for distributing information about the project in the enterprise, establishing when information will be given on which topics. It is also important to document the project itself and the functions of the solution. A user manual can also help make the introduction of the system easier for the end users.

- **Pilot users and the introduction of the system**
  To include the users affected in a practical way from as early as possible it should be possible to organize pilot use of the system. As a result the project will enjoy a higher level of acceptance and the results will be more transparent. Plans should also be made for the *roll-out* in the enterprise.

- **User training**
  Before the system can be implemented productively, there should be training courses for the users who will mainly use the system for the handling of business processes. For technical subjects (for example, systems administration) separate training courses should be conducted.

SAP Solution Architect and SAP Solution Manager

There are two extensive tools for the introduction and operation of mySAP.com solutions in enterprises:

- SAP Solution Architect (business planning and implementation)
- SAP Solution Manager (technical implementation and productive operation)

The *SAP Solution Architect* is a portal for a business-oriented evaluation and implementation of mySAP.com solutions, also allowing for the fast adjustment and improvement of the solutions.

SAP Solution Architect includes the following methods, tools and content:

- AcceleratedSAP methods for planning and executing mySAP.com implementation projects including a procedure model (Roadmap) for all phases of the implementation project
- Best Practices for mySAP.com for the implementation of e-business solutions on the basis of pre-configured systems
- Collaborative Business Maps for cross-enterprise business processes
- E-Business Case Builder for determining ROI (return on investment) during the sales process, that is to say, for calculating the cost-effectiveness of implementing a mySAP.com solution.
- Customizing tools for the individual specification of the mySAP.com implementation
- Authoring environment with which customers and partners can put together their own pre-configured implementation solutions.

The *SAP Solution Manager* is SAP's service portal for technical support of the implementation and productive phase of mySAP.com solutions.

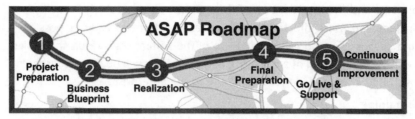

Figure 15.1 ASAP Roadmap (without the CRM phase "feasibility study")

The following services are offered by SAP Solution Manager:

▶ Management of the technical implementation and running of mySAP.com solutions

▶ Guaranteeing the technical running of all central business processes

▶ Monitoring all central business processes (application monitoring)

▶ Monitoring the entire mySAP.com system landscape including interfaces to third party systems (system monitoring)

▶ Access to SAP support services such as

   ▶ *GoingLive Check* (a practically proven method of procedure for the successful start of operation)

   ▶ *Early Watch Service* (proactive system diagnosis)

   ▶ *EarlyWatch Alert* (automated system analysis for optimizing performance and availability)

▶ Access to *SAP Notes Assistant* with up-to-date information, tips and error correction

▶ Remote Support

▶ Service planning for optimizing and maintaining mySAP.com solutions throughout the entire life cycle

A general discussion of all services offered by SAP Solution Architect and SAP Solution Manager would go beyond the capacity of the present work. Special aspects, associated with the introduction of mySAP CRM, do arise though upon examination of the implementation method and the use of pre-configured business know-how. These subjects are dealt with in the next two sections.

AcceleratedSAP for mySAP CRM

AcceleratedSAP (*ASAP*) is SAP's general implementation method for the successful, fast and efficient implementation of SAP software solutions. The advantages of ASAP are:

- Standardization in the implementation of CRM solutions
- Guarantee of successful implementation taking the factors *time*, *budget* and *quality* into account
- Transfer of knowledge within SAP and to customers, consultant partners, and so on

For consideration of the special requirements of CRM implementation projects, a special ASAP version, called *AcceleratedSAP for mySAP CRM* has been developed.

Overview

AcceleratedSAP for mySAP CRM (ASAP for mySAP CRM) is the implementation method developed by SAP for CRM solutions and CRM projects. It is adapted to suit the requirements of CRM and in the main project phases it is based on ASAP for SAP R/3. The components of ASAP for mySAP CRM (process library and road map) are delivered with SAP Solution Architect.

A special implementation method, adapted to the needs of CRM projects is necessary because a CRM project is different to, for example, an R/3 project in essential aspects:

- Difference in technology and system landscape (for example, for mobile sales)
- Different user groups
- Different influence on the internal company organization
- Different roles and project structures
- Customer wishes go beyond standard functions more frequently than happens with SAP R/3

Project Plan for the Implementation of mySAP CRM

The implementation of the CRM solution is supported by ASAP for mySAP CRM with a special roadmap which includes the following phases:

- Feasibility study
- Project preparation
- Business blueprint
- Realization
- Final preparation
- Go live and support

Feasibility Study

An important difference between ASAP for mySAP CRM and standard methods is the consideration of the feasibility study as an important preliminary phase of the CRM implementation project.

This phase takes place when an enterprise has decided on a CRM solution and it must be checked to see to what extent the software covers the functional requirements of the customer. During this phase the customer is supported in drawing up business and IT strategies and in the selection of the relevant processes from a business point of view. The result of this phase is usually a quotation including an estimation of costs (approximate project planning, scheduling, internal and external resource expenditure).

The aims of the feasibility study are:

▶ To understand the customer's business and requirements
▶ To comprehend the customer's business processes
▶ To understand the existing system landscape and the level of customization of installed applications
▶ To compile data on the scale, resources and costs of the project
▶ To work out hardware and software requirements
▶ To reach agreements with the relevant decision makers: Customer, SAP and partners

Project Preparation

This phase covers the planning and preparation of the CRM implementation project. Even if each SAP project is different regarding objectives, scope and priorities, the following, general operations are of considerable importance to the further success of the project:

▶ Generate project charter
▶ Establish the objectives of the project
▶ Clarify the scope of implementation
▶ Set down implementation strategy
▶ Fix a general time schedule for the project and the order to be followed during the implementation
▶ Arrange project structure and project committee
▶ Allocation of human resources
▶ Project kickoff

With a timely clarification of these aspects, a solid basis is created for a successful SAP implementation and the efficient running of the project is assured.

Business Blueprint (Conceptual Design)

The objective of this phase is to document the enterprise's business process requirements, established in a requirements workshop, in a *business blueprint*. Based on this, an overall concept is worked out of how the enterprise wishes to portray its business procedures with the CRM system.

During this phase the following steps are also taken:

▶ Fine tuning of the original project aims and objectives

▶ Implementation of Change Management

▶ Arranging of system environment

▶ Establishing basic scope of the solution

▶ Detailed preparation of the entire project plan and the procedure of the implementation

Realization

The purpose of this phase is to execute the business and process requirements established in the business blueprint. The aim of this phase is the final implementation of the system, an overall test and the release of the system for productive operation.

Realization takes place in two work packages, baseline configuration (main scope) and detail configuration (detail scope). The baseline system is remarkable for the fact that the organization structures are completely configured and the business processes are around 60 % configured. With this method of procedure, after the baseline system has been approved, the details can systematically be processed further.

Final Preparation

The object of final preparation is to conclude the preparation of production including finalizing tests, user training and the drawing up of system management and user support organization. All remaining questions regarding final preparation for going live are cleared up. After the successful completion of this phase productive business processes can run in the CRM system.

Go-Live and Support

The aim of this phase is to progress from the pre-productive environment to productive operation. It is important at this stage to set up user support that will not only be available during the first critical days of productive operation, but that will be available long-term.

During this phase the users get practical experience with the CRM solution. A well-organized user support, to which all users have access, must be provided. This phase also serves to monitor the system transactions and to optimize the overall performance of the system. The end of this phase marks the conclusion of the project.

Employee Roles in the CRM Implementation Project

The use of the ASAP for mySAP CRM method requires the drawing up of a suitable project organization. In addition, for the successful completion of the tasks associated with the method and process steps it is necessary to clearly establish responsibilities.

Below we present an overview of the important roles that are included in a CRM implementation project:

▶ **Project manager**
The project manager is responsible for the project results and the operative management of the project. The project manager foresees deviations in the project and immediately takes corrective measures. In addition, the project manager should understand the systems integration of the business processes in the enterprise environment.

The project manager has decision making authority on issues relating to the project and the budget. He or she passes strategic questions on to the ordering party for reaching mutual decisions.

Depending on the size and complexity of the mySAP CRM implementation, a second project management level can be introduced, if necessary. In this case the project manager would be supported by regional project managers.

▶ **Application consultant**
The application consultant is responsible for ensuring that the software configuration is adapted to suit the business processes and that analysis and report requirements are fulfilled. In addition, he or she imparts application and configuration knowledge to business process team leaders and other team members. The application consultant is entrusted with proven business procedures to be able to offer support in the design. The application consultant also acts as an advisor and if necessary helps the project team in all tasks.

Modifications often lead to open questions in *Change Management*. The application consultant occupies a key position in that he or she supports *Organizational Change Management* with useful information. If legacy data is extracted, close collaboration with the legacy system experts is absolutely necessary.

▶ **Technical consultant**
The technical consultant works together with the project manager and the leader of the technical team in planning the technical requirements and then executes the technical system tasks and customer specific development.

Depending on the scope and complexity of the implementation, this consultant can work in one or several areas, for example, in system administration, database administration, network administration, operating system administration, development of cross-application components or in ABAP development.

In international projects the technical consultant also takes on consultancy management in the following areas:

▶ Country specific business and SAP software requirements

▶ Language or codepage-specific requirements

▶ Dealing with different time zones

Best Practices for mySAP CRM

Best Practices for mySAP CRM pursues the aim of enabling SAP customers to use comprehensive CRM functions as quickly and effortlessly as possible, with the help of pre-configurations.

The main priorities are

▶ Creating the organizational and technical foundations for the efficient realization of new CRM solutions

▶ Ensuring that all business processes to be portrayed in the CRM system are optimally arranged to meet customer requirements

In addition, Best Practices for mySAP CRM allows SAP customers access to e-business knowledge that has been accumulated by SAP and SAP partners in numerous evaluation and implementation projects.

A survey among customers who had used Best Practices, showed that Best Practices dealt fully with the above mentioned requirements. This also covers an analysis of the delivery data of all existing product versions of Best Practices for mySAP.com, of which Best Practices for mySAP CRM is also a part. Up to the end of 2001 over 4,000 delivieres could be listed. One reason for the success of Best

Practices most certainly lies in the fact that due to the increasing complexity of technical and business requirements, it is necessary to fall back on pre-configured systems in order to keep the costs, time and risk involved in an evaluation or implementation project as low as possible.

The components of Best Practices are examined in the following section.

Components of Best Practices for mySAP CRM

The following elements form part of *Best Practices for mySAP CRM*:

▶ **Easy to understand implementation methods**
The Best Practices method is based on the AcceleratedSAP method. It is augmented by additional documents and procedures that help to ensure an optimal use of the condensed expertise.

▶ **Detailed documentation**
The reusable documentation on mySAP CRM is suitable for private study, evaluation and for training project teams and users.

▶ **Complete pre-configuration**
The pre-configured settings make it possible to have integrated core processes up and running in a short space of time. This involves only minimal installation work.

The components of Best Practices for mySAP CRM make it possible to put together an operational prototype of mySAP CRM in the shortest time possible, which is integrated into the customer's existing system landscape. Customer data from existing SAP ERP systems can simply be transferred into the new CRM system. This CRM prototype is fully documented and can be used as a basis for further adjustment and thus for the final implementation and setting in operation.

In this way, customers can also use Best Practices for mySAP CRM to expand an already operational SAP solution with CRM supported business scenarios. This includes both technical and business aspects. In the scope of supply there is, for instance, a widely automated installation process for linking SAP Mobile Sales to the CRM server taking all technical and business aspects into account.

Numerous configuration settings, which ensure that the CRM system components can communicate with each other, are also available with Best Practices. Best Practices for mySAP CRM ensures that all necessary data on products, business partners and pricing conditions contained in an existing SAP R/3 system can be easily transferred to the new solution and at the same time, can be made available to the mobile components.

Pre-Configured Business Scenarios

Best Practices for mySAP CRM offers direct implementation support with the help of the following pre-configured business scenarios:

- ▶ E-selling
  - ▶ Ordering transaction in B2B
  - ▶ Ordering transaction in B2C
- ▶ Sales
  - ▶ Opportunity management and mobile sales
- ▶ Field sales
  - ▶ Customer visit with order entry
  - ▶ Execution of campaigns
- ▶ Interaction Center
  - ▶ Information help desk
  - ▶ Interaction center service
  - ▶ Inbound telesales
  - ▶ Outbound telesales
- ▶ Marketing management
  - ▶ Campaign management
  - ▶ Lead management
  - ▶ Analysis of customer behavior
- ▶ Integrated sales planning (ISP)
  - ▶ ISP for key accounts
- ▶ Specific CRM scenarios for service providers

All the scenarios mentioned are outlined in chapter 8.

Advantages for the Customer

Best Practices for mySAP CRM contains precise descriptions of important CRM business processes and of the corresponding pre-configuration for the fast realization of these processes. There are many and varied areas of usage for Best Practices for mySAP CRM: The product can be used by both medium-sized enterprises looking for a speedy implementation, and by corporate groups wishing to create templates for subsidiaries. It does not matter if the customer already has SAP software installed or is a new customer, Best Practices for mySAP CRM makes it possible to have an e-business solution up and running in a very short time.

The advantages for the customer of Best Practices for mySAP CRM can be summarized as follows:

▶ **Typical beginner mistakes in e-business can be avoided**
Best Practices for mySAP CRM is a tried and tested product and helps to avoid errors in systems, business processes or configuration that usually occur with enterprises new to e-business. Right from the beginning SAP has identified potential sources of error and in Best Practices for mySAP CRM show how they can be avoided.

▶ **Savings of time and money**
Best Practices for mySAP CRM anticipates most general enterprise requirements and necessary project steps. The documentation and configuration is completely reusable and can easily be adapted to meet individual requirements.

▶ **A wealth of knowledge on e-business processes**
Apart from integrated, universal business processes, which make the best possible use of mySAP CRM, Best Practices for mySAP CRM also supplies everything needed for becoming an expert. This includes information on the system landscape, a tried and tested implementation strategy, documented business processes, configuration and documentation, user roles as well as test data and practical examples.

▶ **Easy expansion of enterprise solutions**
Best Practices for mySAP CRM contains an automatic implementation procedure, based on typical customer systems. Best Practices for mySAP CRM can be operated with one or several new mySAP.com components. The linking of SAP Business Information Warehouse and SAP Advanced Planner & Optimizer with mySAP CRM is also automatic. This linking makes it possible to enhance the CRM solution with additional functions such as cross-selling and up-selling or availability check with reservation.

▶ **Faster construction of an operational prototype**
With the help of Best Practices for mySAP CRM it is possible to create an operational, fully documented prototype in just a few days, which can serve as a starting point for the continued implementation.

SAP's mySAP CRM Implementation Project

Thanks to close dealings with customers, SAP has gained a wealth of experience in the management of customer relationships over the years, which has been fed into the SAP product mySAP CRM. This product is now also used within SAP for maintaining customer relationships. The implementation began in the marketing and sales departments, followed by customer service and support.

Internally existing software solutions that SAP had previously used for customer relationship management are successively being replaced by mySAP CRM.

The Customer Engagement Lifecycle (CEL)

SAP's internal *Customer Engagement Lifecycle* describes the individual phases of the relationship of a customer or potential customer with SAP and the individual activities carried out by the different SAP field organizational units such as marketing, sales, consultation, training, customer service, and so on, in order to look after their customers, partners and potential customers in the best possible way and to achieve a high level of customer retention.

The customer engagement lifecycle is organized in the following main phases:

▶ Discovery

▶ Engage

▶ Implementation

▶ Continuous improvement

The following activities form part of the individual phases:

▶ The *discovery phase* includes the acquisition of potential customers and existing customers. During this phase the possiblities and advantages of SAP products should be demonstrated. For this, forms of direct marketing via different channels such as e-mail, telephone, and so on, are available, in addition to the execution of customer and information events.

▶ The *engage phase* is concerned with the sale of software licenses, training, consultation and maintenance. First of all a solution pack that meets each customer's individual requirements is put together in collaboration with the customer. After this has been validated by both sides there is a negotiation phase until a contract is agreed.

▶ The *implementation phase* describes the activities of SAP in supporting the customer during the implementation of the software solution.

▶ In the *continuous improvement phase* the customer is looked after by SAP to such an extent that the added value that the customer hoped to obtain with the implementation of the SAP solution is guaranteed, or even increased. This includes both services that constantly check system availability and also offer support in the adjustment of software to cope with changing conditions and requirements.

The customer engagement lifecycle is thus SAP's internal *Solution Map* for satisfying customer needs. The customer engagement lifecycle is closely linked to the mySAP CRM Solution Map, which describes extensive functions for a general lifecycle of a customer's relationship with an enterprise. In this sense, the customer engagement lifecycle is a SAP-specific, internal development of the mySAP CRM Solution Map.

SAP as a User of mySAP CRM

SAP has implemented its own mySAP CRM software solution to support all the activities of the customer engagement lifecycle. Not only are existing software solutions and all their interfaces replaced, there is also an improvement in processes thanks to the gearing of all activities toward the customer engagement lifecycle.

Marketing Management

The implementation of mySAP CRM began in the marketing department. There were two main objectives to be achieved here:

▶ *First of all*, it had to be possible to establish global strategic goals for SAP marketing. With the help of the global strategic organization the individual countries and regions could develop their own strategies and their operational activities in line with this.

▶ *Secondly*, all activities should comply with the needs of the customer or potential customer, and it should be possible to follow up on all activities. This means that the potential customer must be provided purposefully with information and communication should be established via the channel that the potential customer prefers. To ensure this, all information on potential customers must be available centrally for all actions and channels of communication.

To achieve the global strategic goals the individual regions and countries carry out market potential analyses – with the help of analytical CRM services – in order to plan individual campaigns. This includes both the planning of individual actions within a campaign and budget planning. In addition, statistics (Key Performance Indicators, KPIs) are defined, such as the number of potential customers gained, and so on, and these indicators then serve as a benchmark for the success of the campaign.

Individual campaigns are linked with marketing plans which reflect the strategic orientation of the marketing campaigns. The budgets available for individual campaigns are established as part of a marketing plan. In marketing planning different KPIs can be defined and planned for a campaign so that later, apart from the success of a campaign, it is also possible to check the success of the strategic orientation. The planned campaigns and the budgets planned for them are approved by management using a workflow.

By recording the costs arising, the contacts made with potential customers, and so on, after the end of the campaign, the actual data is then compared with the planned values and the success of the campaign can thus be evaluated. With this, it is possible on the one hand to get an overview of all the activities that take place in the realization of the strategic goals, and on the other hand the success of the campaign can be evaluated regarding the contribution made to overall sales.

For the realization of the second goal, that of communication with the customer irrespective of channel, the introduction of the mySAP CRM solution involves a change from *channel-specific* (e-mail, telephone, and so on) to *theme-specific* campaign planning. In general, a campaign consists of several actions which cover different channels and build successively on one another. With this system it is possible to pre-qualify the possible interest of a potential customer (lead), by which, depending on their reaction to a target group-specific campaign action, the potential customers can be designated a further action in the campaign.

SAP uses the following channels of communication in the execution of individual marketing actions:

▶ There are telephone actions, in which interaction center agents call the customers or potential customers (*Outbound*). With the help of interactive scripting the interaction center agent receives a conversation outline. For this, a profile of the customer or potential customer can be drawn up or, for example, a customer's request to receive informative material can be recorded. The interaction center agent always has access to all information on the person they have to call.

▶ In addition, there are actions which involve the customer or potential customer calling SAP (*Inbound*), in order to, for example, register for events or ask questions on SAP products. The interaction center agent is supported by the mySAP CRM Solution Database for this type of call.

▶ In addition, personalized e-mails can be sent. These can contain different text elements depending on the profile of the customer or potential customer. They can also contain links to SAP information pages on the Internet. It is possible to trace how many e-mail recipients subsequently go to these information pages. It is also possible to link up from an e-mail message to a web form with which customers or potential customers can, for example, register for events or express interest in SAP products. This interest in purchasing is directly evaluated and stored in the CRM system as a lead, and the interest of the customer or potential customer can subsequently be qualified.

- Conventional letters can also be sent to customers or potential customers instead of e-mails. These can be personalized, just like e-mails.
- At trade fairs or conferences, Personal Digital Assistants (PDAs) are used for inquiring about customers' or potential customers' interest in products. The trade fair or conference participant is registered at the stand and entered into mySAP CRM as a potential customer. With the help of their PDA's, SAP employees ask the participants questions and transfer their answers directly from the PDA to the CRM system. Leads are then recorded in mySAP CRM and they are automatically qualified depending on the answers given.

The number and subsequent evaluation (*cold*, *warm*, *hot*) of leads entered in consequence of a campaign is the result that is passed on from marketing to sales.

A workflow informs sales employees of all leads classified as *hot*. Should the sales employees now wish to start further activities, the information on the lead can be transferred to a sales project. The sales project is then automatically entered in the CRM system as an opportunity.

Opportunity Management

The sales cycle for software licenses, consultation, training and maintenance subsequent to marketing measures mainly takes place during the engagement phase of the customer engagement lifecycle.

SAP uses SAP CRM Opportunity Management to direct the sales process. This enables SAP to get an overview of all sales projects and with this, to obtain a forecast of expected sales during different periods. However, it should also help sales employees and the sales project team to carry out the right activities at the right time and to correctly evaluate the chances of success with the potential customer.

Sales assistant

Sales Assistant in Opportunity Management is used for planning the activities that form part of a sales project. SAP has stored their sales methodology here in the form of a catalog of activities, structured according to different sales phases. This catalog of activities is structured closely on the generic sales methodology, delivered by SAP as *Best Practices*.

Irrespective of the phase at which a sales project currently stands, in their 'to-do' lists the sales employees receive certain activities that should be executed during this phase, in line with the SAP sales methodology. They can choose further activities from the catalog or define their own. The catalog of activities can apply globally. The activities generated for an employee related to the current sales phase can, however, be different for individual countries, to take regional and cultural differences into account.

The Sales Assistant is thus like a coach that helps the participants of the virtual sales team to do the right thing at the right time. In addition, an overview of the activities already executed simultaneously gives an overview of the status of the sales project.

Assessment

The assessment function in mySAP CRM Opportunity Management helps SAP management to evaluate correctly the prospects of success of a possible contract conclusion. The members of a sales project team have to answer questions in a country-specific questionnaire. The answers to the questions for each sales project can be seen in Opportunity Management and as such serve as a basis for evaluating the prospects of success.

Buying center

With the Buying Center function, sales employees not only maintain an organizational diagram of the people involved in the sales project on the side of the buyer, in addition, informal relationship types such as *has influence on* and the relationship of the SAP sales project participants with the customer's contact persons are also maintained. This is graphically presented in an organization diagram and all relationships between the people involved in the project can easily be identified in the system. The maintenance of information on informal relationships is very important for a sales project, because they play an important role in the purchasing decision.

The strategy with which a sales project is brought to a successful close is also stored in Opportunity Management. Transparency in each sales project strategy means that there is uniform direction for all activities within the project and conflicting actions should be avoided as a result. Data on competitors, participating partners and the project team itself are also maintained in Opportunity Management. A summary report from Opportunity Management sees to it that management is optimally informed for customer or potential customer visits.

Analytical CRM

All opportunities are comprehensively evaluated with the help of the analytical features of mySAP CRM. Given that each opportunity can be linked with a campaign, the conclusion of an opportunity also forms part of the evaluation of the success of the campaign from which it was originally generated.

Collaborative Opportunity Management

In the future, SAP would also like to work in close collaboration with their partners in the acquisition of new customers. Therefore, with the implementation of mySAP CRM, collaborative opportunity management should also be carried out with SAP's partners. A pilot project of this has already been started.

Both SAP employees and also partners should be able to enter an opportunity in the CRM system using a form on the Internet. An e-mail sent by workflow informs the relevant employees both at SAP and at the partner's enterprise of the opportunity, so that it can be further qualified. Using partner determination in the CRM system it is also possible to decide on the sales employees that should carry out contractual negotiation – both on the side of SAP and that of the partner – in the event that the further qualification gives a positive result. In this case the selected sales employees are also informed by e-mail.

The sales employees involved decide if they want to carry out the sales project together and handle the opportunity accordingly. An information page on joint opportunity projects gives an overview of the participating contact partners on the side of SAP and of the partner and keeps all those involved up to date.

Implementation and Continuous Improvement

The phases *implementation* and *continuous improvement* should also be supported by mySAP CRM, both by the service components and the solution database (see also chapter 7, "Customer Service" on page 112).

Objectives Achieved

The following objectives have been achieved as a result of the global implementation of CRM in SAP:

▶ The previously installed legacy applications were based on interfaces to the SAP back office system, which have now been abandoned. The removal of these interfaces considerably lowers maintenance work and hardware costs.

▶ By harmonizing global processes, while at the same time, still taking regional characteristics into account, a more global view of the individual actions in the CRM process is possible.

▶ The migration of the different, scattered data sources used up to now into the central CRM system means that data quality is significantly higher.

▶ The integration of operational processes with the analytical functions of mySAP CRM means that it is possible to plan processes strategically, with a subsequent analysis of success using KPIs.

Training and Transfer of Knowledge on mySAP CRM

The implementation and putting into operation of mySAP CRM is accompanied by a number of different training offers from SAP, covering the following subject areas:

▶ Business knowledge

▶ CRM application knowledge

▶ CRM technology knowledge

▶ New release knowledge

The following forms of training are offered:

▶ Classroom training courses (traditional form of training in class groups)

▶ Virtual classroom training courses (training via the web to bridge the gap between the teacher and participants)

▶ Netshows (recorded training units, completed with textual and visual information, can be called up on the Internet)

▶ Web-based training courses (didactically prepared training units, produced with the help of various multimedia possibilities, can be accessed via the Internet)

▶ iTutors (screen recording of examples of use for explaining the user interfaces. Interactive queries on knowledge possible)

Additional information sources available are:

▶ IDES (Internet Demo and Evaluation System)

▶ Best Practices for mySAP CRM

▶ AcceleratedSAP for CRM

▶ CRM Knowledge Database (for developers and consultants)

More detailed information on SAP training proposals can be found on the SAP service exchange under *http://service.sap.com*.

16 Technical Component View of mySAP CRM

Key Capabilities With Components and Backend Systems

The following key capabilities were identified in chapter 8:

- ► E-selling (ES)
- ► Field sales (FS)
- ► Interaction center (IC)
- ► Customer service (CS)
- ► Field Service & Dispatch (FSD)
- ► Marketing management (MK)
- ► Sales (SL)

The technical components needed for implementing these key capabilities are summarized in the following overview of the CRM release 3.0. *X* indicates components that are necessary and *(X)* indicates optional components.

Software components for mySAP CRM	Key capability						
	ES	FS	IC	CS	FSD	MK	SL
CRM Server	X	X	X	X	X	X	X
SAP J2EE Engine	X						
SAP Enterprise Portals (formerly SAP Workplace)	(X)	(X)	(X)	(X)	(X)	(X)	(X)
SAP Internet Transaction Server (SAP ITS)	(X)			X	(X)	(X)	(X)
SAP Internet Pricing and Configurator (SAP IPC)	X	X	(X)	(X)	(X)	(X)	(X)
Standalone Gateway	X		(X)				
Internet Sales Web Application Components	X		(X)				
Text Retrieval & Information Extraction (TREX)	X						
Communication Station		X			(X)	(X)	

Table 16.1 Allocation of software components for key capabilities of mySAP CRM

Software components for mySAP CRM	Key capability						
	ES	FS	IC	CS	FSD	MK	SL
Computer Telephony Integration (CTI)			(X)				
Broadcast Messaging Server			(X)				
Mobile Client Software		X			(X)	(X)	
INXIGHT RFC Server	(X)		(X)	(X)			
TeaLeaf	(X)						
SAPMarkets Dynamic Pricing Engine (DPE)	(X)						
SAP Business Connector	(X)						
BackWeb		(X)					
SAP Content Server	(X)		(X)				
Mobile Recovery Manager		(X)					

Table 16.1 Allocation of software components for key capabilities of mySAP CRM (Contd.)

In addition, the following backend systems are available for the individual CRM scenarios. Other ERP systems from other producers can also be used instead of the R/3 system:

Backend systems for mySAP CRM	Key area						
	ES	FS	IC	CS	FSD	MK	SL
SAP Business Information Warehouse (SAP BW)	(X)	(X)	(X)	(X)	(X)	X	(X)
SAP Strategic Enterprise Management (SAP SEM)						(X)	(X)
SAP APO	(X)	(X)	(X)	(X)	X		(X)
SAP liveCache					(X)		(X)
SAP R/3	(X)	(X)	(X)	(X)	(X)	(X)	(X)

Table 16.2 Backend systems for mySAP CRM

Software Components

CRM Server

The CRM server is the logical central SAP system within a CRM system landscape. Technically, it is based on the SAP Web Application Server (see chapter 17, "SAP Web Application Server" on page 272) and offers the following services:

▶ CRM Middleware for synchronizing mobile clients and for integrating applications (see chapter 17, "CRM Middleware" on page 278)
▶ Server applications
  ▶ Sales
  ▶ Customer service
  ▶ Marketing
  ▶ E-selling
  ▶ Interaction center

SAP J2EE Engine

SAP J2EE is a Sun J2EE (Java 2 Platform, Enterprise Edition) compatible application server. It supports Servlets, Java Server Pages (JSP) and Enterprise Java Beans (EJB), among others. In the mySAP CRM Internet sales scenario the Servlet and JSP services of the J2EE Engine are used primarily.

SAP Enterprise Portals (Workplace)

SAP Enterprise Portals offers all users a centralized access to all necessary applications, services and information (see chapter 17, "Portal Infrastructure" on page 270).

SAP Internet Transaction Server

The Internet Transaction Server acts as gateway between traditional SAP GUI applications and web-browser technology. Alternatively, the SAP Web Application Server also supports direct HTTP communication.

SAP Internet Pricing and Configurator

SAP Internet Pricing and Configurator is a tool for interactive product configuration and automatic pricing on the Internet, in the interaction center or on the laptop of a field sales employee. Product variants are configured according to customer wishes – taking dependencies and restrictions into account – and are priced. Trade with end users (B2C), between enterprises (B2B) and with resellers (Business-to-Reseller) are all supported.

SAP Internet Pricing and Configurator is delivered with standardized user interfaces for mobile and Internet users which can easily be adapted to the individual requirements of enterprises. Internet users can choose between SAP ITS (Internet Transaction Server) based interfaces and the new user interface developed with JSP (Java Server Pages).

Thanks to its open architecture SAP Internet Pricing and Configurator can be linked with every product catalog and every shopping basket system.

SAP Internet Pricing and Configurator is made up of the Sales Configuration Engine and the Sales Pricing Engine, both of which are fully implemented in Java and can as such be run on different platforms.

SAP Internet Pricing and Configurator forms part of the mySAP CRM business scenarios of e-selling, Field Sales and Interaction Center.

Standalone Gateway

With the help of Standalone Gateway, non-SAP system RFC's (Remote Function Calls) can be received by SAP systems.

Internet Sales Web Application Components

Java applications that come into play for the Internet sales scenario on the In-Q-My Application Server or another J2EE server.

Text Retrieval & Information Extraction (TREX)

TREX is a tool for

▶ Searching for documents
▶ Structuring large quantities of electronic documents by means of a classification procedure
▶ Extracting relevant information from a document (text mining)

The following TREX components are of particular interest within the context of mySAP CRM:

▶ Index Management Service (IMS)
A tool for indexing any documents in an SAP or CRM environment. Search engines that fulfill the SAP IMS Server API specification (for example, TREX Search Engine), can use IMS indexing for document searches.
▶ TREX Search Engine
A search engine that offers all standard functions of text retrieval. It supports the SAP IMS server API specification.

Communication Station

The Communication Station is based on the SAP COM+ connector that converts mobile device DCOM calls into RFC calls for the CRM server.

Computer Telephony Integration

The goal of CTI (Computer Telephony Integration) is to make the telephone an integral part of computer aided business processes. The necessary foundations are created with the SAP component SAPphone and have the following functions:

▶ Control functions (for example, initiating or forwarding calls)

▶ Processing incoming calls

▶ Call center functions (for example, agent logon)

▶ Campaign support (predictive dialing)

▶ IVR (interactive voice response) support

To send or receive e-mail or fax messages the mySAP CRM system uses the standard SAP interface for e-mail and fax, called SAPconnect. With this interface, mySAP CRM can send and receive messages via different APIs such as the Business Communication Interface.

Broadcast Messaging Server

With the help of the broadcast messaging server messages can be sent to all agents in an interaction center. The Broadcast Messaging Server is a Java application that can be operated either as a stand alone solution or as a Servlet. The client is a Java Applet

Mobile Client software

Mobile Client software includes the following functions:

▶ Mobile sales

▶ Mobile service

▶ Handheld sales

▶ Handheld service

▶ SAP Internet Pricing and Configurator for mobile laptops

INXIGHT RFC Server

The INXIGHT RFC server is needed for using the Solution Database (SDB) and Interactive Intelligent Agent (IIA) in Japanese, Chinese or Korean.

TeaLeaf

TeaLeaf is a tool for analyzing Internet users' online experiences. TeaLeaf allows for the comprehensive recording and storage of all interaction steps taken by the user. The evaluation of the data extracted (identifying trends, dependencies, behavior patterns, and so on) is carried out in close integration with SAP BW.

SAPMarkets Dynamic Pricing Engine

The Java application SAPMarkets Dynamic Pricing Engine supports different dynamic pricing procedures such as auctions and requests for proposal.

SAP Business Connector

SAP Business Connector (SAP BC) is a Java based middleware product for integrating SAP solutions with non-SAP applications on the basis of open XML interfaces. Based on XML/HTML for example, quotations, purchase orders, purchasing contracts, delivery notification or catalog data can be exchanged.

The SAP Business Connector is made up of two components:

▶ BC Server
Constructs XML data structures and proprietor data formats on any other XML-data structures and vice versa

▶ BC Developer
Development tool for defining mapping rules

BackWeb

BackWeb is a third-party component for the collection and focused distribution, through the enterprise, of large quantities of data to desktop and mobile devices. Any format is supported – audio, video, program files, HTML documents, and so on.

BackWeb is used for the optional Infocenter in the Field Sales scenario.

SAP Content Server

SAP Content Server supports the administration of large quantities of documents, for example, the product catalog in Internet Sales scenarios. Smaller document quantities can also be administered on the CRM server itself.

Mobile Recovery Manager

The Mobile Recovery Manager is a tool for the central support team in an enterprise, which helps deal with the exchange of faulty or damaged mobile devices.

Backend Systems

Backend components, used not only by mySAP CRM but also by other solutions, are briefly explained below.

SAP Business Information Warehouse

With the SAP Business Information Warehouse (SAP BW), SAP ensures that decision makers in enterprises have fast and efficient access to all relevant information. SAP BW offers:

▶ Coordinated flow of information from internal and external information sources to individual information users

▶ Data storage and processing

▶ Extensive possibilities for evaluation and data formatting adapted for the end-user

SAP BW is made up of the following elements:

▶ Business Content
  Pre-configured reports and analyses together with information models (InfoCubes) and tools for extracting and formatting data

▶ Business Explorer
  User interface for carrying out data analyses and reports, archived in the Business Explorer Library

▶ Business Explorer Analyzer
  In the event that a data evaluation is needed, which is not covered by a standard report in the Business Explorer Library, an ad-hoc report can quickly be defined with the help of Business Explorer Analyzer.

▶ Administrator Workbench
  SAP BW can easily be implemented, administered and adapted to new applications with the help of the Administrator Workbench.

SAP BW is a component of mySAP BI and serves as the basis for the analytical functions of mySAP CRM.

SAP Strategic Enterprise Management

SAP Strategic Enterprise Management (SAP SEM) is the mySAP BI component for the support of strategic decision making on the part of business management. The key functions of SAP SEM include:

▶ Measurement of performance
▶ Strategy management

- Planning, simulation, budgeting and rolling predictions
- Consolidation
- Shareholder Relationship Management

SAP SEM is installed as an SEM add on, extending SAP BW

SAP Advanced Planner and Optimizer

SAP Advanced Planner and Optimizer (SAP APO) is a comprehensive solution for planning and optimizing all processes along the supply chain. SAP APO forms part of mySAP SCM (Supply Chain Management). The following functional areas are included in SAP APO:

- Demand Chain Planning
- Supply Chain Planning
- Production Planning and Scheduling
- Order Promising and Global Available-to-Promise, ATP
- Transportation Planning and Vehicle Scheduling
- Supply Chain Collaboration
- Supply Chain Control

Powerful optimizing algorithms such as *Mixed Integer Linear Programming* and *Constraint Programming Genetic Algorithm* are implemented in SAP APO for solving different planning and sequence problems (compare [Stadtler 2000]). When executing this procedure it should be borne in mind that the entry of all factors relevant to optimizing can result in very large quantities of information, even in small supply chains. Yet, for the optimizing process all this information must be in the main memory. To deal with this SAP has developed liveCache, a special main memory database for planning and optimizing tasks.

mySAP CRM uses SAP APO for the availability check (Available-to-Promise, ATP).

SAP liveCache

SAP liveCache is a component of SAP APO (Advanced Planner and Optimizer) – the SAP solution for real-time planning and decision making support in the value added chain. SAP liveCache is an intelligent database buffer (cache) for business objects, which helps to significantly improve the performance of APO services, such as availability check (Available-to-Promise, ATP) and production and resource planning.

SAP R/3

mySAP CRM can be operated with SAP's own OLTP (Online Transaction Processing) system SAP R/3 and also with other backend systems. The use of several parallel backend systems is also possible. For this, the standardization of heterogeneous data and key structures must be guaranteed (see also chapter 17, "Master Data Management" on page 283 and "Multiple Backend Installation" on page 284).

17 Technology and System Architecture of mySAP CRM

mySAP Technology – Platform for Open, Integrated e-Business Solutions

SAP has many years of experience not only as a leading business application provider but also as a developer of innovative platform technologies. The multi-level client/server system architecture, introduced by SAP at the beginning of the 1990's in the form of the R/3 system is still considered a milestone in the history of business application systems today [Buck-Emden 1996]. Further decisive steps in the development of SAP technology were EnjoySAP in 1998, with the optimization of user interfaces and the Internet Business Framework in 1999, for cross-component business processes on the basis of open Internet standards.

Building on these long years of practical and development experience, SAP has created a platform for open, integrated e-business solutions in the form of mySAP Technology. The following design principles apply to mySAP technology

▶ Prevision of a powerful development and runtime environment for user-oriented application and interface design and cross-enterprise collaboration

▶ Linking (*syndication*) of different applications and information to create comprehensive e-business solutions which are no longer spatially limited thanks to access via the Internet

▶ Use of open interfaces and standards

▶ Simple integration and collaboration thanks to open access to shared knowledge

▶ Reliability and scalability form the basis for freely-available and high-performance application services

▶ Lowest possible overall costs (Total Costs of Ownership, (TCO) thanks to simple Plug&Play components

Building on these design principles the following core elements are available in mySAP technology:

▶ Portal infrastructure as a further development of SAP's workplace solution

▶ Exchange infrastructure

▶ SAP Web Application Server

▶ Infrastructure services

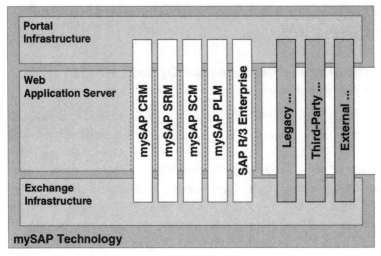

Figure 17.1 Interaction of mySAP Technology and business applications

Portal Infrastructure

SAP's portal infrastructure offers users a shared window to the application and data world of e-business. With the help of portal infrastructure users can navigate smoothly between different applications and data from a single entry point.

The portal infrastructure offered by SAP in the form of the mySAP Enterprise Portals includes the following elements:

▶ **Portal framework**

Services for high performance *aggregation* and *rendering* of information from different sources for user administration and for collaboration between users.

▶ **Presentation component framework**

Provision of mechanisms for user-appropriate, hierarchical organization of information. This includes the use of optimized content elements in portals, displayed as *iViews* and *Worksets*, which are made up of several iViews

▶ **Unification**

Mechanism which permits navigation between different applications without losing the context, that is to say the current local data environment. Unlike process integration, unification cannot be used to link systems at transaction level. Rather, this is a process which helps to relate user data from one system with data in another system. *Drag&Relate* is a good example of this.

Exchange Infrastructure

The ability to integrate different applications is one of the key ingredients of SAP's success. The SAP products R/2 and R/3 are remarkable for their ability to integrate separate business applications locally in a shared database. SAP's aspiration to be able to offer appropriate integration possibilities for systems distributed in enterprises or corporate groups was realized in 1995 with the ALE (Application Link Enabling) procedure. ALE permitted the technical and business integration of distributed R/3 and third party systems via explicit messaging interfaces (Integration via Local Interfaces).

The experience SAP gained with ALE now forms part of the foundation for SAP's new exchange infrastructure, based on open Internet technologies and XML message exchange. The task of this exchange infrastructure is to support the standard-based, and as such, open process-oriented integration of heterogeneous application components in a divided IT environment (*Enterprise Application Integration, EAI*).

The following elements form part of the SAP exchange infrastructure:

▶ **Integration server**
The integration server is responsible for the operational support of collaboration between application components. A core component of the integration server is the *Integration Engine* which has the following tasks:

  ▶ Queuing: temporary buffering of messages

  ▶ Mapping: mapping in different message formats and representations

  ▶ Routing: determining message recipient

In addition to the integration engine, the integration server can offer other services such as analysis applications or central master data administration.

▶ **Integration repository**
The integration repository stores all the knowledge available at the time of system design on possible collaboration between application components.

▶ **Integration directory**
The integration directory records the knowledge available at the time of system configuration on the desired collaboration between the application components. Unlike the integration repository, the information in the integration directory is specific to the installation in question.

▶ **Integration monitor**
The integration monitor permits the monitoring of collaborative processes at runtime.

SAP Web Application Server

The SAP Web Application Server is the technical platform for mySAP CRM and also for other mySAP.com solutions. The SAP Web Application Server represents the natural development of the earlier SAP Basis and as such offers all the familiar strengths of SAP Basis such as high performance, wide reaching scalability and robust operation. In addition, the SAP Web Application Server offers direct integration into the Internet and the parallel support of programming languages ABAP and Java.

The most important components of the SAP Web Application Server are included in the following overview:

▶ Tools for developing and running ABAP and Java based applications

▶ Development environment for web applications, based on an extensive library of pre-defined user interface elements (*Tag Library*) and on server side scripting with Business Server Pages (BSP) and Java Server Pages (JSP). HTML source code can be exchanged with external development tools using the WebDAV (Web Distributed Authoring and Versioning) protocol. In addition a MIME (Multipurpose Internet Mail Extension) repository is available for the integration of multimedia content.

▶ Web programming models, which are based exclusively on server side scripting and pre-defined user-interface elements show a weak point regarding dealing with errors, verifying input and flicker-free screen layout, for example. To improve ease of use and performance, the new web screen technology forms a part of the SAP Web Application Server.

▶ The support of XML documents is also a central component of the SAP Web Application Server. In collaborative environments it is not uncommon to find a number of different XML formats. For transfer between different XML formats, the SAP Web Application Server has access to its own XSLT processor, which can also convert XML documents to ABAP data structures.

▶ For a long time now SAP has used different single byte and double byte codepages as a basis for the different languages used in applications. As only one codepage can be active at a time, the SAP Web Application Server also supports the Unicode codepage, with which applications can be run in any language.

▶ *SAP Webflow*, SAP's web-enabled workflow solution, automates business processes in a flexible and transparent way. SAP Webflow links user tasks using graphic webflow descriptions. This can be between departments, services and systems.

- The *Internet Communication Manager (ICM)* is available as an interface to portal infrastructure, browsers and mobile devices and for integrating message services. Standards such as HTTPS (Secure HTTP), SOAP (Simple Object Access Protocol) and WSDL (Web Service Description Language) are supported by ICM.
- A global system management environment for monitoring and administering all IT components from one place and comprehensive services for software logistics, upgrade support and change management.

An important characteristic of the SAP Web Application Server is its HTTP capacity, that is to say its ability to directly support browser interfaces. The Web Application Server elements related to this are briefly described below.

HTTP Capacity of the SAP Web Application Server

It is possible to gain direct access to the SAP Web Application Server from a web browser without additional software. The basis for this is the *Internet Communication Manager (ICM)*, which accepts HTTP inquiries and can forward them to the appropriate interfaces for further processing. A special Internet Transaction Server (ITS) is no longer necessary in this case. For existing applications with SAP GUI interfaces (for Windows or Java), ITS provides a special communication layer to the web browser.

Java Server Pages

Java Server Pages (JSP) are an extension of Java Servlet technology. As a connecting link between presentation and business logic they enable the preparation of dynamic web pages for the browser user. JSP is a script language that can be embedded in HTML. At runtime script parts are interpreted and executed by the JSP runtime environment.

The mySAP CRM applications E-Selling and SAP IPC have used Java technology from very early on.

Business Server Pages (BSPs)

Business Server Pages is an ABAP (Advanced Business Application Programming)-based script language that enables the software developer to create graphical user interfaces simply, based on HTML templates. In comparison to simple HTML, Business Server Pages presents a much more powerful programming model. For example with the integration of a single BSP tag in the HTML code it is possible to generate a data entry field in the browser at runtime, which can validate user information.

BSP includes elements as simple as the data entry field and also complex presentation elements such as trees or tables that can be sorted.

Custom Tags

Applications based on Business Server Pages can be developed very quickly with the options mentioned above. However if the applications are more complex it often occurs that the user interfaces in HTML and JavaScript are stretched to their limits. If the external appearance of an application has to be adapted, for example, to fit in with the corporate identity, a developer often has to work through large quantities of HTML program code. One possibility for dealing with this is to use *Cascading Style Sheets* (CSS). With Cascading Style Sheets, colors, fonts and sizes can easily be changed in HTML documents.

Alternatively, HTML-like tags (known as Custom Tags) can be developed. Web designers can easily import these into HTML pages. The advantages of custom tags are:

▶ Customer-specific look and feel
▶ Custom tags can be reused in other applications
▶ They are not dependent on a particular web browser
▶ There can be direct links with data from very different sources

The Java Connector

The Java Connector is a development tool for integrating Java applications into mySAP.com solutions. It offers an easy to use programming interface (API) which allows communication in both directions.

Infrastructure Services

Component-oriented system landscapes with many different collaborative services make high demands on infrastructure management. mySAP Technology offers very comprehensive services for this. The most important areas are

▶ Security
▶ Globalization/internationalization
▶ Infrastructure management

Security Services

mySAP Technology offers an integrated security infrastructure for the entire mySAP.com landscape. On the basis of widely used Internet security standards such as

- ▶ HTTPS (Secure HTTP)
- ▶ Secure Sockets Layer (SSL)
- ▶ Lightweight Directory Access Protocol (LDAP)

this infrastructure provides a reliable environment for

- ▶ Central user administration
- ▶ Secure user authentication
- ▶ Single Sign-On
- ▶ Secure communication between all client and server components
- ▶ Secure business transactions

User administration

User administration in mySAP Technology is founded on the central storage of user profiles (*User Accounts*) and user authorizations (*Authorization*) on the basis of roles (groups of content-related activities) and responsibilities (authority to read or modify certain data). The LDAP protocol is supported for communication with central administration in distributed environments.

Authentication and single sign-on

The secure detection of user identities – user authentication – and single sign-on, to avoid repeated logon when using several application systems, are supported by certificates, tickets and connection possibilities for third party products.

- ▶ **Single Sign-On**
  With the single sign-on procedure users only logon once at a central location. All applications and systems that are subsequently called up can request the user authentication from this central location.

- ▶ **Certificates**
  Digital certificates contain identity and public key information for encryptions and digital signatures. They are issued by a central certification authority, with which a user must first register. SAP supports the use of X.509 compatible certificates, and recommends them for critical applications. The *SAP Trust Center Service* issues digital certificates free of charge for SAP customers.

- ▶ **Tickets**
  Tickets are cookies, secured with a digital signature, which pass on logon information to the applications called up. Tickets do not use a public key infrastructure and if necessary, they should be used in conjunction with additional security mechanisms.

Secure communication between systems

mySAP Technology supports the SSL (Secure Socket Layer) standard for HTTPS (secure HTTP) connections between individual system components. Communication between existing mySAP.com components is secured by GSS API (Generic Security Services) with protocols such as Kerberos, Simple Public Key Infrastructure (SPKI) and Windows NT LAN Manager (NTLM).

External access to internal systems can be controlled using firewalls to block individual communication channels (ports). In addition it is possible to use the firewall to check incoming and outgoing data traffic for viruses or sensitive information, for example. In addition, highly sensitive systems should be protected with what are known as demilitarized zones – created by several firewalls – even for internal communication.

Secure business transactions

To ensure the security of business transactions in e-business, mySAP Technology supports digital signatures. These are attached to any business documents to be exchanged and guarantee their authenticity, integrity and friendliness (non-repudiation). Additionally, the content of business documents can be encrypted.

Auditing Framework

IT security involves two prerequisites:

▶ The definition and implementation of a comprehensive security strategy
▶ Proof that all processes are run in accordance with this security strategy

Particularly in collaborative business scenarios, it is not sufficient to check the security architecture continuously merely within the enterprise itself. All business partners must also be included in the verification procedures. To perform this task, SAP, together with partners, has developed the Auditing Framework.

Globalization Services

Every global e-business solution must be geared toward both local and international business processes. This includes the support of the enterprise's official languages and currencies as well as support of different local languages, local time zones, local currencies and local business procedures and regulations.

All of the abovementioned globalization requirements are fulfilled by mySAP Technology. In addition, several languages can be used parallel to each other in a single application. Different character sets and Unicode are supported.

Management of the IT Landscape

mySAP Technology has access to all necessary tools and technologies for the comprehensive mangagement of the IT landscape – from planning, installation and going-live through to the day to day operation and continuous change management. Distributed, heterogeneous system landscapes can be centrally monitored and controlled from a single location with the help of mySAP Technology. In addition, system management tools from other producers can be integrated using open interfaces.

mySAP CRM Architecture

Overview

mySAP CRM is a software solution that constantly builds on the system services of mySAP Technology. In more detail, this means:

▶ CRM server applications, including CRM Middleware, are created on the basis of the SAP Web Application Server.

▶ Users can access mySAP CRM using the services of mySAP Enterprise Portals.

▶ The services of mySAP Exchanges and CRM Middleware are available for process oriented integration with other applications.

▶ All of the infrastructure services of mySAP Technology are freely available for mySAP CRM, including security services, globalization services and management of the IT landscape.

Figure 17.2 shows how mySAP CRM is embedded in mySAP Technology.

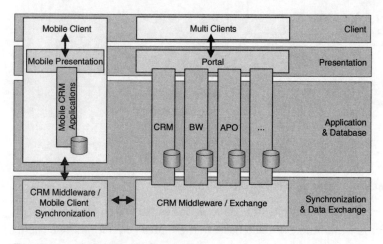

Figure 17.2 mySAP CRM system architecture

CRM Middleware

The exchange of messages between the CRM server and any SAP or non-SAP systems is handled by CRM Middleware. One of the most outstanding features is the synchronization of mobile clients with each other and with the central CRM database.

CRM Middleware is an integral component of the mySAP CRM solution. The server element of CRM Middleware is installed on the SAP Web Application Server, together with the CRM server components. It is therefore not a separate installation and there is no need for a separate server for CRM Middleware.

CRM Middleware is made up of the following core elements:

▶ Central Middleware services for controlling the flow of messages and the synchronization of mobile clients (replication).

▶ CRM-Plug-In, which must be installed in the SAP R/3 backend system (if there is one) for communication with the CRM server.

▶ Communication Station for the conversion of DCOM calls from mobile clients to RFC calls for the CRM server.

▶ Connection Handler, which must be installed in each mobile client for communication with the CRM server (this forms part of Mobile Application Installation).

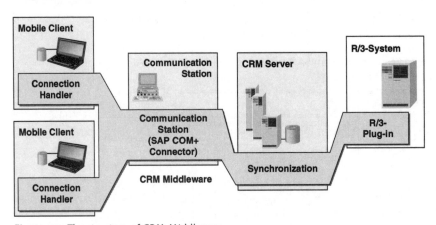

Figure 17.3 The structure of CRM Middleware

Synchronization Services for Mobile Clients

The synchronization of mobile clients is done by the consolidated database (*CDB*), a logical database within the CRM database. In the CDB all data for mobile clients are archived in consolidated form.

A publish and subscribe mechanism is available for synchronizing mobile clients. Subscriptions are maintained centrally in the *Administration Console* of the CRM server. The following synchronization possibilities are available:

▶ Bulk replication
▶ Intelligent replication
▶ Dependent replication
▶ Realignment

With *bulk replication*, all documents of a certain type are sent to all sites that have subscribed for this document type.

With *intelligent replication*, certain selection criteria can be defined so that a site only receives selected documents of a particular type, for example, only customers from a particular country.

With *dependent replication*, dependencies between messages can be taken into account. A mobile laptop user can, for instance, receive all customers in his or her sales region together with all corresponding (dependent) activities.

Realignment involves a re-distribution of business data to mobile clients. This is necessary when the distribution model changes (for example, if a field sales employee is assigned a new sales area) or if business data changes (for example, if a customer moves). The need for realignment is identified by CRM Middleware and is carried out automatically.

Sites and Adapters

The CRM Middleware message services can be used by any systems (sites) – from a mobile system – a laptop only linked temporarily with the CRM server – to a permanently linked backend system such as SAP R/3. Corresponding adapters are needed to convert incoming messages and forward them. The following types of site are supported:

▶ **SAP R/3**
Data exchange occurs with the help of the adapter framework in the CRM server and the CRM Plug-In in the SAP R/3 system

▶ **SAP Business Information Warehouse**
Data exchange between SAP BW and the CRM server is done using the BW Adapter. Any other sites exchange messages with SAP BW using the CRM Middleware flow control.

▶ **Non-SAP application systems**

The External Interfaces Adapter (XIF) offers interfaces based on XML and IDoc for communication with non-SAP systems. In addition, special formats such as RosettaNet, xCBL, EDIFACT, ANSI X.12 and ODETTE are supported using the corresponding sub-systems.

▶ **Mobile clients**

Mobile clients normally only link up with the CRM server temporarily. When data has to be replicated to mobile clients it is buffered in the consolidated database (CDB). If a mobile client is linked to the CRM server the data is transferred from the consolidated database to the client and, if necessary, vice versa.

Flow Control and BDocs

Flow control in CRM Middleware accepts business messages such as sales orders, customers and activities from the sending system and forwards them to the recipient or recipients. Business messages are transported within CRM Middleware in the form of *BDocs* (*Business Documents*) which must comply with certain format rules. Each BDoc has a BDoc type that determines its data segment structure.

BDoc type descriptions contain no implementation details whatsoever. BDoc messages can thus be presented in different ways, for example, as ADO (ActiveX Data Object) record sets on laptops, as internal tables on the CRM server or in an XML format for non-SAP systems.

BDoc types are divided into the following classes:

▶ *Messaging BDocs* for the exchange of messages between CRM server applications and other fixed applications. These messages are not archived in the consolidated database.

▶ *Synchronization BDocs* for the exchange of messages between CRM server applications and mobile clients. These messages are archived in the consolidated database.

In addition, there are *Mobile Application BDocs*, which are only used locally by the mobile clients.

BDocs are defined with the help of the BDoc Modeler and are stored and administered in the BDoc Repository. Using BDoc Modeler one or more Synchronization BDocs can be assigned to a Messaging BDoc. Conversion services in CRM Middleware take care of the necessary mapping.

Data Exchange With Backend Systems

CRM Middleware includes the following services for the support of data exchange with backend systems:

▶ Initial data exchange between the CRM server and SAP R/3 and non-SAP systems.

▶ Delta data exchange between the CRM server and SAP R/3 and non-SAP systems.

▶ The synchronization of customizing data between the CRM server and SAP R/3

▶ Data exchange between the CRM server and non-SAP systems on the basis of XML messages. The following business objects are supported:

  ▶ Business partners, hierarchies, relationships

  ▶ Sales orders, activities

  ▶ Products (inbound)

  ▶ Conditions (inbound)

  ▶ Invoices (outbound)

▶ File-based initial data exchange to the CRM server

  ▶ Initial data transfer from non-SAP systems with the help of the SAP Data Transfer Workbench using the XIF adapter's IDoc interface.

  ▶ Initial data transfer from non-SAP systems which can provide data as ASCII files.

Monitoring Services

The Middleware Cockpit offers central monitoring functions for monitoring:

▶ Message flow

▶ Queues

▶ Adapter framework

▶ Message exchange with mobile clients

▶ Performance

In addition there is integration with the Alert Monitor in the mySAP Technology infrastructure services.

Mobile Engine

The *Mobile Engine* (*ME*) is a platform-independent runtime system for mobile application scenarios – online and offline. With the help of Mobile Engine, business applications can run offline on mobile devices, for example, Personal

Digital Assistants (PDAs) and laptops and transaction data can be synchronized with any SAP or non-SAP system at a later point in time.

Mobile Engine is fully integrated in the development and runtime environment of SAP. It is made up of the following elements:

▶ Java Plug-In on the mobile devices

▶ ME server components

▶ ME Public Interface

▶ ME SyncLayer

▶ MicroITS

▶ Deployment components

The Java Plug-In is a Java VM for mobile devices.

The Mobile Engine server components include a compact web server and a Servlet engine.

The Mobile Engine Public Interface supports the integration of individual Plug-Ins and offline enhancements in mobile devices and these devices can then access all Mobile Engine services, for example, local data retention and synchronization.

The SyncLayer offers data synchronization services between mobile devices and an SAP system.

The MicroITS offers a special runtime environment for mobile applications.

The deployment components of Mobile Engine provide central administration functions for user administration and application distribution. All offline applications are monitored by the deployment console. In addition, information on device type/ID and software versions is forwarded to the participating systems.

Configuration and Installation of mySAP CRM

Overview

Basically the same rules and procedures apply for the configuration and installation of mySAP CRM as for other mySAP.com solutions based on mySAP Technology. For mySAP CRM installations the hardware equipment needed can also be determined with the help of the *Quick Sizer Tool*, which SAP has developed for mySAP.com solutions in collaboration with hardware partners.

A complete presentation of all the subjects related to the configuration and installation of mySAP CRM would go beyond the scope of this book. Please refer to *SAP CRM Master Guide* which offers comprehensive reference to additional configuration and installation documents for all required components [SAP 2001a]. More detailed information on the operation of mySAP CRM can be found, for example, in [SAP 2001b].

Three themes that are of particular interest regarding the use and operation of mySAP CRM will be briefly outlined here. On the one hand there is the running of several mySAP.com components with a single database and on the other, there is the linking of several backend systems to one mySAP CRM system.

One Database Installation

Distributed IT system landscapes with application components such as ERP, CRM, SCM and Data Warehouse on different servers, each with their own databases, offer advantages regarding the flexibility, availability and scalability of the individual systems, but they also involve a whole range of administrative disadvantages:

▶ Costly maintenance of several or different operating and database systems

▶ The implementation of high availability solutions is difficult

▶ Backup and restore synchronization involves a lot of work

▶ Greater hardware requirements

To cope with these disadvantages it is possible to install several mySAP.com components such as SAP CRM, SAP APO, SAP BW, SAP SEM and SAP R/3 in such a way that they share one common physical database system (one database installation). In early projects the following savings have been made by doing this:

▶ 10 % less hard disk requirement

▶ 30 % less backup hardware costs (tapes, tape drives, disk drives)

▶ 40 % less backup administration costs

Figure 17.4 shows the different possibilities for the installation of mySAP.com components.

Master Data Management

The management of shared master data in distributed, heterogeneous application environments is very demanding. As a solution for this SAP has developed a central *Master Data Management* (MDM), that makes it possible to handle master data in distributed environments in a standardized, consolidated way and also

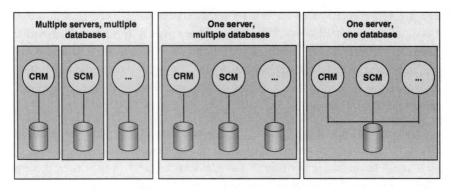

Figure 17.4 Installation options for mySAP.com components

supports demanding collaborative applications such as Distributed Order Management (see chapter 12, "The Next Step: Distributed Order Management" on page 206). SAP's Master Data Management is based on mySAP Exchange Technology and uses XSLT mapping (Extensible Stylesheet Language Transformations) for mapping between different XML object representations.

Multiple Backend Installation

Many enterprises want to link their CRM system with several backend systems because, for example, they have a separate backend system installed for each region or each enterprise area.

SAP supports this requirement as part of CRM 3.0 for harmonized backend systems. This means that shared data can work with similar table keys, or that an appropriate mapping procedure is available. In a second step, this strategy is generalized further with the use of shared master data servers (Master Data Management) and mySAP Exchange technology.

In this connection it should be mentioned that today many SAP R/3 customers run different independent business units (for example, plants, sales organizations, and so on) with their own company codes on a shared SAP R/3 system. These R/3 customers have the possibility of implementing customer relationship management for all business units with a single mySAP CRM system.

Bibliography

[Bader 2001] Günther Bader, *SAP and Dun & Bradstreet Partner to Provide Business Information at the Touch of a Button*, SAPinsider, Vol. 2, No. 4, October-December 2001

[Blattberg 2001] Robert C. Blattberg, Gary Getz, Jacquelyn S. Thomas, *Customer Equity*, Harvard Business School Press, Boston, Massachusetts, 2001

[Bond 1999] B. Bond, D. Burdick, C. Eschinger, D. Miklovic, K. Pond, *C-Commerce: The New Arena for Business Applications,* Gartner Group, 1999

[Boulanger 2000] David Boulanger and Peggy Menconi, *SAP CRM is Finally Ready for Your Short List*, AMR Research, The SAP Advisor, August 2000

[Brandenburger 1996] A. M. Brandenburger, B. J. Nalebuff, *Co-opetition*, Doubleday, New York, 1996

[Brenner 2001] Walter Brenner, *Ausgewählte Tendenzen im Informationsmanagement*, University of St.Gallen, Institute of Computing for Business, 2001

[Brinkmann 2001] Sandra Brinkmann, Axel Zeilinger, *SAP R/3 Financial Accounting: Making it Work for Your Business*, SAP PRESS, Addison-Wesley, Harlow, England, 2001

[Buck-Emden 1996] Rüdiger Buck-Emden, Jürgen Galimow, *The SAP R/3 System – A Client/Server Technology*, Addison-Wesley, Harlow, England, 1996

[Butler 1997] P. Butler; T. W. Hall, A. M. Hanna, L. Mendonca, Auguste, B., Manyika, J., Sahay, A., *A Revolution in Interaction*, The McKinsey Quarterly, Number 1, 1997

[Clark 2000] Sam Clark, *Putting Marketing Wheels on the Customer Life Cycle*, META Group, Delta, ADS 886, July 20, 2000

[Close 2001] Wendy Close et al., *CRM at Work: Eight Characteristics of CRM Winners*, GartnerGroup, Research Note AV-13-9791, June 19, 2001

[Curry 2000] Jay Curry, *The Customer Marketing Method*, Free Press, 2000

[Diez 2000] W. Diez, *Wenn das Internet als Verkäufer arbeitet*, Harvard Business Manager, Volume 22, No. 1, 2000

[Fritz 2000] Franz-Josef Fritz, *The Internet Business Framework – The Foundation for SAP's Collaborative Business Scenarios*, SAPinsider, October-December, 2000

[Fritz 2001] Franz-Josef Fritz, *From "SAP Basis" to "SAP Web Application Server" – It's Much More Than Just a Name Change!*, SAPinsider, Vol. 2, No. 3, July-September 2001

[Hack 2000] Stefan Hack, *Collaborative Business Scenarios – Wertschöpfung in der Internetökonomie*, in: Scheer, A.-W. (Ed.): E-Business – Wer geht? Wer bleibt? Wer kommt? 21. Saarbruck symposium on industry, services and administration 2000. Physica-Verlag, Heidelberg, 2000

[Hammer 1993] Michael Hammer, James Champy, *Reengineering the Corporation*, HarperCollins, New York, 1993

[Homburg 2000] Christian Homburg, *Customer Relationship Management*, Arbeitspapier M52, University of Mannheim, 2000

[Kagermann 2001] Henning Kagermann, Gerhard Keller, *mySAP.com Industry Solutions: New Strategies for Success with SAP's Industry Business Units*, SAP PRESS, Addison-Wesley, Harlow, England, 2001.

[Kalakota 1999] Ravi Kalakota, Marcia Robinson, *e-Business – Roadmap for Success*, Addison Wesley Longman, Reading, Massachusetts, 1999

[Kalakota 2001] Ravi Kalakota, Marcia Robinson, *M-Business: The Race to Mobility*, McGraw-Hill, 2001

[Kaplan 1996] Robert S. Kaplan, David P. Norton, *The Balanced Scorecard: Translating Strategy into Action*, Harvard Business School Press, 1996

[Kimbell 2001] Ian Kimbell, *Deciphering "SAP", "mySAP.com" and "mySAP"*, SAPinsider, Vol. 2, No. 4, October-December 2001

[Kumar 2001] Anil Kumar et al., *Beyond CRM – Realizing the Customer Value Promise*, McKinsey&Company, 2001

[Lassmann 2000] Jay Lassmann and David Paris, *CRM in the Call Center and Contact Center*, Gartner Group, Tutorial DPRO-93666, November 21, 2000

[Lübke 2001] Christian Lübke, Sven Ringling, *Personalwirtschaft mit mySAP Human Resources*, SAP PRESS, Galileo, Bonn, 2001

[Martin 2000] Wolfgang Martin, *Real-Time Marketing: Beyond Campaign Management*, META Group, Delta, ADS 909, October 13, 2000

[McKenna 1995] Regis McKenna, *Real-Time Marketing*, in: Harvard Business Review, Jul/Aug 1995, Vol. 23, No. 4

[META 1999] META Group and IMT Strategies, *Customer Relationship Management Study*, Sep 22, 1999

[Morris 2000] Henry Morris, *Analytic Applications Market Forecast and Analysis, 2000–2004*, IDC Report 23498, December 2000

[Muther 2001] Andreas Muther, *Customer Relationship Management – Electronic Customer Care in the New Economy*, Springer, Berlin, 2001

[Nelson 2000] S. Nelson, *Customer Service is the Most Important CRM Function*, Gartner Group, Research Note SPA-11-7680, Nov 9, 2000

[Nelson 2001] S. Nelson, J. Kirkby, *Seven Reasons Why CRM Fails*, Gartner Group, Research Note COM-13-7628, August 20, 2001

[Newell 1997] Frederick Newell, *The New Rules of Marketing: How to Use One-to-One Relationship Marketing to Be the Leader in Your Industry*, Irwin Professional Publishing, 1997

[Newell 2001] Frederick Newell, *Loyalty Rules!: How Today's Leaders Build Lasting Relationships*, HBS Press Book, 2001

[Peppers 1993] Don Peppers, Martha Rogers, *The One to One Future: Building Relationships One Customer at a Time*, Doubleday, New York 1993

[Peppers 1997] Don Peppers, Martha Rogers, *Enterprise One to One – Tools for Competing in the Interactive Age*, Doubleday, New York, 1997

[Peppers 1999] Don Peppers, Martha Rogers, *The One to One Manager*, Doubleday, New York, 1999

[Pine 1993] Joseph B. Pine, *Mass Customization: The New Frontier in Business Competition*, Harvard Business School Press, Boston, Massachusetts, 1993

[Porter 1986] M. Porter, *Competitive Advantage*, Harvard Business School Press, Boston, MA, 1986.

[Rapp 2000] Reinhold Rapp, *Customer Relationship Management*, Campus, Frankfurt/Main, 2000

[Reicheld 1996] Frederich F. Reichheld, *The Loyalty Effect: The Hidden Force behind Growth, Profits, and Lasting Value*, Harvard Business School Press, 1996.

[SAP 2000] SAP, *mySAP.com Collaborative Business Scenarios*, SAP AG, WhitePaper, Walldorf, 2000.

[SAP 2001] SAP AG, *A Business View of mySAP CRM*, SAP White Paper, Walldorf, 2001

[SAP 2001a] SAP AG, *SAP CRM Master Guide*, Walldorf, 2001

[SAP 2001b] SAP AG, *mySAP Technology for Open E-Business Interaction – Overview*, SAP White Paper on mySAP Technology, Walldorf, 2001

[SAP 2001c] SAP AG, *IT Landscapes: Architecture and Life-Cycle Management of Distributed Environments*, SAP White Paper on mySAP Technology, Walldorf, 2001

[SAP 2001d] SAP AG, *Analytical CRM*, SAP White Paper, Walldorf, 2001

[Schneiderman 2001] Nathan Schneiderman, Adrienne Yih, *The Emerging Face of Customer Relationship Management*, Wedbush Morgan Securities, Industry Report, August 2001

[Siebel 1996] Tom Siebel, Michael Malone, *Virtual Selling*, The Free Press, New York, 1996

[Siemers 2001] Hans-Heinrich Siemers, *Holistic CRM: The Key to Optimizing Customer Value, Service, and Retention*, SAPinsider, April-June 2001

[Simon 2001] Hermann Simon, *Die vielen Irrtümer im E-Business*, Manager Magazin, Nr. 9, September 2001

[Sinzig 2001] Werner Sinzig, *SAP SEM Drives Strategies Into Operational Practice*, SAPinsider, January 2001

[Slywotzky 1998] Adrian J. Slywotzky, Dave J. Morrison, *The Profit Zone: How Strategic Business Design Will Lead You to Tomorrow's Profits*, Random House 1998

[Spang 2000] K. Spang, *Customer Relationship Management*, Current Analysis, Market Assessment, Nov 13, 2000

[Stadtler 2000] Hartmut Stadtler, Christoph Kilger (Eds.), *Supply Chain Management and Advanced Planning – Concepts, Models, Software and Case Studies*, Springer, Berlin/Heidelberg, 2000

[Thompson 2001] Ed Thompson, Wendy Close, *ERP Vendors Are a Safe Choice for CRM, but Not for All*, Gartner Group, Research Note M-13-3257, 18 April 2001

[Vering 2001] Matthias Vering et al., *The E-Business Workplace: Discovering the Power of Enterprise Portals*, John Wiley & Sons, New York, 2001

The mySAP CRM Team of Authors

The following colleagues have contributed to this book as authors:

Achim Appold

Achim Appold studied business management and holds an MBA. In 2001 he was appointed Country Manager of the SAP CRM Regional Group. Before this, Achim Appold was business development manager at the SAS Institute, senior consultant for Mobile Sales and CRM at Kiefer & Veittinger Information Systems and at SAP CRM Consulting.

Stephan Brand

Stephan Brand, an industrial engineering graduate, has worked with SAP since 1996. He was manager of the Asia/Pacific regional CRM group and in October 2000 he took over the tasks of assistant to executive board member Dr. Peter Zencke. His responsibilities include, among other things, the integration of office productivity tools with mySAP CRM.

Dr. Rüdiger Buck-Emden

Dr. Rüdiger Buck-Emden has a degree in computer science. Since 1990 with SAP, he has held different management positions in the areas of strategic planning, development and product management, including the work of assistant to executive board member Prof. Hasso Plattner. He is also Vice President for the area of CRM Architecture & Technology. Dr. Rüdiger Buck-Emden has written many text books and other publications.

Christian Cole

Christian Cole has worked at SAP for five years and to date has worked in the areas of quality management, implementation consulting and product management for retail and CRM. He also works in the field of mySAP CRM Workforce Management, particularly in the areas of integration and analytics. Christian Cole studied biology and chemistry at university.

Christopher Fastabend

Christopher Fastabend joined SAP AG in 1998 as product manager for mySAP CRM Marketing. Before joining the company he worked with the CRM specialists Kiefer & Veittinger Information Systems in Mannheim. Christopher Fastabend holds a bachelor's degree in industrial engineering and an MBA.

Dr. Jörg Flender

Dr. Jörg Flender is product manager for mySAP CRM and apart from product development he is also responsible for the internal implementation of mySAP CRM at SAP. Dr. Jörg Flender joined SAP in 1995 and first worked in SAP internal application development and as a consultant for the area of logistics. He later worked as project manager for SAP internal e-commerce and Employee Self-Service projects.

Alison Gordon

Alison Gordon has worked with SAP since 1996. As technical writer for mySAP CRM Sales, she documents the areas of Activities Management, Sales Management and Support as well as the CRM content in SAP Business Information Warehouse. Alison Gordon studied German and Spanish in Great Britain and has an MA in Translating and Interpreting.

Tomas Gumprecht

Tomas Gumprecht is an IT graduate and works as product manager for mySAP CRM Service. He is responsible for international brand position, roll-in and roll-out, coordinating market demands with development, and the documentation and translation of mySAP CRM Service. He joined SAP in 1993 and since then he has worked on the development of software for utility companies, the development of software for service management/ maintenance and in mySAP CRM product management.

Stefan Hack

Stefan Hack holds the position of Vice President for SAP Solution Lifecycle Management. He is responsible for tools and content for the support of the solution-oriented implementation of the mySAP.com platform (SAP Solution Architect). In addition he looks after the development of methods for the modeling, documentation and implementation of cross-enterprise business processes (Collaborative Business). Before joining SAP Stefan Hack was a senior consultant with KPMG Peat Marwick and senior associate at McKinsey. Stefan has a degree in industrial engineering and an MBA.

Dr. Volker Hildebrand

Dr. Volker Hildebrand is the director of product management at SAPMarkets, Inc., a 100 % subsidiary of SAP AG in Palo Alto, California. Previous to that he was head of product management for e-selling solutions at SAPMarkets Europe and a member of the management team of the CRM business unit at SAP AG. His career at SAP began in 1998 in sales, where he helped build the CRM Software sales area. Before joining SAP Volker Hildebrand worked as an assistant to Prof. Jörg Link at the universities of Frankfurt and Kassel, where he obtained a doctorate in the area of customer relationship management. He has been the author or co-author of several books and numerous articles in specialist journals and collections.

Frank Israel

With a degree in business studies, Frank Israel holds the position of senior pre-sales consultant for mySAP CRM. Before taking up this position he was a consultant at Kiefer & Veittinger Information Systems and at SAP CRM Consulting, in the area of capital goods/high-tech.

Fabian Kamm

Fabian Kamm studied business management and holds an MBA. Since 1996 he has worked at Kiefer & Veittinger Information Systems, then at SAP as a consultant and project leader throughout Europe in various different CRM projects. Fabian Kamm today holds the position of senior consultant at SAP, specializing in mySAP CRM Sales and CRM implementation methods and tools.

Stefan Kraus

Stefan Kraus studied business management. From 1992 to 1996 he was a consultant for the implementation of industry-specific software solutions for profitability and sales accounting at many different enterprises. He subsequently joined SAP as product manager, responsible for Profitability Analysis. In the beginning of 2000 Stefan Kraus was appointed product manager for analytical mySAP CRM.

Mark Layden

Mark Layden is Vice President world wide, responsible for mySAP CRM Workforce Management. He was a founding member of Campbell Software Inc. (Chicago), leader in the area of workforce management solutions for the retail and service industries, until the company was taken over by SAP. As president of SAP Campbell he was responsible for integrating the strategies, processes and development of both companies. Mark Layden studied economics at Harvard.

Claudia Mairon

Claudia Mairon studied business management at the university of Mannheim, specializing in marketing, international management and psychology. While still a student she already worked in different areas of SAP AG. On completion of her studies she worked first of all in product management of EnjoySAP and later in the area of product management in mySAP Workplace. Since 2000 she has worked in strategic product management for e-selling solutions at SAPMarkets Europe.

Wolfgang Ölschläger

Wolfgang Ölschläger is product manager for the mySAP CRM area of Mobile Sales. In collaboration with customers and developers, he works out product requirements which then serve as a basis for further planning and development at SAP. Wolfgang Ölschläger is an economics graduate and has over ten years experience in consultancy, product management and in business development for Sales Force Automation and CRM. He joined SAP in 1998 from the Mannheim CRM specialists Kiefer & Veittinger Information Systems.

Jörg Rosbach

Jörg Rosbach, BEng. studied mechanical engineering at the technical university of Karlsruhe and the ETH in Zurich, specializing in production engineering. He came to SAP in 1994, first as a consultant then as a corporate marketing manager for the area of CRM. In June 1999 Jörg Rosbach was appointed product manager for mySAP CRM Sales.

Ingo Sauerzapf

Ingo Sauerzapf, board member of quipus AG, Heidelberg, has worked with SAP Basis themes, ABAP/4 development and Internet technology for many years. He worked for SAP SI and e-SAP.de as a consultant before founding quipus AG with three other colleagues. Together they successfully use their SAP know-how in various different e-business projects.

Dr. Thomas Weinerth

Dr. Thomas Weinerth has worked in SAP product management for Best Practices for mySAP CRM for two years. Before that he worked at the university of Mannheim as a researcher in the area of CRM. Thomas Weinerth obtained a doctorate in the area of marketing and organization and has degrees in economics and psychology.

Peter Wesche

After studying mathematics and numerical analysis Peter Wesche worked in several commercial concerns before turning to the area of IT. He has worked at SAP AG in Walldorf since 1987, first in application programming for retailing and then in product management. Since the middle of 2000 he has worked in CRM as Vice President in the area of Mobile Business and is responsible for all SAP mobile applications in all areas.

Rainer Zinow

Rainer Zinow is a business management graduate and over the last 10 years he has held various management positions at SAP AG. His responsibilities have included the creation of the SAP IBM Competence Center, the international (business) coordination of SAP training offers and the direction of the area of Knowledge Management. Rainer Zinow also worked as assistent to Dietmar Hopp, chairman of the executive board. He is currently Vice President responsible for mySAP CRM Interaction Center.

Index